Criminal Law

BUTTERWORTHS CORE TEXT SERIES

Criminal Law

Second Edition

Nicola Padfield
BA (Oxon), Dip Crim (Cantab), DES (Aix-Marseille),
Barrister-at-Law,
Fellow in Law, Fitzwilliam College, Cambridge

Butterworths
London, Edinburgh, Dublin
2000

United Kingdom	Butterworths, a Division of Reed Elsevier (UK) Ltd, Halsbury House, 35 Chancery Lane, LONDON WC2A 1EL and 4 Hill Street, EDINBURGH EH2 3JZ
Australia	Butterworths, a Division of Reed International Books Australia Pty Ltd, CHATSWOOD, New South Wales
Canada	Butterworths Canada Ltd, MARKHAM, Ontario
Hong Kong	Butterworths Asia (Hong Kong), HONG KONG
India	Butterworths India, NEW DELHI
Ireland	Butterworth (Ireland) Ltd, DUBLIN
Malaysia	Malayan Law Journal Sdn Bhd, KUALA LUMPUR
New Zealand	Butterworths of New Zealand Ltd, WELLINGTON
Singapore	Butterworths Asia, SINGAPORE
South Africa	Butterworths Publishers (Pty) Ltd, DURBAN
USA	Lexis Law Publishing, CHARLOTTESVILLE, Virginia

A CIP Catalogue record for this book is available from the British Library.

ISBN 0 406 91602 0

Printed in Great Britain by Cromwell Press, Trowbridge, Wiltshire

Visit Butterworths LEXIS *direct* at: http://www.butterworths.com

Preface to the second edition

What has happened in the last two years? On the Parliamentary front, politicians seem to be vying with each other to see who can be 'tougher' on law and order, but this is not yet having much of an impact on substantive criminal law (except perhaps delaying the enactment of a criminal code as Parliament spends its limited time on measures which the Government consider more attractive to the electorate). But it's not all gloomy: the Home Office Consultation Paper on reforming the law of Involuntary manslaughter (May 2000) may be a sign that the Government is edging slowly towards some essential reforms. The Law Commission remains busy, and this new edition refers to some of their more recent work, such as the 1999 Consultation Paper on Fraud and Deception.

This edition was completed in May 2000, which means we have been able to include some important recent developments (B v DPP, for example) but have missed others (the House of Lords' decisions in *Hicks* and *Smith* are both expected imminently). Such is the nature of studying law: you can only take a snap shot at one particular moment in time. A new Lord Chief Justice (Lord Woolf) was appointed this month and it remains to be seen what impact he will have on the development of the criminal law.

I should like to express my thanks to the other contributors to this series (especially to Chris Willmore for her advice on chapter 13 of this book) and to the team at Butterworths who have combined energetically to launch the series so successfully. Meanwhile, whilst delighted that the series has been well received by students, may I repeat my request set out in the earlier Preface for comments and criticisms.

Nicky Padfield
Fitzwilliam College,
Cambridge CB3 0DG

Preface to the first edition

This books forms one of the first to be published in Butterworths' Core Text Series. The idea for the series sprang originally from Butterworths themselves and from Nick Johnson, now Director of the Legal Practice Course at Oxford. Butterworths wanted to produce a series of books which provided value for money, were brief, but which did not over-simplify the subject matter. Law can be made simple, but not without intellectual dishonesty. The challenge to the authors in this series has been to write at several levels simultaneously, to strip their subject to its core while continuing to point out the intellectual challenges and difficulties within it.

It is a 'core' law series in several senses:

(i) the books are short

(ii) they seek to identify the fundamental principles of the subject

(iii) they concentrate on the most important, key topics within the subject.

This book therefore seeks to provide a different sort of criminal law textbook. The criminal law needs to be reduced to its core for a number of reasons. Parliament is in the habit of adding more and more offences to the statute book, and the core is in danger of being lost from sight. The subject is notoriously unclear, with appellate decisions regularly shifting the already unsteady foundations of criminal liability. The book investigates the core of criminal law by looking at various central concepts and offences. The main target audience is the student who is largely working on her own. I have sought to cover the subject in standard textbook fashion, but also to graft into it the elements of a case book: substantial statute and case law quotation should enable the student to get to the heart and core of the subject, and references to academic analyses and to law reform proposals are intended to point the student in the direction of the many challenges and difficulties of the subject. Doubtless many readers will take issue with the choice of material: given the constraints imposed by the need to produce a short book, much has been omitted, and much is doubtless dealt with more briefly than will satisfy the purist.

The style of the book is deliberately brief and core-like. Certain abbreviations have been routinely used in order to save space and for ease of presentation. Where cases have been summarised, the text is slightly indented for ease of reference. Sometimes after the name of the deciding court (HL, CA etc), a judge's name is mentioned. This is because he (almost never she) gave the main or only judgment or speech. If a judge's name appears later in the summary, it is because I have chosen to highlight what was said by one judge in particular. I make no apology for frequent references to individual judges: it is after all the judges who are making and interpreting the law. The student may well find the large amount of knowledge she is required to digest easier to learn once she has 'got to know' judges individually: the subject comes alive when you are able to think, 'Aha, Lord Goff again', or 'I'm not surprised that Lord Mustill held that, given his views in …'. It also impresses examiners if a candidate can say, 'as Lord Diplock said in *Caldwell* …', rather than the prosaic 'as the House of Lords said in *Caldwell*' or the rather feeble 'as *Caldwell* decided'. An examiner is more likely to give a candidate the benefit of the doubt when he is not sure if something has been understood, if the candidate has made it very clear elsewhere that she had an accurate understanding.

The choice of subjects is not entirely arbitrary: the books within the series all cover the syllabus of the external London LLB course. However, I have chosen to add chapters on sexual offences, public order, and environmental offences simply to help illustrate difficulties in identifying the fundamental 'core' of the subject.

The additional reading at the end of each chapter is necessarily highly selective. Within the text there are also references to some of the leading textbooks: Smith and Hogan, Glanville Williams, Ashworth and Allen. Students who have access to law reports and periodicals will be well rewarded if they keep up-to-date by browsing through new cases and articles as they appear. The main criminal law journal remains the Criminal Law Review: students are well advised to read Professor Sir John Smith's monthly commentaries on recent cases: he provides excellent reviews of the key issues as well as pointers towards possible reforms and improvements. If, as a student, you can follow these arguments, you will know you are doing fine! As well, periodicals such as the Cambridge Law Journal, the Modern Law Review, the Law Quarterly Review and the Journal of Criminal Law regularly publish short commentaries on key cases. The practioners short monthly newsletter Archbold News also gives up-to-date information. Another technique for understanding the criminal law: take this book and read it in the public gallery of your local Crown Court or Magistrates' Court: then you will not forget the impact and importance of the subject as it affects people's lives.

It is hoped that the Core Text Series will be a success - a useful aid to study. Work has already started on the next edition of this book. Please send comments and criticisms of this edition to the author.

Nicky Padfield
Fitzwilliam College,
Cambridge CB3 0DG

Contents

Table of abbreviations

Throughout this book, a number of abbreviations are used to save space and to make the text more concise:

CA	Court of Appeal (Criminal Division)
CAA	Criminal Attempts Act
CC	Crown Court
CCCR	Court of Crown Cases Reserved
CDA	Crime and Disorder Act
CJA	Criminal Justice Act
CJPOA	Criminal Justice and Public Order Act
CLA	Criminal Law Act
CLB	Criminal Law Bill
CLRC	Criminal Law Revision Committee
CMAC	Courts Martial Appeals Court
CYPA	Children and Young Persons Act
D	Defendant
DC	Divisional Court (of the Queen's Bench Division of the High Court)
DCC	Draft Criminal Code
HL	House of Lords
LCJ	Lord Chief Justice
LJ	Lord Justice
MC	Magistrates' court
OAPA	Offences against the Person Acts
P	Prosecution
RTA	Road Traffic Act
SOA	Sexual Offences Act
SO(A)A	Sexual Offences (Amendment) Act
TA	Theft Act
T(A)A	Theft (Amendment) Act 1996
V	Victim

A number of leading textbooks are also referred to in the text:

Allen	Allen's *Textbook of Criminal Law* (5th edition, 1999)
PCL	Ashworth's *Principles of Criminal Law* (3rd edition, 1999)
S & H	Smith and Hogan's *Criminal Law* (9th edition, 1999)
TCL	Glanville Williams' *Textbook on Criminal Law* (2nd edition, 1983)

Table of statutes

List of cases

CHAPTER ONE

Introduction

SUMMARY
This chapter attempts to put criminal law in its context: to look at the aims and ambit of the criminal law; and the criminal justice system within which it is applied. The student is encouraged to think about some key principles and values which will help in the evaluation of the offences and defences described later in the book.

1.1   It is relatively easy to distinguish criminal law from other areas of law: criminal law involves a description of the behaviour which makes a person liable to punishment by the state. Thus a crime is a legal wrong, which may result in punishment. However, it is more difficult to work out the exact boundaries. For example, where does criminal law end and civil law take over? If I refuse to pay the plumber who mends my dripping tap, he may either sue me in the civil courts for non-payment of a civil debt, or he may seek to get the police to initiate a criminal prosecution alleging that I obtained his services by deception. In other areas, the boundaries may be blurred because the extent to which someone should be held to be blameworthy may be unclear: if a doctor treats you appallingly and causes your death, should she be prosecuted? Another example might be the meaning of the word 'dishonestly'. A person is not guilty of theft unless he or she acted 'dishonestly': are you dishonest if you see £50 in the street and you decide to keep it? Not all crimes are perceived to be immoral: some are merely 'regulatory', as we shall see particularly when we look at environmental crimes (chapter 13). In any case, it is difficult to agree on a 'shared morality'.

1.2   In order to identify the proper boundaries of the criminal law, it is useful to identify certain fundamental principles. Ashworth's *Principles of*

Criminal Law (PCL) is a pioneering assessment of the criminal law through the identification of key principles. For Ashworth, the **principle of autonomy** lies at the foundation of criminal liability. Individuals in general have the capacity and free will to make meaningful choices, and this individual autonomy should be respected by others and the legal system. He also selects other key principles which should be at the heart of the criminal law:

- the principle of welfare, of upholding the common good

- the principle of prevention of harm to others

- the principle of minimal intervention: the law should not criminalise too much behaviour

- the principle of social responsibility: society requires a certain level of co-operation between citizens

- the principle of proportionate response: the response of the criminal law should be reasonably proportionate to the harm committed or threatened

- the non-retroactivity principle: a person should not be convicted or punished except in accordance with a previously declared offence

- the thin-ice principle: those who skate on thin ice can hardly expect to find a sign denoting the precise spot where they will fall in

- the principle of maximum certainty: people should have fair warning about the criminal law

- the principle of fair labelling: offences should be labelled so as to reflect the seriousness of the law breaking

- the principle of strict construction: ambiguities in criminal law should be construed in favour of the defendant

- the presumption of innocence: a principle of procedural fairness that D should be presumed innocent until proved guilty.

1.3 In a recent essay, Ashworth (2000) has identified four interlinked principles which form the principled core of the criminal law:

Ashworth's principled core of the criminal law
- the criminal law should be used, and only used, to censure persons for substantial wrongdoing
- criminal laws should be enforced with respect for equal treatment and proportionality
- persons accused of substantial wrongdoing ought to be afforded the protections appropriate to those charged with criminal offences; ie at least the minimum protections declared by Articles 6.2. and 6.3. of the European Convention on Human Rights
- maximum sentences and effective sentence levels should be proportionate to the seriousness of the wrongdoing.

Throughout this book, the student is encouraged to think about the principles behind individual crimes. These principles sometimes clash and conflict, and they are often not openly acknowledged by the judges and commentators. But by applying the sort of approach that Ashworth suggests, you will find it much easier to judge and evaluate the criminal law. 'General principles of criminal law' may include the general principles discussed in chapters 2 and 3 of this book; they may also include the more fundamental principles of criminal justice discussed by Ashworth.

Purposes of criminal law

1.4 Despite the value of these fundamental principles, it remains important to try and work out the purpose of the criminal law. When you have read about people being prosecuted for anything from aiding and abetting suicide to outraging public decency, you may well want to ask some fundamental questions about what the criminal law is seeking to achieve. Here are some ideas:

The criminal law seeks

• to enforce moral values

• to punish those who deserve punishment

- to protect the public from harm

- to reform the offender

- to deter offenders and potential offenders

- to educate people about appropriate conduct and behaviour

- to preserve order

- to protect vulnerable people from exploitation and corruption.

Many writers have sought to find a primary aim. However, it may be that you decide that the criminal law should seek to achieve a combination of the above, but giving different priorities to different aims in different contexts. Most law courses separate out the study of punishment from the study of criminal law, but the two are inevitably intertwined and you may find it useful to read a book on theories of punishment (eg Walker (1991); Walker and Padfield (1996)).

The relationship between law and morals

1.5 The question whether the law should be used to penalise immoral behaviour has been endlessly debated. A classic example of the debate is that between Professor Hart and Lord Devlin in the 1960s, provoked by the recommendation of the Wolfenden Committee to decriminalise homosexual acts between consenting adults (which happened in the SOA 1967). Devlin, a retired Law Lord, argued that society cannot live without morals, and that its morals are those standards of conduct which the reasonable man approves. The law was needed to enforce morality. Hart, on the other hand, argued that not only was there no such thing as a moral consensus, but neither was there any evidence that those who deviate from conventional sexual morality are in other ways hostile to society. Devlin's stand depends on there being some common shared morality (which he thinks can be found in the jury room). Yet current debates on some subjects, such as abortion or euthanasia, suggest that there is no easily accessible common thread of morality. Currently, it seems to be widely accepted that the criminal law should not criminalise certain activities that many might consider immoral as long as they don't

4

happen in public. Yet is this distinction between that which happens in public and in private tenable?

1.6   Whose morality is to be enforced? It is likely to be the morality of those in power. The enactment of new offences (such as criminal trespass introduced in the CJPOA 94; employing those without the right to work, in the Asylum and Immigration Act 1996 or breach of an anti-social behaviour order, in the Crime and Disorder Act 1998) remind us that it is the Government of the day which has the power to define the limits of the criminal law. The role of the jury, magistrate and judge is limited by the statutory framework within which they work. New crimes are often added to the statute book, and few are removed. It is important for the student to consider whether there is too much criminal law, and an application of key principles allows an assessment of whether the body of criminal law needs to be stripped back to its core.

1.7   A modern version of the Hart/Devlin debate is to be found in the speeches of the HL in *Brown* (1994). What is instructive is the different attitude of the majority and minority judges to the question of whether the criminal law should be used to uphold morality:

> *Brown* (1994) A group of sado-masochists committed acts of violence against each other for the sexual pleasure they got from giving and receiving pain. They were convicted of offences against s 20 and s 47 of the OAPA 1861, and received sentences of imprisonment. HL (by a majority of 3 to 2): upheld the CA's decision to reject their appeals. Lord Templeman, in the majority, said:

>> The violence of sado-masochistic encounters involves the indulgence of cruelty by sadists and the degradation of victims ... Society is entitled and bound to protect itself against a cult of violence. Pleasure derived from the infliction of pain is an evil thing. Cruelty is uncivilised.

> Lord Mustill (dissenting) disagreed:

>> The issue before the House is not whether [D]s' conduct is morally right, but whether it is properly charged under the Act of 1861. When proposing that the conduct is not rightly so charged I do not invite your Lordships' House to endorse it as morally acceptable ... What I do say is that these are questions of private morality; that the standards by which they fall to be judged are not those of the criminal

5

law; and that if these standards are to be upheld the individual must enforce them upon himself according to his own moral standards.

Consider which way you would have decided this issue before reading on to **1.24**, which considers the ECHR's approach.

Grading crimes

1.8 So far we have discussed some of the difficulties involved in marking the outer limits of the criminal law. As difficult is the challenge of grading individual crimes according to their relative seriousness. This is equally important, since we seek to punish people appropriately according to the gravity of their offence. While we can easily agree that murder is worse than assault, is it necessarily worse than manslaughter? There is no one scale of seriousness. A common measure is the seriousness of the harm caused. Thus, it can be argued that I am more culpable if I kill you than if I merely wound you, whatever my intent. Certainly, we seem to blame the drunk driver who kills someone more than we blame the drunk driver who happily doesn't happen to hit anyone. But how do you work out which harms are worse than others? Von Hirsch and Jareborg (1991) have developed a scale based on the extent that the harm affects someone's living standards, but the complexities of real life suggest that there are other possible dimensions to help measure offence seriousness. Another measure of culpability might be the intent of the offender. I am more culpable if I intend to kill you and do so, than if I cause your death merely by being careless. Grading crimes according to what happens is somewhat arbitrary: concentrating on the state of mind of the offender may be fairer. Yet this too may be unfair as we cannot enter other people's minds – you are still likely to judge me by the external appearances of my act, whatever my innermost thoughts. When we come to look at individual crimes, we will see that they are graded in various ways by Parliament in different contexts, and that different words are used to describe the required guilty state of mind (see chapter 3).

1.9 How narrowly should individual crimes be sub-divided? For example, culpable homicides are currently divided into murder and manslaughter, but English law does not distinguish first degree and second degree murder or manslaughter. The Law Commission in 1996 recommended that manslaughter should be sub-divided into reckless killing and a more minor offence of killing by gross carelessness (see **8.38**). Are greater subdivisions such as this useful? One can argue that the law is already over-precise. Glazebrook wrote a stimulating article in 1969 arguing that we could live without a law of attempt by defining substantive crimes more widely: thus rape would not be unlawful sexual intercourse, but an assault committed with sexual intent. Then there would be no need for a crime of attempted rape. This raises a question of fair labelling: since people understand rape to be unlawful sexual intercourse, there are compelling reasons to define it in law in this way. Some crimes may indeed be too wide: indecent assault includes anything from forced oral sex to bottom-pinching (see **10.16**), and robbery is now defined to include mere handbag snatching (see **11.21**): has this diluted too much an otherwise serious offence?

Criminal law in context: the criminal justice process

1.10   The criminal law is not a neat theoretical system: it needs to work in practice. After reading this book you may conclude that the criminal law is in something of a state of chaos, because, in studying criminal law, we often concentrate on the most difficult and controversial areas. It is therefore worth reminding ourselves that courts up and down the country are today dealing with many criminal prosecutions with little difficulty. Most disputes in criminal trials concern questions of fact not questions of law (though distinguishing law from fact can be very difficult: see **5.24**). Of course, many crimes are never discovered, or reported to the police. A high proportion of known offenders are never prosecuted, but may be formally or informally cautioned by the police. If someone is to be prosecuted, then this prosecution is likely to be initiated by the police. Many of the difficulties in this subject are created by the charging practices of individual officers. Thus, one of the difficulties we will explore is whether someone who tricks their victim into giving them possession of their goods is guilty of theft (see *Gomez* at **11.9**) as well as guilty of obtaining by deception. This difficulty would never have become an issue of criminal law if the police charged such suspects with obtaining by deception and not with theft. Thus, the criminal law can be tidied up by better policing and not just by clarification from appellate judges at the other end of the process. Of course not all crimes are dealt with by the police: we will look briefly at the role of environmental agencies in prosecuting crime in chapter 13.

1.11 If the police have decided to charge someone with a criminal offence, the prosecution will then be conducted by the Crown Prosecution Service (CPS). The CPS follow the guidance of the Code for Crown Prosecutors as well as their own policy manuals. Thus a case may be dropped because the CPS decide there is insufficient evidence to proceed to trial, or because the public interest does not demand a prosecution: the offence may be trivial, or there has been a long delay between the offence taking place and the date of the trial, for example. You may well be surprised when reading some of the cases discussed in this book that the case was ever prosecuted at all, or you may wonder why the CPS did not choose to amend a criminal charge at an early stage. The CPS has been much criticised in its 15-year life and current reforms are attempting to reinforce the role of the CPS at any early stage in criminal investigations (see Padfield (2000)).

1.12 Criminal cases will be tried in either the Crown Court (CC) or magistrates' court (MC). Offences can all be categorised according to their mode of trial. Offences may be indictable (ie triable by a jury in a CC); summary (ie triable by magistrates (lay or stipendiary in a MC); or triable either way. The Criminal Justice (Mode of Trial) (No 2) Bill 2000 seeks to remove the defendant's ability to elect for trial in the Crown Court in either way offences, making the decision instead one for the magistrates, a move aimed at saving money and cutting delays in the criminal justice process. The categorisation of offences should have little impact on the general principles of criminal liability, being most relevant to procedures before or at trial. However, it would be wrong to assume that these procedural differences have no effect on substantive issues of criminal law. Appeals from MCs are generally heard in the CC and are rarely reported, and so there is very little judicial guidance on the interpretation of, for example, driving offences, or of minor assaults. A procedure exists for MCs or CCs to state a case for the opinion of the Divisional Court of the Queen's Bench Division of the High Court, and this procedure is used not infrequently to clarify points of law, especially in cases heard in MCs: in 1998, there were 188 appeals by way of case stated heard in the Divisional Court (the figure for 1995 was 243), of which over half were successful. Note which of the cases that you come across in this book were decided by the DC, and consider which party appealed and why. It may also be that the HL do not take minor offences as seriously as they should, sometimes appearing to ignore the general principles that such cases may raise. Thus, Spencer (1984) 43 CLJ 10 suggests that cases such as *Lawrence* and *Morris* reflect the HL's opinion that theft was inadequately important to merit detailed consideration in the HL, and this exacerbated the problems experienced in defining the word 'appropriation' (see **11.9**). You should be aware that the vast majority of cases you look at in criminal law are decisions of the Court of Appeal, which is dealing with appeals from trials in Crown Courts. The only ground for allowing an appeal against conviction is that the Court thinks that the conviction is 'unsafe' (s 2 CAA 1968 as amended by the CAA 1995).

The rules of procedure and evidence

1.13 This book ignores most of the rules of procedure and evidence. Yet it should not be forgotten that these rules may well have more influence on whether someone stands trial and indeed on whether they are convicted, than the substantive rules of criminal law. Bear in mind that, in practice, lawyers may well be more concerned to argue points of criminal evidence and procedure than in arguing points of substantive criminal law. In a trial, arguments about the admissibility of certain evidence (can a witness give certain oral evidence or was it inadmissible hearsay; was a confession gained by oppression and should it therefore be excluded) may have crucial importance in securing an acquittal or a conviction. Similarly, rules of procedure (can the judge's guidance on a possible sentence be sought before D enters a plea of not guilty, for example) have enormous impact. Similarly, questions about the burden of proof (who has to prove what) are crucial.

This book follows the traditional pattern of criminal law courses in this country by leaving the study of evidence and procedure to other texts, but the wise student would keep an eye on the wider issues at stake in the criminal process. While studying criminal law, visit a court and consider what a small proportion of the court's time is spent in considering details of substantive criminal law.

The role of the jury

1.14 The most serious cases are eventually tried by a judge and jury, and it is worth considering the impact that trial by jury has had on the development of the criminal law generally. It is often suggested that it was the reluctance of juries to convict drivers who killed of manslaughter which resulted in the creation of the more minor offence of causing death by reckless driving. Jackson and Doran (1995) compare the process of trial by judge alone with that of the trial by jury. They conclude that trials throughout the common law world are still dominated by rules and practices designed for a lay fact-finding tribunal, even though many no longer have trials by jury. Even in England few cases result in jury trial: most of the minority of cases which reach the CC result in guilty pleas, and there is no trial.

1.15 The existence of a system of trial by jury can allow the law to be less precise than perhaps it should be. In **11.13** we examine the meaning of the word 'dishonesty' in the criminal context. Juries are told by judges that it is an ordinary word which should be given its ordinary meaning. Yet how is a jury to decide whether someone who keeps a £50 note, found in the street, is acting dishonestly? This raises the question whether the jury should merely decide questions of disputed fact (the defendant is lying: he did not intend to tell the police the next day about the £50 note, otherwise why would he have already gone on a spending spree that afternoon?), or whether they have some wider function as a barometer of public morality (is keeping property found lying in the street wrong?). There are ardent supporters of trial by jury: for example Devlin (1991), Houlder (1997), who suggest that the jury provides a democratic veto on law enforcement. Can this really be so in a system where the less than 3% of all criminal cases are tried in the CC, and even then the minority of these cases are contested?

Sentencing

1.16 In many ways it makes little sense to study criminal law without studying sentencing. In practice, the public is more interested to know the punishment imposed on an offender rather than the label of the offence applied: it may indeed be more important to know that someone got three years' imprisonment for a wounding than in knowing the precise legal label applicable to their offence. However, this does not mean that the offences themselves should not be appropriately distinguished, as Ashworth's fair labelling and other principles makes clear (see **1.5**).

1.17 In the case of most offences, Parliament has laid down a statutory maximum penalty. Thus, the maximum possible penalty for rape is life imprisonment, for theft, seven years. Prosecutors may be influenced as much by ideas about the suitable sentence as by the definition of the offence itself. Thus, since an offence under s 20 of the OAPA 1861 (inflicting grievous bodily harm) has the same maximum penalty (five years) as an offence under s 47 (occasioning actual bodily harm), there is little reason for the prosecution to set out to prove the more serious offence. Since a life sentence of imprisonment is available for manslaughter as well as for murder, prosecutors may be happy to accept a guilty plea to manslaughter. The law on provocation has proved controversial recently: this may be simply because prosecutors are increasingly reluctant to let killers 'get away with' manslaughter and so more borderline cases are being considered by courts. Indeed, specific defences to murder such as provocation and diminished responsibility evolved at a time when the death penalty existed. It may be argued that if the penalty for murder were changed from a mandatory life sentence to a discretionary one, the debates on the borderline between murder and manslaughter would lose their urgency. This book therefore sometimes includes comments on the sentences imposed, since these may be a key to understanding the evolving definition of the offence itself.

Sources of criminal law

1.18 Many offences (especially recent offences) have been created by statute, but others have simply evolved through the common law. This means that definitions have evolved slowly through judgments stretching back over the centuries. The obvious example is murder: traditionally defined as 'unlawful killing with malice aforethought', the individual elements in this definition have to be explored by reference to many cases, some recent, some ancient. Judge-made law is in fact based on only a very small pool of cases: only the cases of those who the police have chosen to charge, who have been convicted and who have chosen to appeal are likely to reach the appellate courts.

Figure 1: Crown Court trials

Year	No of trials	% not guilty pleas	Percentage of those pleading not guilty acquitted
1995	89,000	24%	40%
1998	75,815	39%	64%

Figure 2: Appeals against conviction

Year	No of applications for leave to appeal	% of appeals actually heard which were allowed
1995	2,393	33%
1998	2,099	42%

1.19 Most of the cases discussed in this book are decisions of the CA and HL: classic examples of appellate decisions. When an appellate court allows an appeal, it is not saying that D is necessarily innocent, just that his conviction was unsafe. For example, in *Quick* (1973) (see **4.11**), the CA quashed the conviction of the diabetic nurse not because they thought he was not guilty, but because it was unsafe to allow his conviction to stand. The jury might well have rejected the defence of automatism, but it was wrong to let the conviction stand when they did not have the chance to consider a possible defence. Until very recently, retrials were exceptionally rare in English law, and they are still very unusual (see Fig 1). It seems to have been accepted that it is wrong to make D face a retrial, and of course it is very expensive. Should they be more readily used, especially in cases where the CA feels D is probably guilty?

Figure 3: Number of retrials ordered by the Court of Appeal[1]:

	1989	1990	1991	1992	1993	1994	1995	1996	1997	1998
No of retrials	1	3	15	12	20	51	52	53	33	73

1.20 Other cases we look at will be DC decisions (appeals by way of case stated (see **1.12**)) as well as a few A-G's References, where the prosecution refer an acquittal with which they are not happy. Although the original acquittal will not be affected by the result of the appeal, the procedure allows the higher courts the opportunity to review a wider variety of case than simply those of aggrieved convicted offenders. It also allows them to 'sit on' a wrong ruling on a point of law before it becomes widespread.

1.21 The principle of non-retroactivity (see **1.5**) means that people should only be found guilty of crimes which were known to be criminal

---

1   Source for all statistics in this chapter: Judicial Statistics (HMSO; 1998).

at the time that D committed his offence. One of the dangers with judge-made law is that it has retroactive effect. Much of the controversy which surrounded the case of R (1992) (see **1.24; 10.12**) concerned the question whether the HL went too far in extending the law of rape to husbands who had sex with their wives without their consent. Whilst few people today would argue that such activity should not be criminal, many considered that it was more appropriate for Parliament rather than the judiciary to change the law: even though R might have argued that at the time when he raped his wife, his act was not an offence in English law, the HL was able to uphold a change in the law with retrospective effect.

1.22 Another danger is that some common law offences remain vaguely defined, perhaps offending against the principle of maximum certainty. Consider two examples concerning the offence of outraging public decency:

> *Gibson* (1990) D1 exhibited at D2's art gallery an exhibit of a model's head from which were hung earrings made out of (real) freeze-dried human foetuses (the message being that women allegedly wear their abortions as lightly as they wear their earrings). They were convicted of outraging public decency, contrary to the common law. CA: upheld their convictions. Despite the paucity of reported cases, there was undoubtedly a common law crime of outraging public decency.

> *Walker* (1996) D was convicted of outraging public decency when he exposed his penis to two girls in the sitting room of his house. CA (Laws J): allowed his appeal. The act had not been committed in a place where there was a real possibility that members of the general public might witness it. A more appropriate charge might have been indecent assault or under the Indecency with Children Act 1960.

Should an offence such as outraging public decency exist? It seems unlikely nowadays that the courts would evolve new crimes since it is accepted that Parliament is the appropriate body to create new offences. Parliament is democratically accountable, and has the opportunity to seek expert advice (see **1.27**) prior to its debates.

The Human Rights Act 1998

1.23 The European Convention on Human Rights has been part of English law for many years, but until now the aggrieved citizen has had to pursue her claim in the European Court of Human Rights (ECHR) in Strasbourg. The Human Rights Act 1998 has incorporated the Convention into domestic law: from 2 October 2000 these Convention rights will become part of the underlying principles of our criminal law. Here are extracts from some relevant articles:

Article 6:

(1) In the determination of his civil rights and obligations or of any criminal charge against him, everyone is entitled to a fair and public hearing within a reasonable time by an independent and impartial tribunal established by law ...

(2) Everyone charged with a criminal offence shall be presumed innocent until proved guilty according to law.

(3) Everyone charged with a criminal offence has the following minimum rights:
(a) to be informed promptly, in a language which he understands and in detail, of the nature and cause of the accusation against him;
(b) to have adequate time and facilities for the preparation of his defence;
(c) to defend himself in person or through legal assistance of his own choosing or, if he has not sufficient means to pay for legal assistance, to be given it free when the interests of justice so require;
(d) to examine or have examined witnesses against him and to obtain the attendance and examination of witnesses on his behalf under the same conditions as witnesses against him.
(e) to have the free assistance of an interpreter if he cannot understand or speak the language used in court.

Article 7:

No one shall be held guilty of any criminal offence on account of any act or omission which did not constitute a criminal offence under national or national law at the time when it was committed.

Article 8:

Everyone has the right to respect of his private and family life, his home and his correspondence ...

Article 10:

Everyone has the right to freedom of expression ...

Article 11:

Everyone has the right to freedom of peaceful assembly ...

1.24   Even before the incorporation of the ECHR into domestic law, the Court has had an important influence. The following are simply examples:

SW v United Kingdom; CR v United Kingdom (1996) Both applicants had been convicted of the rape/attempted rape of their wives before their marriages had been legally ended. They relied on art 7, since at the time of their convictions it had been widely accepted that marital rape was not a crime (see *R*, discussed at **1.21** and **10.12**). ECHR: held unanimously that the essentially debasing character of rape was so manifest that the results of the decisions of the CA and HL, that the applicants could be convicted of rape and attempted rape, could not be said to be at variance with the object and purpose of art 7, namely to ensure that no one should be subject to arbitrary prosecution, conviction or punishment. Furthermore, the abandonment of the unacceptable idea of a husband being immune against prosecution for the rape of his wife was in conformity with the fundamental objectives of the Convention, the very essence of which was respect for human dignity and human freedom.

Laskey, Jaggard and Brown v United Kingdom (1997) The applicants had been convicted of offences under the OAPA 1861 arising out of sado-masochistic acts (see **1.7** above). ECHR: held unanimously that there had been no violation of art 8.

> One of the roles which the state is unquestionably entitled to undertake is to seek to regulate, through the operation of the criminal law, activities which involve the infliction of physical harm. This is so whether the activities in question occur in the course of sexual conduct or otherwise. ... it is evident from the facts established by the national courts that the applicants' sado-masochistic activities involved a significant degree of injury or wounding which could not be characterised as trifling or transient ... the national authorities

were entitled to consider that the prosecution and conviction of the applicants were necessary in a democratic society for the protection of health within the meaning of art 8(2) of the Convention.

One judge, Judge Pettiti, wished to expand the first paragraph quoted above, by noting

to regulate and punish practices of sexual abuse that are demeaning even if they do not involve the infliction of physical harm.

The Human Rights Act 1998 will certainly result in a flood of litigation. However, it should not be seen as a cure for all ills: the Convention is dated, and may do little to protect suspects' rights, especially in the crucial time before they ever arrive at the police station (see Sharpe (1997).

Reform and codification

1.25 Criminal law evolves slowly through the courts. Many of the key cases are subtly shifting the boundaries of the criminal law as it adapts to modern ideas of appropriate behaviour. Such change may be inadequate both because of its slow speed and because one has to wait for the 'accidents of history' which cause a relevant case to reach the higher court. Imagine that the HL felt that the time had come to decide that women who have sex with men by deceit should be guilty of rape (at present, only men can commit rape): could the courts change the law? Not only would it be argued that such a fundamental change in the law could only be enacted by Parliament, but that a court cannot invent a suitable case in which to change the law. We would need a woman to be prosecuted and to be convicted by a jury, so that an appeal could reach the higher courts. Perhaps the most interesting fact about *R* (see **1.21**) was that the husband was prosecuted in the first place, and that the jury convicted him, given that it was widely accepted at that time that the law did not penalise marital rape.

1.26 Law reform is no easy business. Choose a subject on which you have strong opinions: euthanasia, abortion, possession of cannabis: try and draw up a water-tight proposal in the shape of a Bill that you would like to present to Parliament. The Criminal Law Revision Committee (CLRC) was set up in 1959, by the then Home Secretary, Lord Butler 'to be a standing committee to examine such aspects of the criminal law of

England and Wales as the Home Secretary may from time to time refer to the Committee, to consider whether the law requires revision and to make recommendations'. But its members gave their services voluntarily and part-time, and only dealt with topics specifically referred to them by the Home Secretary. When Lord Gardiner became Lord Chancellor in 1963, he took the post on condition that a Law Commission, a permanent body outside Government, be set up to keep the law up to date. The CLRC's Report on *Conspiracy to Defraud* (1986; Cmnd 9873) was their final piece of work, and they ceased to meet after that.

The Law Commission

1.27   Section 3(1)of the Law Commissions Act 1965 provides that the Law Commission was established to

> take and keep under review all the law ... with a view to its systematic development and reform, including in particular the codification of such law, the elimination of anomalies, the repeal of obsolete and unnecessary enactments, the reduction of the number of separate enactments and generally the simplification and modernisation of the law.

Since that time, the Law Commission has published many reports, some of which have been implemented. There will be frequent reference in this book to such reports. Perhaps the most exciting project was the Draft Criminal Code (DCC), which was laid before Parliament in 1989. The Law Commission summarise the advantages of codification under the following heads:

(i) The constitutional arguments for codification

(ii) Accessibility and comprehensibility

(iii) Consistency

(iv) Certainty

1.28   Although this has not been enacted students may find it useful to look at the DCC. It was published in two volumes, one being the Code itself and the other a commentary to the Law Commission's proposals. The Law Commission, and the small group of senior academic criminal lawyers who produced the first draft, were at pains to draw up a Code of what the law is rather than a Code of what the law should be. The task of reducing the principles of criminal law of England and Wales to one neat Bill was immense, and the Law Commission's frank comments on how they reached the definitions they did, provide a useful commentary on key issues in criminal law. They had the support and help of many within the criminal justice system in putting together the report, which therefore had widespread support. But Parliament's time is scarce, and criminal law is controversial. The Government has not found the time (or the inclination?) to enact the DCC, and so the Law Commission in the 1990s has produced a wealth of smaller bills dealing with only parts of the criminal law in the hope that Parliament may find the time to act on these smaller and less time-consuming Bills.

1.29 The normal practice for the Law Commission is to produce a Consultation Paper, to which interested people are encouraged to respond, and then a Report. Throughout this book there will be references to many of the more important papers and reports to emerge from the Law Commission since the 1989 DCC:

- Law Com No 218 (1993): Legislating the Criminal Code: Offences against the Person and General Principles

- Law Com Consultation Paper No 134 (1994): Consent and Offences against the Person

- Law Com Consultation Paper No 139 (1995): Consent in the Criminal Law

- Law Com No 229 (1995): Legislating the Criminal Code: Intoxication and Criminal Liability

- Law Com 237 (1996): Legislating the Criminal Code: Involuntary Manslaughter

- Law Com Consultation Paper No 155 (1999): Legislating the Criminal Code: Fraud and Deception

Students with enough time on their hands may find it useful to read these reports: they include not only proposals for reform, but useful summaries of current difficulties and dilemmas. But there are few signs that Parliament is ready to take up these projects. In recent years, the Government has had little enthusiasm for tidying up and improving the criminal law, preferring to concentrate on procedural and sentencing matters. Appellate judges will still have a vital role in keeping the criminal law up to date even after a Criminal Code becomes law, but until that time reform of the law remains largely in their hands.

1.30   This is in stark contrast with most other countries which nowadays have a basic criminal law in statutory or codified form. A Code may mean a coherent re-statement of a body of law, or merely a compilation or collection of existing laws. In France, there has been a Code Pénal since 1810, though a new one, passed in 1992, came into force in 1994. Indeed, most European countries have a penal code: the penal codes of Denmark, Finland, France, Germany, Greece, Italy, Norway, Sweden and Turkey are all discussed in Law Com No 139. Nowadays most English-speaking (ie common law) countries also have a codified system of criminal law, at least to the extent that there is a basic criminal statute. The first common law code to be enacted was Macaulay's Indian Penal Code produced in 1837, and enacted in 1860. In the USA, each state has its own criminal law, often much influenced by the American Law Institute's Model Criminal Code produced in 1985. Despite valiant attempts by the Law Commission, there is still little sign of a criminal code reaching the statute book in England and Wales (or Scotland). Many chapters in this book will re-echo this author's wish to see the Government act.

Further reading

Ashworth *Principles of Criminal Law* (3rd edn, 1999)

Devlin *The Enforcement of Morals* (1965)

Devlin, 'The Conscience of the Jury' (1991) 107 LQR 398

Glazebrook 'Should we have a law of attempted crime?' (1969) 85 LQR 27

Hart *Law Liberty and Morality* (1963)

Houlder 'The Importance of Preserving the Jury System' [1997] Crim LR 875

Jackson and Doran *Judge without Jury: Diplock Trials in the Adversary System* (1995)

Padfield *The Criminal Justice Process: Text and Materials* (2nd ed, 2000)

Sharpe 'The European Convention: A Suspects' Charter?' [1997] Crim LR 848

von Hirsch and Jareborg 'Gauging Criminal Harms: a Living Standard Analysis' (1991) 11 OJLS 1

Walker and Padfield *Sentencing: Theory, Law and Practice* (2nd edn, 1996)

Walker *Why Punish?* (1991)

Self-test questions

1. What (if any) are the general principles underpinning the criminal law?

2. Can you explain the relationship between criminal law and morals? Is there any identifiable shared morality nowadays?

3. Why do you think that criminal law is usually studied independently of sentencing, or of criminal procedure and evidence?

4. Is it the role of the Court of Appeal to re-think the jury's decision? If not, what is the function of an appellate court?

5. Consider the arguments for and against codification of the criminal law.

CHAPTER TWO

The conduct element of a crime

SUMMARY
Most crimes require a criminal 'act': this chapter seeks to answer these questions: what is a *voluntary* act (cf automatism)? can one distinguish acts from omissions? Why is a person generally not liable for her failure to act? Note carefully the exceptions to this general rule, particularly the cases where the courts recognise a *duty* to act: what are the rules of causation? A person may cause a consequence which was perhaps unintended and unforeseen. Both factual causation (*but for* causation) and legal (or imputable) causation must be proved. Not all offences require an act: the existence of a *state of affairs* may be sufficient to impose liability. Are such offences drafted too widely?

Actus reus and mens rea

2.1 It has been conventional to divide crimes into two elements: *actus reus* (Latin for guilty act) and *mens rea* (guilty mind), and any crime can be chopped into these elements. For example, murder is the intentional killing of a human being. The *actus reus* of murder is the killing and the *mens rea* is the intention. However, these ambiguous Latin terms may lead to confusion since the *actus reus* or guilty act may include:

(i) a voluntary act, or omission, or a state of affairs,

(ii) as well as particular consequences, and/or

(iii) particular circumstances.

2.2 Thus murder is a crime which requires that D does an act which causes death (the prescribed *consequence*). A person is not guilty of having sex with a girl under 16 unless P proves the *circumstance* of the offence that she was indeed under 16. We will return to the problem of distinguishing the *actus reus* of a crime in chapter 5, when we look at the difficulty of distinguishing the offence (*actus reus*) elements of a crime from its defence elements. It is worth wondering for a moment why we group the circumstances and consequence requirements of an offence under the one label '*actus reus*'. Robinson (1993), for example, points out that by grouping them (as well as the supporting doctrines of causation, voluntary act, omission and possession) under the same heading, we gain no special insight into a characteristic or function that the various doctrines may share. However, having acknowledged the limitations of the labels, this book will continue to use terms which most commentators have adopted as convenient shorthand. Different commentators will define and categorise crimes differently, but the student should be able to distinguish different sorts of criminal conduct:

- act or conduct crimes (those crimes which need no consequence, but are complete as soon as D does a certain act) eg wounding; rape.

- consequence or result crimes (the conduct must bring about a proscribed consequence) eg murder; criminal damage.

- situational crimes (where neither an act or a consequence is necessary) eg possessing illegal drugs.

Voluntary acts

2.3 D's act must be conscious and voluntary. In chapter 4, we consider the defences of insanity and automatism. D may argue that he is not guilty of a crime because his mind was not in control of his actions. From D's point of view, it is better to treat questions of automatism as relevant to the *actus reus*, not *mens rea*: if it is treated as a question of *mens rea*, then D's recklessness can negate any possible argument based on automatism. The same will not be true if automatism is seen as a way of proving that an essential part of the *actus reus* is missing. Defining a voluntary act is no easy business:

Broome v Perkins (1987) D, a diabetic, drove home for five miles very erratically in a hypoglycaemic state. There was evidence that he may not have known what he was doing. Magistrates dismissed a charge of driving without due care and attention against him on the grounds of automatism. DC (Glidewell LJ): remitted the case to the magistrates with the direction to convict. Since D was exercising some control over his bodily movements, his actions were not 'automatic' and 'involuntary'. D had to adduce evidence that his mind was not controlling his limbs (ie of no control) before he could be acquitted.

Antoine(2000) D was charged with murder, and it was argued that he was unfit to plead (see **4.6**). Under the Criminal Procedure (Insanity) Act 1964, s 4A(2) it was then necessary for a jury to decide if 'he did the act or made the omission charged against him as the offence'. The judge ruled that the jury would have to be satisfied that the Crown had proved both *actus reus* and *mens rea*, but that the defence of diminished responsibility (see **8.9**) was not available. HL (Lord Hutton): The defence of diminished responsibility was not available; the jury only need be satisfied that D committed the *actus reus*. D could raise the defences of accident, self-defence or mistake, (which normally raise issues concerning *mens rea*) only if there was 'objective evidence' from a witness that raised an issue under one of the defences.

2.4   When the Law Commission were drawing up the DCC (see **1.27**), they were concerned to find a formula which would lead to the acquittal of someone such as the D in *Broome v Perkins* (subject to the question of prior fault). Clause 33(1) therefore provides that

A person is not guilty of an offence if -
(a) he acts in a state of automatism, that is, his act-
　(i) is a reflex, spasm or convulsion; or
　(ii) occurs while he is in a condition (whether of sleep, unconsciousness, impaired consciousness or otherwise) depriving him of effective control of his act; and
(b) the act or condition is the result neither of anything done or omitted with the fault required for the offence nor of voluntary intoxication.

The DCC test appears to be more 'lenient' than that of *Broome v Perkins*, under which D must be convicted if he shows some control over his actions. The DCC definition would lead to his acquittal if he did not have effective control over his actions. Does this allow the court to acquit him if they judge him not to need punishment?

Liability for omissions

2.5 The person who commits a crime by a failure to act may be as culpable as the person who deliberately acts. Yet English law has traditionally been reluctant to impose liability for omissions because of a fear that this would throw too wide the net of the criminal law. As Lord Diplock said in *Miller* (1983), 'The conduct of the parabolic priest and Levite on the road to Jericho may indeed have been deplorable but English law has not so far developed to the stage of treating it as criminal'. In **2.12** we will consider whether a bolder approach to liability should be applied, but first the situations in which D may or may not be guilty simply for a failure to act will be examined.

2.6 Crimes cannot be committed by omission if the statute creating the offence requires action:

> *Ahmad* (1986) A landlord made major structural alterations to a flat but then took no steps to complete them. He was convicted under the Protection from Eviction Act 1977 of 'doing acts calculated to interfere with [V's] peace and comfort'. CA: D's conviction was quashed since he had not done 'acts' merely by failing to finish the alterations and so leaving the premises uninhabitable.

2.7 Other statutes, on the other hand, use terms which make clear that the person will be guilty if they 'cause' a consequence to happen whether by act or omission. Thus, s 85 (1) of the Water Resources Act 1991 provides that

> a person contravenes this section if he causes or knowingly permits any poisonous, noxious or polluting matter or any solid waste matter to enter any controlled waters (see **13.7**).

The DCC deliberately defines homicide offences in terms of 'causing death' rather than 'killing', and specifies that under the Code such results may be caused by omission (see **8.7**).

2.8 With common law offences, the position is particularly difficult. Although the basic rule is that D is not generally liable for a failure to act there are a number of ways of avoiding this limitation. One way to explain liability for an omission is to describe a series of acts and events as one continuous act:

> *Fagan v Metropolitan Police Comr* (1969) D stopped his car accidentally on a policeman's foot, but then refused to move it for several minutes. He was convicted of assaulting the police officer in the execution of his duty. DC: upheld his conviction. D's conduct in driving the car on to the foot and leaving it there should be viewed as a continuous act: once he developed a guilty mind, the crime was committed. Note the dissenting judgement of Bridge J, who argued that D had done no act after driving on to the foot which could constitute an assault: allowing the wheel to remain on the foot was merely an omission for which there was no liability.

2.9 This case illustrates the principle that the *actus reus* and *mens rea* should be contemporaneous. In *Fagan*, D developed the guilty mind after he had done the culpable act. The problem may also arise where D no longer has the guilty mind when he does the relevant act:

> *Meli v R* (1954) D beat up V in a hut, and then threw him over a cliff, believing him to be dead. Medical evidence showed that V died from exposure at the bottom of the cliff and not from the beating. D therefore argued that his act of causing death (throwing V over the cliff) was not accompanied by *mens rea*. PC: upholding the conviction, the whole matter was one transaction which should be regarded as a single course of conduct.

> *Le Brun* (1992) D hit his wife, V, on the jaw. She fell unconscious. Attempting to carry her home, he dropped her and she died of a fractured skull caused when her head hit the pavement. CA (Lord Lane CJ): dismissed his appeal from his conviction for manslaughter. 'The act which causes death and the necessary mental state to constitute manslaughter need not coincide in point of time'.

2.10 *Duty to act* It is more common (and perhaps easier) to create liability for an omission by proving that D was under a duty to act. Such duties arise in a number of different ways:

25

(i) A person who creates a dangerous situation may be under a duty to act to remove the danger:

> *Miller* (1983) D fell asleep holding a lit cigarette. He was awoken by a small fire, and merely moved to a different room without attempting to put out the fire. HL: upheld his conviction for arson. Lord Diplock's main speech is worth studying. He deprecates the use of the expression *actus reus*, and compares the different academic analyses which explain liability in these circumstances. Whilst he prefers JC Smith's 'duty theory' to Glanville Williams' adoption of the continuing act theory, he suggests the term 'responsibility theory' as it may be easier to explain to a jury.

Few would disagree with the conclusion of this case, though Ashworth does ask whether it is objectionable on grounds of retroactivity and lack of warning (see PCL page and **1.5**).

(ii) A duty may arise from a special relationship such as that of parent/child, or doctor/patient.

(iii) If D voluntarily undertakes a duty, then a failure to undertake that duty may result in liability.

> *Gibbins and Proctor* (1918) V's father and his mistress starved him to death. CCA: upheld their convictions for murder.

> *Stone and Dobinson* (1977) Ds, a man and his mistress, made little attempt to seek medical attention for V, his sister, who died whilst a lodger in their care. CA (Geoffrey Lane LJ): upheld their convictions for manslaughter. The jury were entitled to find that the duty to care had been assumed, and once V became helplessly infirm, they had a duty either to summon help or to care for her themselves.

(iv) If a duty to act is created by statute, then failure to fulfil that duty will result in criminal liability. Thus a positive duty is imposed by s 1 of the CYPA 1933 on parents and those who are legally responsible for children to provide food, clothing, medical aid and lodging for their children, creating the offence of wilful neglect.

(v) A contract with a third party may give rise to a general duty to act.

Pittwood (1902) A railway crossing guard opened the gates to let a vehicle through, but then forgot to shut them again. V, a man in a cart, was hit and killed by a later train. Taunton Assizes: Wright J: there was clearly misfeasance since D directly contributed to the accident. A man may incur criminal liability from a duty arising out of a contract.

However, although this case is often quoted as illustrating contractual liability resulting in criminal liability for omissions, it could just as well be seen as an example of (i) above.

2.11 Distinguishing between an act and an omission can itself be difficult. Medical treatment is a good example: when a doctor turns off a life support machine he would appear to do an act which causes death, whereas if he doesn't replace an empty drip bag he merely omits to do something. Smith & Hogan, having asked whether the ending of a programme of dialysis is an omission, while switching off a ventilator is an act, conclude that 'it seems offensive if liability for homicide depends on distinctions of this kind; but it appears to be so' (at page 49).

Airedale NHS Trust, ex p Bland (1993) A patient had been in a persistent vegetative state (PVS) for more than two years, and his parents supported the hospital in its application to be allowed to turn off his life support machine. HL: unanimously held that if the doctors did so in this case, they would not be criminally liable. Students might like to read Hoffman LJ's judgment in the CA (he was the only judge to explore the moral issues in depth). The HL agreed that doctors were not obliged to continue care and treatment where it was no longer in the patient's best interests, accepting that nasal feeding was treatment. Indeed, 3 of the 5 Law Lords called for Parliamentary intervention in this area, but none has yet been forthcoming (see Helme and Padfield (1993)).

The HL's reasoning is not entirely convincing. Not only is the distinction between causing death and allowing someone to die dubious (see *Re B* (1981); *Re J* (1991)); the case does not explore the question of intent adequately. It might be more helpful if the courts were prepared to hold that a doctor in these circumstances has fulfilled her duties, and that there is therefore no *actus reus* on which to base liability.

2.12 Is it time to widen liability for omissions? Ashworth (see (1989) 105 LQR 424) has suggested that the law should move towards a 'social responsibility' view of criminal liability, recognising certain duties of citizenship and equally recognising the limits on what it is fair to ask of citizens. Thus he suggests that it is appropriate to penalise those who fail to take steps towards law enforcement or who fail to assist those in sudden peril. Glanville Williams responded at (1991) 107 LQR 86 by defending individualism. He believed that there is a moral distinction between killing and letting die which the law should recognise.

2.13 Later we shall see (at **11.39**) that people can be deceived by silence – is this a form of liability by an omission?

> *Firth* (1989) D, a consultant obstetrician, omitted to inform his hospital that he had been treating private patients at his NHS hospital and had therefore avoided being billed for NHS beds and facilities. CA (Lord Lane CJ): upheld his conviction for an offence under s 2(1)(c) TA 1978. If it was incumbent upon him to give the information to the hospital and he deliberately refrained from doing so, with the result that no charge was levied either upon the patients or upon himself, the wording of the section is satisfied. 'It mattered not whether it was an act of commission or omission'.

Causation

2.14 Many crimes require a certain consequence to have been caused by the criminal act. Thus, in murder or manslaughter, the act must cause death. For how remote a consequence of my act should I be held responsible? The rules have become relatively clear in homicide offences, and can be applied generally throughout the criminal law where *mens rea* is required. We will see later that some crimes do not require *mens rea*. These 'strict liability' offences (see **3.38**) may deal differently with the question of causation. This will become particularly obvious in chapter 13 which explores environmental offences.

First, factual causation must be established: it must be proved that the death would not have resulted 'but for' the accused's conduct.

White (1910) D was indicted for the murder of his mother having put cyanide in her drink intending to kill her. Medical evidence showed that she had died of heart failure before drinking the poisoned drink, and he was convicted of attempted murder. CA: dismissed his appeal (and upheld his sentence of penal servitude for life).

The case is a useful example of 'but for' causation: the cyanide did not kill her, and so even though he intended to kill her and she died, he could not be guilty of murder.

2.15 In manslaughter cases (see **8.31**) questions of factual causation are often swallowed up within a discussion of dangerousness. As we shall see, D is guilty of manslaughter if he intentionally does an unlawful and dangerous act which causes death. It must be dangerous in the sense that all sober and reasonable people would realise that the act would subject the victim to the risk of harm. The question is often how much knowledge of the circumstances should be attributed to this fictional bystander: contrast these two cases:

Dawson (1985) Three Ds wearing masks, one carrying a replica gun and another carrying a pickaxe handle, attempted to rob a petrol station. They fled when the attendant, V, pushed an alarm, but V later died of a heart attack. CA (Watson LJ): quashed their convictions for manslaughter. A key element in the decision was the fact that it was not suggested that any of the Ds knew that V had a weak heart. (All three were also convicted of offences of robbery and attempted robbery, and their sentences of $7^1/_2$ to $9^1/_2$ years' imprisonment were upheld).

Watson (1989) D and another man burgled the house of a man aged 87, who died of a heart attack 90 minutes later. CA: upheld their conviction for manslaughter: Ds knew of the old man's frailty, even though they only discovered it once they had broken in.

2.16 *Legal (or imputable) causation* This 'but for' test is not enough on its own, since it might lead to the conviction of the morally innocent: A invites B to her house, and B is murdered on the way. Clearly A is not guilty of murder. The obvious reason is that she has no guilty mind or guilty intent. But the law seems to go further and often seems to suggest that A has not even 'caused' B's death. There are several additions to the 'but for' test, often referred to as questions of legal, or as Glanville Williams would prefer, 'imputable' causation (see TCL, page 381). As you read the following paragraphs, ask yourself why it is that causation is not established independently of culpability.

2.17   D must have performed a culpable act. Thus, in a 'result crime', the culpable act must have caused the result, and in a 'conduct crime', the culpable act is the culpable element in the conduct.

> *Dalloway* (1847) V, a child, ran in front of D's cart and was killed. D was not holding the reins, but had left them lying loosely on the horse's back. D was acquitted after Earle J had summed up to the jury that if they thought that he could not have saved the child by pulling the reins, they must acquit him: ie he was only guilty if his neglect in not holding the reins had been the cause of death. The presence of the cart caused the child's death, and not the negligent driving. There was no causal connection: the child would have been killed even if he had been driving carefully.

2.18   D's act must be more than a minimal cause of the result.

> *Cato* (1976) D injected V with a heroin compound at her request. V died. CA: upheld D's conviction for manslaughter. Lord Widgery CJ: 'As a matter of law, it was sufficient if the prosecution could establish that it was a cause, provided it was a cause outside the *de minimis* range, and effectively bearing upon the acceleration of the moment of the victim's death'.

Ashworth points out that the court in *Cato* may have been using causal arguments to circumscribe the law of manslaughter: 'if the offence charged had been a crime of intention in which D's intention had been proved, the court would probably have taken a broader view' (PCL, page 127). What is *de minimis*? In *Hennigan (1971)* the CA held that the trial judge was wrong to direct the jury that D was not guilty if he was less than one-fifth to blame.

> *Dyson* (1908) D's child, V, died of injuries he received from D more than a year before his death. V was dying of meningitis and would have died within a short time despite his injuries. CA: quashed D's conviction for manslaughter since V had not died within a year and

a day of his injuries (this is no longer the law: see **8.4**). The fact that V's death was an imminent event was not the reason for quashing the conviction: D's act had accelerated death.

2.19   In clause 17(1), the DCC puts the test this way:

> ... a person causes a result which is an element of an offence when –
> (a) he does an act which makes a more than negligible contribution to its occurrence; or
> (b) he omits to do an act which might prevent its occurrence and which he is under a duty to do according to the law relating to the offence.

Glanville Williams (1989) argued that this definition fails because it 'does not give even the barest indication that a question of moral responsibility or justice is involved' (at page 397). For him, clause 17(a) is open to the criticism that it fails to distinguish between factual and imputable causation. He preferred to redraft the clause in the following way:

> (1) Subject to the other provisions of this section, a person causes a result which is an element of an offence when he does an act which
> (a) in fact causes or contributes to its occurrence, and
> (b) is not too remote, too trivial or too accidental to have a just bearing on the doer's liability or on the gravity of his offence.

To those who object to the word 'just' in this definition, he responds that it makes clear that a question of justice is involved, which enables the tribunal to exercise a degree of discretion.

2.20   A *novus actus interveniens* which absolves the defendant of liability. Examples include:

(a) outrageously incompetent medical treatment:

> *Jordan* (1956) D stabbed V who died eight days later in hospital when the wound had largely healed but after the V had been wrongly injected with a drug and a large quantity of liquid which caused his death. CCA: D's conviction for manslaughter was quashed since the medical treatment was 'palpably wrong'.

> *Cheshire* (1991) D shot V in the thigh and stomach whilst they were arguing in a fish and chip shop. V died not of the wounds, but of a

tracheotomy performed whilst he was in hospital to help him breath. CA: upheld his conviction for murder.

Even though negligence in the treatment of the victim was the immediate cause of his death, the jury should not regard it as excluding the responsibility of the accused unless the negligent treatment was so independent of his acts, and in itself so potent in causing death, that they regard the contribution made by his acts as insignificant (per Beldam LJ).

How does one reconcile these two cases? There is a clear hint in *Cheshire* that Ds should not avoid liability for the consequences of their acts just because of the actions of doctors. Why is this? In an appropriate case, D could in any case be found guilty of attempted murder or of wounding.

(b) acts of the victim. Sometimes V's own act may be said to break the chain of causation. However, it is more common for the courts to hold that D 'must take his victim as he finds him', and apply the 'thin skull rule'. Thus even if there is something unusual about V's physical or emotional make-up such that the consequence is much more serious than D could have foreseen, he may still be liable:

Holland (1841) V refused to have his finger amputated after he had been wounded by D, despite a surgeon's advice that this was the best form of treatment. He died of lockjaw (tetanus). KB: convicted D of murder.

Blaue (1975) D stabbed a Jehovah's Witness, who refused a blood transfusion and died. CA: upheld D's conviction for manslaughter. Lawton LJ:

It has long been the policy of the law that those who use violence on other people must take their victims as they find them. This in our judgement means the whole man, not just the physical man. It does not lie in the mouth of the assailant to say that his victim's religious beliefs which inhibited him from accepting certain kinds of treatment were unreasonable. The question for decision is what caused her death. The answer is the stab wound. The fact that the victim refused to stop this end coming about did not break the causal connection between the act and the death.

Williams (1992) V, a hitch-hiker, having been threatened by Ds, jumped out of their car and died of his injuries. CA (Stuart-Smith LJ): quashed D's conviction for manslaughter. D was guilty if V's attempted escape was proportionate to the threat, that is to say, that it was within the ambit of reasonableness and not so daft as to make it his own voluntary act which amounted to a *novus actus interveniens*.

In judging whether V acted reasonably, the jury should take in to account 'any particular characteristic of the victim and the fact that in the agony of the moment he may act without thought and deliberation'.

Notman (1994) D charged at a policeman, V, who injured his own ankle when attempting to trip D up. CA: upheld D's conviction for assault occasioning actual bodily harm.

In many cases, the 'thin skull rule' may lead to no injustice since D may not be convicted if he does not have the *mens rea* for the unusual consequence: D may only be convicted of murder, for example, if he intended to kill or cause grievous bodily harm. But is it right in principle that someone is held responsible for consequences more serious than they could have foreseen? Does it stretch the principles of causation too far?

(c) naturally occurring unpredictable events:

Allen (in his *Textbook on Criminal Law*, 3rd ed, at page 40) provides the example of D rendering V unconscious and leaving him in a building which is then blown up by a bomb planted by terrorists. In this case, D will not be held to have caused D's death.

2.21 These rules of imputable or legal causation have developed because of a reluctance to convict of homicide someone who is not considered adequately blameworthy. Thus Glanville Williams writes

when one has settled the question of but-for causation, the further test to be applied to the but-for cause in order to qualify it for legal recognition is not a test of causation but a moral reaction. The question is whether the result can fairly be said to be imputable to the defendant ... If the term cause must be used, it can best be distinguished in this meaning as the 'imputable' or 'responsible' or 'blameable' cause, to indicate the value-judgment involved (TCL, page 381).

2.22 Why should a value judgement be involved? As Norrie (1991) points out, causation can only be explained by taking into account the social context within which people act. But is this necessarily the case? If policy considerations are to affect criminal liability, they could as well be reserved for the *mens rea* element. Glanville Williams poses the troubling example of tobacco companies: can they be prosecuted for manslaughter in causing the death of smokers? His answer is clear: no, they do not 'cause' death. But even in manslaughter, liability does not necessarily follow just because causation is established: some kind of *mens rea* has to be proved, involving perhaps the running of an unjustifiable risk (see **8.28**). Largely for autonomy reasons perhaps, English law appears to say that the risks taken by tobacco companies are justifiable. But these policy questions could be dealt with as part of the *mens rea* of the offence, and need not necessarily be treated as questions of causation. To return to the example given earlier of A and B, A did not intend to kill, nor was it virtually certain that B would be killed when A invited her to visit her house. What is the problem with accepting that A's invitation was one of the causes of B's death? Commenting on the interaction of causation and culpability, Ashworth talks of 'the puissance of culpability over causation' (PCL, page 127). Questions of culpability dominate even questions of causation.

2.23 So far we have been looking at causation issues in relation to homicide cases. Interestingly the courts seem to have taken a different attitude in crimes of strict liability (see **3.38**). Thus, in pollution cases, the courts have treated the word 'causing' in a much more straightforward way, perhaps because the courts are less interested in these cases with questions of blameworthiness than with the idea of making the polluter pay:

> *Alphacell Ltd v Woodward* (1972) Pumps in a settling tank became blocked and the tank overflowed, allowing polluted water to escape into a stream. D, the company who operated the settling tanks, were convicted of causing polluting matter to enter a stream. HL: upheld their conviction.

> > I consider ... that what or who has caused a certain event to occur is essentially a practical question of fact which can best be answered by ordinary common sense rather than abstract metaphysical theory (per Lord Salmon).

We will look more at environmental crimes in chapter 13. For the moment, simply bear in mind that there is no easy answer to causation issues. Is it wiser to leave the issue as a question of fact for the jury, or should judges advise them on causation as a matter of law?

State of affairs

2.24 Some offences require neither an act or an omission, but merely a status or a state of affairs.

> *Larsonneur* (1933) D was deported from Ireland and brought reluctantly into this country by the police. CCA: upheld her conviction for 'being found in the UK', contrary to the Aliens Order 1920.

> *Winzar v Chief Constable of Kent* (1983) The police removed D from a hospital where he was found drunk and put him in the street. He was then charged with 'being found drunk on the highway'. DC: upheld his conviction.

These cases have been widely criticised: what act of D's caused him or her to commit the crime? But it is the wide drafting of the offence which is at fault rather than its interpretation by the courts. Similarly with drug possession offences, which normally require only that D possessed the substance voluntarily. Thus s 5 of the Misuse of Drugs Act 1971 provides simply that 'it is an offence for a person to have a controlled drug in his possession'.

2.25 Even where no knowledge is required in respect of the nature of what D possesses, D must know that he possesses something:

> *Warner v Metropolitan Police Comr* (1969) D was charged with possessing drugs contrary to the Drugs (Prevention of Misuse) Act 1964. She believed the stuff she possessed was scent. HL: upheld her conviction. Lord Wilberforce: the jury must make the decision whether, in addition to physical control, D has, or ought to have imputed to him the intention to possess, or knowledge that he does possess, what is in fact a prohibited substance. If he has this intention or knowledge, it is not additionally necessary that he should know the nature of the substance.

However, in most crimes, the state of affairs or surrounding circumstances are only one part of the *actus reus*. There will be an 'act' as well. For example, s 20 of the SOA 1956 involves taking an unmarried girl under the age of 16 out of the possession of her parent or guardian against the parent or guardian's will. Here the surrounding circumstances are that the girl must be unmarried, under 16, in the possession of her parent or guardian, and that they do not wish her to leave. The guilty act narrowly defined is simply the 'taking' of the girl. As we shall see in the next chapter, different *mens rea* requirements may apply to different elements of the *actus reus*.

Further reading

Norrie, 'A Critique of Criminal Causation'(1991) 54 MLR 685

Padfield, 'Clean Water and Muddy Causation' [1995] Crim LR 683

Glanville Williams, '*Finis* for *Novus Actus?*' (1989) Camb LJ 391

Robinson 'Should the criminal law abandon the *Actus-Reus-Mens rea* distinction?' in *Action and Value in Criminal Law* (eds Shute, Gardner and Horder)(1993)

Self-test questions

1. As Dee sneezes, she hits Phil in the face. He develops a black eye: would English law say that Dee 'caused' the injury?

2. The parents of a severely handicapped baby instruct the doctors in the hospital where she is born to give her no treatment. They say that if she is not allowed to die, they will not take her home and care for her. The doctors agree to withdraw treatment, and the baby dies. Consider the criminal liability of both the parents and the doctors.

3. Dee stabs Phil causing him serious but not necessarily fatal injuries. A surgeon gives him an experimental form of treatment which fails to stop the bleeding. Phil dies. Medical experts say that with the

benefit of hindsight the treatment was probably wrong. Discuss Dee's criminal liability.

4. David rapes Violet who is a member of a religious group which emphasises the value of virginity at marriage. Overcome by shame, Violet commits suicide. Discuss the criminal liability of David.

CHAPTER THREE

Criminal states of mind

SUMMARY

This chapter examines various states of mind which may lead to criminal liability:

Intention: Intention is not the same as motive. Distinguish direct intent from inferred intent: an intent may be inferred when the consequence is virtually certain to follow from what D does, even if D did not want it to happen (*Nedrick*).

Knowledge and belief: wilful blindness may constitute knowledge.

Recklessness: For many years recklessness was interpreted subjectively (*Cunningham*) ie D is reckless if he consciously takes a risk; now the concept is interpreted objectively in some contexts (eg criminal damage: *Caldwell*). D is objectively reckless if he gives no thought to an obvious risk. The concept therefore has to be examined carefully in different contexts.

Negligence: Distinguish gross negligence from mere negligence ie carelessness.

Strict liability: common in 'regulatory' offences, this means that D may be guilty even though he did not know that he was doing wrong.

3.1 The criminal law should penalise the blameworthy. In the last chapter we looked particularly at those harms, or acts, which may lead to criminal liability. The emphasis of this chapter is on the mental element in crimes, often known by the Latin expression *mens rea*, or guilty mind. *Mens rea* means something very different in relation to different crimes. As Lord Simon said in *DPP v Majewski* (1977), the *mens rea* is ... the state of mind stigmatised as wrongful by the criminal law which, when compounded with the relevant prohibited conduct, constitutes a particular offence.

Some crimes need intention as the *mens rea*, some recklessness, others a different state of mind (or none at all). In some crimes, the relevant *mens rea* extends to the whole of the *actus reus*, in others to only part. Different elements of a crime may have different *mens rea* requirements. For example, s 15 of the TA 1968 defines the common offence of obtaining property by deception. Whereas the 'main' part of the *mens rea* may be the intention to permanently deprive another person of their property, s 15(4) makes clear that the deception itself may be deliberate or reckless. And some concepts (such as recklessness) are interpreted very differently in different contexts. The key questions to be kept in mind throughout this chapter is whether the criminal law gets it right: decide whether you believe the 'right' people are considered blameworthy.

Intention

3.2 Intention is used in relation to consequences: thus, a person may be said to intend the consequence of his actions if he wants them to happen. This is true whether or not it is likely to happen. For example, liability for criminal attempts depends on intent (see **7.8**). If you shoot at me wanting to kill me and miss, you will still be guilty of attempted murder whether you were standing next door to me or a hundred metres away. This meaning of intent is often referred to as 'direct intent'.

3.3 A person's motive, or reason, for doing something is usually not relevant to liability (though good motives may result in lower sentences).

> *Steane* (1947) D, a British subject, broadcast propaganda for the Germans during the Second World War. He said he had done it simply to save his wife and children who were still in Germany. He was convicted of intentionally doing acts likely to assist the enemy. CCA (Lord Goddard): allowed D's appeal. If on the totality of the evidence there is room for more than one view as to D's intent, the jury should be directed that it is for P to prove the intent to the jury's satisfaction. They would not be entitled to presume a criminal intent if circumstances were consistent with an innocent intent such as a desire to save his wife and children.

This case has been much criticised because the court appeared to quash the conviction on the ground that D may have lacked *mens rea*. Would it be more appropriate to say that he did have the necessary intent, but that he had the benefit of the defence of duress (see **5.13**)?

3.4 The following case (which was not a criminal one) also poses problems in distinguishing motive from intent:

> *Gillick v West Norfolk and Wisbech Area Health Authority* (1986) P sought judicial review of a Department of Health memorandum which said that in exceptional cases a doctor could prescribe contraceptive pills to a girl under the age of 16 without informing her parents. HL: held that the memorandum was not unlawful. A child becomes increasingly independent as she grows older and the law does not recognise any rule of absolute parental authority until a fixed age. The *bona fide* exercise by a doctor of his clinical judgment negated the *mens rea* which would be an essential ingredient of an offence under s 6 (intercourse with a girl under 16) or s 28 (causing or encouraging under-age sex) of the SOA 1956.

The main interest of the case lies in the failure of the judges to be very clear as to why any such doctor would not be aiding and abetting unlawful sexual intercourse (ie intentionally helping the boyfriend commit the offence). Is it because:

(i) the doctor has a defence of necessity? or because

(ii) the 'intent' necessary for aiding and abetting is a different sort of 'direct intent'? The case is discussed further at **5.20** and **6.18**.

3.5 Another example of the relationship between intent and motive is found at **7.19**: in *Yip Chiu-cheung v R* (1994) the PC decided that a drugs dealer could be guilty of conspiring with an undercover drug enforcement officer: even where the undercover agent is acting courageously and with the best of motives (trying to break a drugs ring), he nonetheless 'intends' to commit the offence of importing illegal drugs through customs. Lord Griffiths made clear that a good motive is not itself a defence given that all the ingredients of the offence are present.

3.6 *Oblique intent* Someone may also 'intend' the consequence of his act even if he does not necessarily want it to happen, where he knows that the consequence is virtually certain to happen. His culpability may be as great: if I blow up an aeroplane simply to claim insurance on the cargo, not caring whether or not the pilot is killed, do I intend to kill the pilot? A little statutory help is to be found in s 8 of the CJA 1967:

> A court or jury, in determining whether a person has committed an offence –
> (a) shall not be bound in law to infer that he intended or foresaw a result of his actions by reason only of its being a natural and probable consequence of those actions; but
> (b) shall decide whether he did intend or foresee that result by reference to all the evidence, drawing such inferences from the evidence as appear proper in the circumstances.

3.7 Many of the difficult cases have arisen in the context of murder, since D is only guilty of murder if she intends to kill or cause grievous bodily harm (see also **8.2**).

> *Hyam v DPP* (1975) D poured petrol through the letterbox of the house of her rival and set fire to it. In the resulting house fire, two girls were killed. HL (by a majority of 3 to 2): upheld her conviction for murder, though the three judges in the majority appeared to give different reasons for their decision. According to Lord Cross, mere foresight of probability was enough to allow the jury to infer intent, whereas Viscount Dilhorne felt that foresight of high probability was more appropriate. Lord Hailsham stated that foresight of probability or high probability were too vague, and he concluded that D could be said to intend death if she 'intended to create a risk of death or serious bodily harm'. Lords Diplock and Kilbrandon dissented.

3.8 This case caused a decade of uncertainty, exacerbated by the fact that there were five separate speeches in the HL. It also seemed for a while after *Hyam* that intention might mean different things in different contexts. Two cases reveal the CA's attempts to limit the application of the wide definition of *Hyam*:

> *Mohan* (1976) D drove his car at V, a policeman, in order to escape. V jumped out of the way, but D was charged with, and convicted of, attempting to cause bodily harm to the police officer. CA: quashed his conviction. In order to prove an attempt to commit a crime (see **7.4**), P has to prove a specific intent ie a decision by D to bring about,

so far as it lay within his power, the commission of the offence which it was alleged that he had attempted to commit. It was not sufficient to establish that he knew or foresaw that the consequences of his act would be likely to be the commission of the completed offence: a reckless state of mind was not sufficient.

Belfon (1976) D attacked V with a razor causing him serious injury, and was convicted of wounding with intent to do grievous bodily harm contrary to s18 of the OAPA 1861 (see **9.2**). CA: quashed his conviction on the basis that the fact that D had foreseen that serious harm was likely to result from his acts, or that he had been reckless whether such harm would result, did not constitute the necessary intent.

3.9 Even in murder cases, there was much disquiet, though the issue was not faced again by the HL for another decade:

Moloney (1985) D shot V, his step-father, dead in a drunken game. He was convicted of murder. HL: unanimously agreed that the murder conviction should be replaced by one of manslaughter. Lord Bridge, giving the leading speech, held that murder is a crime of intention only. Intention should have the same meaning throughout the criminal law, and a judge should leave it where possible to the jury's good sense to decide whether D acted with the necessary intent without any elaboration or paraphrase of what is meant by intent. D's foresight of the probability of a consequence does not of itself amount to intention but may be evidence of it. D could be said to intend death where (i) death was a natural consequence of D's voluntary act and (ii) D foresaw that consequence as being a natural consequence of his act.

This decision had the advantage of getting rid of the confusion between probability and intention, but was itself very ambiguous. What is or is not a natural consequence of shooting at someone? It was hardly surprising that within a year the HL had revisited the issue:

Hancock and Shankland (1986) Ds, on strike during a miners' strike, dropped a concrete block off a motorway bridge intending to frighten V, a taxi driver taking strike breakers to work. V was killed, and Ds were convicted of murder. HL (Lord Scarman gave the only speech):

43

upheld CA's decision to substitute a manslaughter verdict. Lord Scarman suggested that the 'natural consequence' test of *Moloney* was too wide, concluding that the guidelines to juries require a reference to probability. They also require an explanation that the greater the probability of a consequence the more likely it is that the consequence was foreseen and that if that consequence was foreseen the greater the probability is that that consequence was also intended. But juries also require to be reminded that the decision is theirs to be reached upon a consideration of all the evidence.

3.10 The point did not reach the HL again for another decade, as the courts seem to accept that a workable definition of intent had been achieved:

Nedrick (1986) D poured paraffin through the letter box of the house of a woman against who he had a grudge, and set fire to it. A child was killed, and D was convicted of murder. CA: reduced his conviction to manslaughter. Lord Lane CJ held that

(A) When determining whether the defendant had the necessary intent, it may therefore be helpful for a jury to ask themselves two questions.
(1) How probable was the consequence which resulted from the defendant's voluntary act?
(2) Did he foresee that consequence? If he did not appreciate that death or serious harm was likely to result from his act, he cannot have intended to bring it about. If he did, but thought that the risk to which he was exposing the person killed was only slight, then it may be easy for the jury to conclude that he did not intend to bring about that result. On the other hand, if the jury are satisfied that at the material time the defendant recognised that death or serious harm would be virtually certain (barring some unforeseen intervention) to result from his voluntary act, then that is a fact from which they may find it easy to infer that he intended to kill or do serious bodily harm, even though he may not have had any desire to achieve that result.
(B) Where the charge is murder and in the rare cases where the simple direction is not enough, the jury should be directed that they are not entitled to infer the necessary intention, unless they feel sure that death or serious bodily harm was a virtual certainty (barring some unforeseen intervention) as a result of the defendant's actions and that the defendant appreciated that such was the case.
(C) Where a man realises that it is for all practical purposes inevitable

that his actions will result in death or serious harm, the inference may be irresistible that he intended that result, however little he may have desired or wished it to happen. The decision is one for the jury to be reached upon a consideration of all the evidence. (Lettering added by Lord Steyn in *Woollin* (see below).)

3.11   Buxton (1988) called the position post-*Nedrick* an 'admittedly fragile equilibrium'. However, the question whether judges should make any attempt to define an ordinary word such as 'intention' at all was revisited by the House of Lords in *Woollin*:

> *Woollin* (1999) A was convicted of the murder of his three-month-old baby. The Crown's case had been that in throwing the baby against something hard he must have realised that what he was doing was virtually certain to cause serious injury. HL: allowed his appeal.

> > In my view Lord Lane's judgment in *Nedrick* provided valuable assistance to trial judges. The model direction is by now a tried-and-tested formula. Trial judges ought to continue to use it ... First, I am persuaded by the speech of my noble and learned friend, Lord Hope of Craighead, that it is unlikely, if ever, to be helpful to direct the jury in terms of the two questions set out in (A). I agree that these questions may detract from the clarity of the critical direction in (B). Secondly, in their writings ... Glanville Williams, JC Smith and Andrew Ashworth observed that the use of the words 'to infer' in (B) may detract from the clarity of the model direction. I agree. I would substitute the words 'to find.' Thirdly, the first sentence of (C) does not form part of the model direction. But it would always be right for the judge to say, as Lord Lane put it, that the decision is for the jury upon a consideration of all the evidence in the case.

We will see later that when judges are summing up to juries on the meaning of the word 'dishonestly' (see 11.13), they advise them to give the word its ordinary meaning. Even here, a certain freedom is given to the trial judge to decide in an individual case how much of a definition of 'intention' he or she should give to the jury.

Clause 18(b)(ii) of the DCC states that for Code purposes,

> a person acts ... 'intentionally' with respect to -
> (i) a circumstance when he hopes or knows that it exists or will exist;
> (ii) a result when he acts either in order to bring it about or being aware that it will occur in the ordinary course of events.

Does this sum up the position today, or is this a wider definition than that to be found in *Nedrick/Woollin?*

3.12 *Specific intent* As well as referring to direct and oblique intent, students will find many references to specific intent, particularly in the context of crimes in respect of which drunkenness may be a defence. In essence, drunkenness may be used to show that D did not have the required *mens rea* in crimes of specific intent (see **4.18**). But beware: the terms specific and direct intent are not magic formulae, and you may find some judges/writers using them interchangeably.

3.13 *Ulterior intent* A final form of intent is referred to as ulterior intent: where there is an additional *mens rea* requirement of the crime which is not directly related to an ingredient of the *actus reus:* For example,

(i) s 18 of the OAPA 1961: Causing grievous bodily harm with intent to do grievous bodily harm or with intent to resist arrest.

(ii) s 9(1)(a) of the TA 1968: Burglary by entering a building with intent to steal, inflict grievous bodily harm, rape or cause damage.

Here the word 'intent' bears the same meaning as it does in murder (see above).

Knowledge and belief

3.14 Many crimes require that D should 'knowingly' do something. Even 'wilful blindness' may constitute 'knowledge': English law treats someone as knowing something if, being pretty sure that it is so, he deliberately avoids asking questions which might confirm the fact. D must normally be judged on the facts as he believes them to be (though some mistakes must be reasonable if they are to absolve D from liability: see **5.27**).

> *Taaffe* (1984) D thought he was importing illegal currency into England. Importing currency was not at the time illegal, but D was in fact importing cannabis. He pleaded guilty to 'being knowingly concerned in the importation of cannabis resin, contrary to s 170(2) of the Customs and Excise Management Act 1979' after the judge

ruled that he would have to direct the jury to convict. HL: upheld the decision of the CA to allow the appeal. D was judged on the facts as he believed them to be, ie that he was importing currency. His mistake of fact that importing currency was unlawful could not convert an innocent act into a criminal offence.

3.15 Clause 18 of the DCC provides that

a person acts -
(a) knowingly with respect to a circumstance not only when he is aware that it exists or will exist, but also when he avoids taking steps that might confirm his belief that it exists or will exist.

To illustrate this test, the Law Commission give the example of D who is handed a packet by E. The packet contains heroin. D chooses not to open the packet and therefore does not see what it contains. If D believes it to contain heroin, he is 'knowingly' in possession of heroin.

3.16 Knowledge and belief are obviously close relations, but knowledge implies that the belief is correct whereas a belief may be mistaken. Thus, a belief that the goods are stolen is a necessary ingredient in the offence of handling stolen goods, contrary to s 22 of the TA 1968 (see **11.44**). Boreham J said in *Hall* (1985):

Belief, of course, is something short of knowledge. It may be said to be the state of mind of a person who says to himself: 'I cannot say I know for certain that these goods are stolen, but there can be no other reasonable conclusion in the light of all the circumstances, in the light of all that I have heard and seen'.

Recklessness

3.17 Someone is reckless if he or she takes unjustified risks. Recklessness is the necessary *mens rea* for many offences: rape, criminal damage, arson, assault, wounding ... Perhaps it is simply the huge variety of offences which rely on recklessness as the basis of the necessary guilty mind which has given rise to the difficulties in its definition. The degree of risk will vary from offence to offence, and a person may be reckless in respect of acts, circumstances or consequences (see **2.2**).

3.18 *Subjective recklessness* This is the least controversial interpretation of the word:

> *Cunningham* (1957) D tore a gas meter from the wall of an unoccupied house in order to steal the money in the meter. Escaping gas seeped through the wall to the next door house where V was partially asphyxiated. D was convicted of maliciously administering a noxious thing contrary to s 23 of the OAPA 1961 (see **11.30**). CCA: quashed his conviction. The Court specifically adopted Professor Kenny's statement that in any statutory definition of a crime 'malice' must be taken not in the old vague sense of 'wickedness' in general, but as requiring either (i) an actual intention to do the particular kind of harm that in fact was done, or (ii) recklessness as to whether such harm should occur or not (ie the accused has foreseen that the particular kind of harm might be done, and yet has gone on to take the risk of it). It is neither limited to, nor does it indeed require, any ill-will towards the person injured.

3.19 Another illustration of this test at work is *Stephenson*, though this case has probably been overruled by *Caldwell* (see **3.22**):

> *Stephenson* (1979) D went to sleep in a haystack and lit a fire to keep warm. He was charged with arson under s 1 of the Criminal Damage Act 1971. The only evidence for the defence was a consultant psychiatrist who said that D had a long history of schizophrenia and was quite capable of lighting a fire to keep warm without taking the danger into account. CA (Geoffrey Lane LJ): quashed his conviction. D was in a mental condition which might have prevented him from appreciating the risk which would have been obvious to any normal person, and this should have been left clearly to the jury.

3.20 The HL in *Savage* (1992) confirmed that this is the test which is applied to all offences under the OAPA 1861 which specify 'maliciously' (see **9.10**). It also applies to rape, where the D must be proved to have been reckless whether the victim was consenting:

> *Satnam Singh* (1983) Two Ds had sex with a 13-year-old girl in the back of a car. She had accepted a lift with them, but said she had tried to stop them having sex with her. Both Ds said that they thought she was consenting. CA (Bristow J): allowed their appeals against their convictions for rape.

In summing up a case of rape which involves the issue of consent, the judge should, in dealing with the state of mind of the defendant, first of all direct the jury that before they could convict of rape the Crown had to prove either that D knew the woman did not want to have sexual intercourse, or was reckless as to whether she wanted to or not. If they were sure he knew she did not want to they should find him guilty of rape knowing there to be no consent. If they were not sure about that, then they would find him not guilty of such rape and should go on to consider reckless rape. If they thought he might genuinely have believed that she did want to, even though he was mistaken in his belief, they would find him not guilty. In considering whether his belief was genuine, they should take into account all the relevant circumstances (which could at that point be summarised) and ask themselves whether, in the light of those circumstances, he has reasonable grounds for such a belief. If, after considering those circumstances, they were sure he had no genuine belief that she wanted to, they would find him guilty. If they came to the conclusion that he could not care less whether she wanted to or not, but pressed on regardless, then he would have been reckless and could not have believed that she wanted to, and they would find him guilty of reckless rape ...

3.21 Yet this meaning of reckless may be part way towards the *Caldwell* objective definition of recklessness (see **3.22**). Has someone who couldn't care less whether a woman consents considered the possibility that she does not consent? Whilst it may be true that such a man should be guilty of rape, the test seems a bit wider than that laid down in *Cunningham*. Another offence which requires recklessness as to a surrounding circumstance is TA 1968, s15: where someone by deception dishonestly obtains property belonging to another with the intention of permanently depriving the other of it, he is guilty of an offence (see **11.35**). The deception itself may be intentional or reckless. Thus D may represent as true that which he is aware may or may not be true. If it turns out to be untrue, then he will have deceived someone. Presumably he would not be guilty if he represents as true that which he believes to be true, but which he ought as a reasonable man to have known was false.

3.22 *Objective recklessness* One of the dangers with a subjective test is that D may well lie, and it is impossible for a jury to enter his mind. Sometimes, too, D may not see obvious risks which the jury may well think that he should have seen. For these reasons, it seems, the courts have developed an alternative view of recklessness in some offences:

> *Metropolitan Police Comr v Caldwell* (1982) D, who was very drunk, set fire to a hotel, and was convicted of arson under s 1(2) of the CDA 1971. HL: upheld his conviction (though note Lord Edmund Davies dissent, with which Lord Wilberforce concurred). Lord Diplock:
>
>> a person charged with an offence under s 1(1) of the CDA 1971 is 'reckless as to whether any such property would be destroyed or damaged' if (1) he does an act which in fact creates an obvious risk that property will be destroyed or damaged and (2) when he does the act he either has not given any thought to the possibility of there being any such risk or has recognised that there was some risk involved and has nonetheless gone on to do it ...Neither state of mind seems to me to be less blameworthy than the other; but if the difference between the two constituted the distinction between what does and what does not in legal theory amount to a guilty state of mind for the purpose of a statutory offence of damage to property, it would not be a practicable distinction for use in a trial by jury.

3.23   This test was clearly not intended to apply only to criminal damage since Lord Diplock applied it in a case of causing death by reckless driving (which is no longer an offence: see **8.39**) on the very same day:

> *Lawrence* (1982) D drove his motorbike at 80 m.p.h. on a busy urban road, and was convicted of causing death by reckless driving. HL (Lord Diplock): upheld CA's decision to quash his conviction:
>
>> An appropriate instruction to the jury on what is meant by driving recklessly would be that they must be satisfied of two things: first, that the defendant was in fact driving the vehicle in such a manner as to create an obvious and serious risk of causing physical injury to some other person who might happen to be using the road or of doing substantial damage to property; and second, that in driving in that manner the defendant did so without having given any thought to the possibility of there being any such risk or, having recognised there was some risk involved, had nonetheless gone on to take it.

3.24   The key difference to *Caldwell* was simply that in *Lawrence* the risk is required to be 'serious' as well as 'obvious'. To what other crimes does *Caldwell* recklessness apply? For a time, it formed part of the test for manslaughter (see the discussion of the HL's decision in *Seymour* (1983) and that of the PC in *Kong Cheuk Kwan v R* (1985) at **8.34**), but since Lord Mackay's speech in the HL in *Adomako* (1995) there must be some doubt as to whether recklessness is any longer an appropriate *mens rea* concept to apply in manslaughter cases (see **8.36**).

3.25 This objective test of recklessness can be extraordinarily harsh in its operation:

> *Elliott v C* (1983) D, a 14-year-old girl with learning difficulties, poured white spirit in a shed and lit it. Magistrates acquitted her, holding that the risk of destroying the shed was not obvious to her. DC (Goff LJ), while admitting that D's conduct was not reckless in the ordinary sense, said that the test was whether the risk was obvious to a reasonably prudent person:
>
>> This is a case where it appears that the only basis upon which the accused might be held to have been reckless would be if the appropriate test to be applied was purely objective – a test which might in some circumstances be thought justifiable in relation to certain conduct (eg reckless driving), particularly where the word 'reckless' is used simply to characterise the relevant conduct. But such a test does not appear at first sight to be appropriate to a crime such as that under consideration in the present case, especially as recklessness in that crime has to be related to a particular consequence.

Goff LJ went on to consider the proposed qualification to Lord Diplock's *Caldwell/Lawrence* principle that Professor Glanville Williams had made in (1981) 40 CLJ 252, that D should only be regarded as having acted recklessly by virtue of his failure to give any thought to an obvious risk that property would be destroyed or damaged, where such risk would have been obvious to him if he had given any thought to the matter. However, Goff LJ concluded that it would not be consistent with Lord Diplock's reasoning to impose any such qualification.

3.26 Perhaps a more just interpretation of *Caldwell* would be Glanville Williams' approach, sometimes called a 'conditionally subjective' approach or a *via media*: the court would ask whether D had the capacity to make himself aware of the risk. The issue was discussed again in

Stephen Malcolm R (1984) D, a 15-year-old boy, threw home-made petrol bombs outside a girl's bedroom, intending to frighten her. CA (Ackner LJ): upheld his conviction under s 1(2)(b) of the CDA 1971 for criminal damage 'being reckless as to whether life was endangered'. Because the HL had not given leave to appeal in *Elliott*'s case, they should be taken to have rejected the argument that it would be right to inquire whether a person of D's age and with his characteristics would have appreciated the relevant risk. Since the risk would have been obvious to the reasonable man, it was irrelevant that D did not know of the risk.

3.27 If D believes that there is no risk at all, he may not be even *Caldwell* reckless. This is the so-called lacuna, or loop-hole in recklessness. However, it is rare for a D to succeed on this point:

Chief Constable of Avon and Somerset v Shimmen (1986) D, a skilled practitioner of Korean self-defence, was larking around with friends, having spent the evening in a pub and a club. Meaning to show how well controlled he was, D kicked out towards a shop window meaning to miss it by two inches. The window broke, and he was charged with and convicted of criminal damage. D argued that by reason of his skill he had satisfied himself (albeit mistakenly) that the window would not break, and so was not reckless. QBD: directed the magistrates to convict. Where D perceives a risk and believes he has minimised it, he has not excluded the risk of it completely and so falls within Lord Diplock's definition.

Merrick (1996) D removed electrical cable from the ground, leaving it exposed for six minutes before he took steps to make it safe. He pleaded guilty to damaging property being reckless as to whether life would be endangered after the trial judge ruled that any precautions taken to eliminate the risk of endangering life must, to provide a defence, be taken before the danger was caused. CA: dismissed his appeal. No lacuna appeared on the facts of this case: there is a clear distinction between avoiding a risk and taking steps to remedy a risk which has already been created.

3.28 True 'lacuna' cases will be very rare. D has to prove some specific fact on which he was mistaken which would have excluded the possibility of any risk. In any case, is the person who makes this mistake necessarily less culpable than the person who fails to see the risk in the first place? The HL returned to a discussion of objective recklessness in

> *Reid* (1992) D 'undertook' another car whilst driving on the inside lane of a dual carriageway and crashed into a taxi driver's rest hut which protruded six feet into the road. His passenger was fatally injured. D was convicted of causing death by reckless driving (an offence since replaced by causing death by dangerous driving; see **8.39**) after the trial judge summed up in terms of Lord Diplock's speech in *Lawrence* . HL: dismissed his appeal. Whilst the substance of Lord Diplock's formulation in *Lawrence* is apt to cover the generality of cases, it was not always necessary to use it. In some cases when the only relevant issue is one of disputed fact it may not be necessary to use it at all. In others it may require to be modified or adapted to suit the circumstances of the case. Lord Goff and Lord Ackner discussed examples of dangerous driving which might not be reckless: if D drove down a one-way street carefully but in the wrong direction in the mistaken belief that it was a two-way street, for example. Lord Goff points out that in split second decisions when engaged in a dangerous activity like driving, you may be more culpable if you fail to see obvious risks than if you see them and take them.

Lord Ackner was confident that recklessness in its ordinary meaning includes not only rashness but also heedlessness. Using the example of a diver who dives onto someone in a swimming pool, he said to prove recklessness,

> what must be shown is no more than that a reasonable man, in the defendant's position, performing the very act which the defendant intentionally performed, would have realised that he was exposing another or others to an appreciable risk of injury or damage to property.

3.29 *Reform* Given the fine distinctions discussed above, it is perhaps not surprising that the drafters of the DCC preferred a subjective definition of recklessness. Clause 18 provides that

a person acts – ...
(c) 'recklessly' with respect to -
    (i) a circumstance when he is aware of a risk that it exists or will exist;
    (ii) a result when he is aware of a risk that it will occur; and it is, in the circumstances known to him, unreasonable to take the risk.

Despite the enthusiastic support of the HL in *Reid* (1992) for the wider *Caldwell* definition, the future of objective recklessness must be in doubt. Whilst it seemed for a time in the 1980s that it might become the dominant interpretation of the word, it now seems to be applied only to criminal damage.

Negligence

3.30 It can be argued that negligence is not a state of mind since it is merely a failure to comply with the standards of the reasonable man, but since it is the fault element required for some offences, it falls to be considered here. For example, RTA 1988, s 3 defines the offence of 'driving without due care and attention', an offence clearly based on negligence. Negligence provides an objective standard which does not vary according to D's individual characteristics. Some statutes provide a 'no-negligence' defence, with the consequence that negligence will satisfy the requirements of the offence. Thus, SOA 1956, s 6(3) provides a defence to the offence of having unlawful sexual intercourse with a girl under the age of 16 for a person under the age of 24 who has not previously been charged with a similar offence if he 'believes her to be of the age of 16 or over and has reasonable cause for the belief'. An offence created where D 'did not know and had no reason to suspect' in effect penalises D for negligence: Ashworth and Blake in [1996] Crim LR 306 point out that such offences raise important questions in relation to the burden of proof and the presumption of innocence.

3.31 Most importantly, 'gross' negligence can be the basis for liability for manslaughter. The following test was laid down by Lord Hewart CJ in *Bateman* (1925):

> the facts must be such that, in the opinion of the jury, the negligence of the accused went beyond a mere matter of compensation between subjects and showed such disregard for the life and safety of others as to amount to a crime against the State and conduct deserving punishment.

3.32 It seemed during the 1980s that this test of 'gross negligence' was going to be replaced in manslaughter cases by a test of objective recklessness (see *Seymour* (1983); *Kong Cheuk Kwan v R* (1985) at **8.34**), but the HL has now confirmed that gross negligence may be sufficient:

Adomako (1995) D, an anaesthetist, failed to notice that an oxygen tube had become disconnected and V, the patient, died. P alleged that D had been grossly negligent in not noticing the obvious signs of disconnection and in failing to see that the alarm on the ventilator was not switched on. HL: upheld D's conviction for manslaughter. Lord Mackay:

> In cases of criminal negligence involving a breach of duty it is a sufficient direction to the jury to adopt the gross negligence test ... it is not necessary to refer to the definition of recklessness in *Lawrence* (1982), although it is perfectly open to the trial judge to use the word 'reckless' in its ordinary meaning as part of his exposition of the law if he deems it appropriate in the circumstances of the particular case ...The essence of the matter which is supremely a jury question is whether, having regard to the risk of death involved, the conduct of the defendant was so bad in all the circumstances as to amount in their judgment to a criminal act or omission.

Thus Lord Mackay wishes to leave a value judgment in the hand of juries: was this behaviour bad enough to justify a manslaughter conviction? We will return to this case at **8.36** in the context of an analysis of the law of manslaughter. Do you think that the key ingredient of such a serious offence should be defined more clearly?

Transferred malice

3.33   If a person by mistake or bad judgment causes injury to the wrong person or property, he may still be guilty of the offence he intended. Thus there is no problem in convicting D of the murder of A when he intended to kill B, or of wounding C when he intended to wound E: the doctrine of transferred malice or transferred intent applies:

Latimer (1886) D aimed a blow at X with a belt, but by mistake hit V. CCCR (Lord Coleridge CJ): upheld his conviction for unlawful wounding, under s 20 of the OAPA 1861. 'He had an intent to do an unlawful act, and in carrying out that intent he did injure a person; and the law says that, under such circumstances, a man is guilty of maliciously wounding the person actually wounded'.

Mitchell (1983) D assaulted a man aged 72 in a Post Office queue. The man fell on to V, an elderly lady of 89 who died of the injuries she suffered. CA: upheld his conviction for manslaughter. Staughton LJ: 'We can see no reason of policy for holding that an act calculated to harm A cannot be manslaughter if it in fact kills B'.

A-G's Reference (No 3 of 1994) (1998) D stabbed his girlfriend who he knew to be pregnant. The girlfriend recovered, but V, her baby, was born prematurely as a result of the wound and died after 120 days. The trial judge held that D could not be convicted of murder or manslaughter and ordered D's acquittal. HL: D was rightly acquitted of murder. Since there was no evidence that D intended to injure the foetus or the child, it would be straining the concept of transferred malice too far to apply it in these circumstances: it would require the malice to be transferred not once but twice, namely from the mother to the foetus and from the foetus to the child. (However, manslaughter could have been committed: see **8.3**; **8.22**.)

3.34 These cases cause no problem because the definition of the offence is wide enough to cover the situation in hand: in *Latimer*, D wounded someone and it doesn't matter that he was striking out at someone else. However, *mens rea* will not necessarily transfer from one offence to a different one:

Pembliton (1874) D picked up a large stone to throw it at someone with whom he was fighting and broke a window. CCCR (Lord Coleridge CJ): quashed his conviction for malicious damage. The jury had found that he had intended to hit someone, but this was not adequate *mens rea* for malicious damage, which required foresight of damage to property, not foresight of damage to people:

> as they have found that he threw the stone at the people he had been fighting with intending to strike them and not intending to break the window, I think that the conviction must be quashed.

Ellis (1986) Ds were participating in importing large quantities of cannabis in secret compartments in cars, and were charged with being knowingly concerned in the fraudulent evasion of the prohibition on the importation of a controlled drug. Their defence was that they thought they were importing prohibited pornography. CA: dismissed their appeal: an intention to import a prohibited substance is the sufficient *mens rea* for importing both a controlled drug of class A and for the separate offence of importing a class B drug, and this would extend to an intention to import other prohibited substances such as pornography.

3.35 What is important is an analysis of the precise fault required for the offence charged. We will return to the problem when we look at the liability of accomplices (chapter 6). If the accomplice encourages violence against a particular victim and the principal deliberately chooses another victim not contemplated by the accessory, the accessory will not be liable. If the accomplice encourages violence against a particular victim, and the principal misfires, then the accomplice will still be liable because the principal has tried to do what the accomplice encouraged. The doctrine of transferred malice applies.

Vicarious liability

3.36 Generally, criminal liability is personal. This can be contrasted with the position in tort, where employers are usually liable for the torts of their employees committed in the course of their employment (see Hedley *Tort* (2nd ed, 2000)). In criminal law, one person is not generally be liable for crimes committed by another:

> *Huggins* (1730) The warden of Fleet prison was acquitted of murder when V's death had been caused by his incarceration in an unhealthy cell.

Thus, in criminal law vicarious liability is exceptional. The exceptions include:

(i) two rare common law offences: public nuisance and criminal libel. Whether such offences should continue to exist was raised at **1.22**.

(ii) 'extensive' or 'extended' construction of statutes. This normally occurs in employer/employee situation where the employer is held to be strictly liable for the offence. Thus words such as 'sell', 'use' or 'possess' may be interpreted as applying both to the person who actually sells, and to the principal on behalf of whom he is acting. This is further discussed at **3.38** below.

(iii) the delegation principle: this is found most frequently in cases relating to licensees. The courts have interpreted some offences requiring knowledge so as to permit the conviction of the manger of premises on the basis of the acts of someone to whom he has delegated responsibility.

Allen v Whitehead (1930) D employed a manager to run a cafe in London. He instructed the manager not to allow prostitutes to gather on the premises, but was convicted of knowingly permitting prostitutes to remain in a place of refreshment contrary to s 44 of the Metropolitan Police Act 1839, even though his manager had flouted his instructions.

3.37 This 'delegation principle' was regarded as anomalous by the HL in *Vane v Yiannopoulous* (1965). Certainly it is extraordinarily harsh on a D who has done all that he can to comply with the law. The enactment of the DCC would lead to its abolition.

Strict liability

3.38 Those offences which do not require proof of *mens rea* in respect of one or more elements of the *actus reus* are known as crimes of strict liability. Liability is rarely absolute: general defences will normally apply. Common law offences of strict liability include public nuisance, criminal libel and blasphemous libel. Although prosecutions for these offences are very rare today, they are not unknown:

Lemon and *Whitehouse v Gay News* (1979) The Editor and publishers of Gay News published a poem which described homosexual acts done with the body of Christ after his death and described his alleged homosexual practices in his lifetime. They were convicted of blasphemy. HL: dismissed their appeal. The harm was done by the intentional publication, whether or not D intended to blaspheme. Lord Diplock dissented, arguing that there was no justification on grounds of public order or public morals for arguing that the common law offence of blasphemy should impose strict liability.

3.39 However, most examples of strict liability offences are statutory, and they are numerous. Ashworth and Blake (1996) consider that of the 540 serious offences dealt with in Archbold (the practitioner's main guide to criminal pleading, evidence and practice) in 1995, 123 had a strict liability element. Most such offences are considered to be regulatory, applying to particular trades, for example, but many can result in significant periods of imprisonment. Ashworth and Blake comment that if Parliament is free to impose strict liability as and when it wishes, the presumption of innocence rings hollow: they point out that the Canadian courts have invalidated most strict liability offences for which imprisonment is a possible penalty.

The following two cases are traditional illustrations of the difficulties which the courts face in this area:

Cundy v Le Cocq (1884) The Licensing Act 1872, s 13 made it an offence for any licensed person to sell intoxicating liquor to a drunken person. D was convicted even though he was not aware that the person he was serving was intoxicated. QBD: upheld his conviction. The words of the section amounted to an absolute prohibition on the sale of alcohol to the drunk, and the existence of a bona fide mistake as to the condition of the person served was no answer to the charge, but only a matter for the mitigation of the penalty imposed.

Sherras v de Rutzen (1895) The Licensing Act 1872, s 16(2) of the prohibits a licensed victualler from supplying liquor to a police constable who is on duty. D was convicted, although he reasonably believed that police constable was off duty. QBD: quashed the conviction. It would be straining the law to say that a D who was acting in the bona fide belief that the constable was off duty, and who had reasonable grounds for that belief, was guilty of an offence for which he was liable both to a penalty and to have his license endorsed.

3.40   Another leading case on strict liability is

Prince (1875) D was convicted of taking an unmarried girl under the age of 16 out of the possession of her parents. It was accepted that he had reasonable grounds for believing that she was over 16. CCCR (16 judges!): The conviction was upheld since strict liability applied in relation to the girl's age. However, Bramwell B (with whom six other judges agreed) said that his judgement gave full scope to the doctrine of *mens rea*: had D believed that he had the father's permission, or that she was in no one's possession, then he would have had no *mens rea*.

But now see

> *B (a minor) v DPP* (2000) D, aged 15, sat next to V, a 13-year-old girl on a bus. He asked her several times to perform oral sex with him, and she repeatedly refused. His defence was that he honestly believed she was over 14, but when the magistrates ruled that this was no defence to a charge under s 1 of the 1960 Act, he changed his plea to guilty. HL (unanimously): allowed D's appeal. Where Parliament failed to specify the mental element required, it was not a necessary implication that it was the intention of Parliament that liability should be strict so that an honest belief as to the age of the child would not be a defence. *Prince* (1875) was a 'relic from an age dead and gone' (Lord Hutton) and could be ignored as concerning a different offence and a different statute. P must prove that D knew that, or was reckless whether, the child was under 14.

Although this case is only about the Indecency with Children Act 1960, it must have important implications for other cases on strict liability.

3.41 Parliament is still creating many 'regulatory offences', and it is often difficult to decide whether strict liability applies. Where Parliament has not made it clear whether strict liability is intended, the courts should start from the presumption that Parliament did not intend to punish a blameless person:

> *Sweet v Parsley* (1970) D rented a farm house, but sub-let it to students. Police found cannabis at the farm, and she was charged and convicted of 'being concerned in the management of premises used for the purpose of smoking cannabis resin', contrary to the Dangerous Drugs Act 1965, s 5(b). HL: quashed her conviction. Lord Reid: 'Whenever a section is silent as to *mens rea* there is a presumption that, in order to give effect to the will of Parliament, we must read in words appropriate to require *mens rea*'. He distinguished quasi-criminal offences, where the presumption of *mens rea* might be more easily rebutted, from truly criminal acts where the stigma attached to conviction was greater.

60

3.42 This decision should not be seen as the death knell of strict liability:

> *Pharmaceutical Society of Great Britain v Storkwain* (1986) D pharmacists dispensed prescribed drugs to someone who gave a forged prescription. D acting in good faith and on reasonable grounds, believed the prescriptions were valid. They were convicted of selling medicines without an appropriate prescription, contrary to the Medicines Act 1968, s 58. HL: upheld the conviction since it was clear from the 1968 Act that Parliament must have intended that the presumption of *mens rea* was inapplicable to s 58(2).

It can be difficult to anticipate when the courts will decide that an offence is one of strict liability. One of the difficulties arises from the courts' attempts to distinguish between truly criminal acts and those which are illegal only because the public welfare so demands.

> *Harrow London Borough Council v Shah* (1999) D's shop assistant sold a lottery ticket to a person who he reasonably believed to be 16, but who was in fact under that age. Div Ct (Mitchell J): upheld his conviction. This was not a 'truly criminal act' but one which in the public interest was prohibited under a penalty. The offence imposed strict (and vicarious) liability.

In other cases, the courts seem somehow to avoid the problem by concentrating on some other issue. Thus, in **2.23** the problems of causation were raised. The 'common-sense' approach of the HL to questions of causation in *Alphacell Ltd v Woodward* (1972) distracted from the need for a discussion of strict liability.

3.43 There are many arguments for creating offences of strict liability:

- Protectionism/social defence.

- People who run businesses should do so properly.

- Guilty people should not escape conviction because of lack of proof/ evidence.

- Strict liability offences are easier to enforce.

- People may be deterred by the knowledge that offences are strict liability.

- It obliges people to adopt high standards.

- It saves court time: people plead guilty.

- A person who creates a risk and takes a profit from that risk should also pay for the adverse consequences.

However, there are perhaps stronger counter-arguments:

- Liability should not be imposed on those who are not blameworthy.

- It is wrong to penalise those who have taken all proper care.

- It is inefficient, merely delaying an analysis of fault until the sentencing stage.

- There is no evidence that it raises standards.

- It may put small business at an unfair risk.

3.44 The arguments are summed up well by Thomas (1978):

> The effect of imposing strict liability is not necessarily to eliminate fault as a requirement of liability, but to delegate to the enforcer both the responsibility of deciding what kind of fault will in general justify a prosecution (with the certainty of conviction) and the right to determine whether in the circumstances of the particular case that degree of fault is present. The main objections to the concept of strict liability are thus procedural rather than substantive, and the questions to be addressed to the proponent of a statute creating an offence of strict liability are: 'Why is it not possible to incorporate into the definition of the offence the nature of the fault which is likely in practice to be required as a condition precedent to prosecution, and why is it not possible for the existence of this fault to be determined in accordance with the normal process of law?'.

We will see again in chapter 13 on crimes against the environment that one consequence of the law's tough stance in imposing strict liability is that wide discretion is then given to the prosecuting body: despite the appearance of a law which imposes liability without fault, in practice a prosecution is unlikely to take place unless the company is perceived to be genuinely blameworthy. While the arguments against strict liability imposed on individuals seem strong, there may be different arguments applicable to corporate liability, a subject to which we shall return in the next chapter.

3.45 *Reform* The DCC accepts that *mens rea* should be presumed in clause 20:

> (1) Every offence requires a fault element of recklessness with respect to each of its elements other than fault elements, unless otherwise provided.

This clumsy clause means that strict liability can only be imposed if Parliament expressly or by necessary implication so provides. In the Commentary to clause 20, the Law Commission say that they thought it would be inappropriate to make the presumption displaceable only by express provision. There is no guidance on when the courts should decide that Parliament 'plainly implied' that an offence is one of strict liability. The Law Commission give the example of an offence of causing polluting matter to enter a watercourse created after the Code comes into force. In the absence of any provision to the contrary the offence requires (a) an intention to cause the matter to enter the watercourse or recklessness whether it will do so, and (b) knowledge that the matter is a pollutant or recklessness whether it is. This puts a heavy onus on Parliamentary draftsmen to make their message clear.

Further reading

Ashworth and Blake, 'The Burden of Proof and the Presumption of Innocence' [1996] Crim LR 306

Brady, 'Recklessness' (1996) 15 Law and Philosophy 183

Buxton, 'Some Simple thoughts on Intention' (1988) Crim LR 484

Duff *Intention, Agency and Criminal Liability* (1990)

Leigh *Strict and Vicarious Liability* (1982)

Thomas, 'Form and Function in the Criminal Law', in *Reshaping the Criminal Law* (ed Glazebrook)

Glanville Williams, 'The Unresolved problem of recklessness' (1988) 8 Legal Studies 74

Self-test questions

1. Dee bakes Phil a birthday cake. Intending to kill him, she puts poison in the cake. Phil takes the cake home and eats it. Dee then has second thoughts and goes to Phil's home where she finds him seriously ill. She calls an ambulance, but Phil dies before it arrives.

2. Dee wishes to collect the insurance money on her house, so sets fire to it knowing that Phil might be asleep upstairs. Would English law say that she intended to kill Phil?

3. Dee is sleeping rough and spends three nights in an old barn. She is freezing cold and sets fire to a pile of old rubbish in the barn. The fire gets out of control so Dee leaves to find somewhere else to sleep. The barn is destroyed. Medical evidence says that Dee has a mental age of 8. Is she reckless?

4. If a patient dies due to medical incompetence, how incompetent does a doctor have to have been before a jury may judge him to have been grossly negligent, and therefore guilty of manslaughter?

5. Is the imposition of strict liability ever justified?

CHAPTER FOUR

Incapacitating conditions

SUMMARY

Childhood: Children under the age of 10 cannot be convicted of a crime. The CDA 1998 abolished (or reversed?) the doctrine of *doli incapax* which had allowed a sliding scale of responsibility for those aged 10-14.

Insanity: *M'Naghten* Rules: D is not guilty by reason of insanity if he has 'a defect of reason, from disease of the mind, as not to know the nature and quality of the act he was doing; or, if he did know it, that he did not know he was doing what was wrong'. Note the problem of providing satisfactory legal/medical definitions of mental disorder.

Intoxication: Conflicting policy issues: D is guilty of most crimes if he commits them when drunk, but his drunkenness may show he did not have the necessary 'intent' for other crimes (eg murder; theft). The Law Commission recommend in 1996 maintaining this '*Majewski* rule'.

Corporate liability: distinguish cases where the company is vicariously liable for the crimes of others, from cases where the company is itself liable.

Introduction

4.1 Neither childhood nor insanity are properly described as defences: it is the child's status as a child which prevents him or her being guilty of an offence. It is a key characteristic, her 'abnormal condition', which excuses her from liability. It is worth noting that, although a child or an insane person may not be blameworthy, such a person may still be 'punished' in some sense: a person not guilty by reason of insanity may still be compulsorily detained in a mental hospital, a 'criminal' child may still be subject to care proceedings. In the case of a child, the law has evolved a sliding scale of criminal responsibility (see **4.2**). With the insane, it is the lack of autonomy in the sense of a lack of ability to make effective choices which makes D not guilty, but there is no sliding scale (except when it comes to sentencing). However, this lack of ability may be caused by

(i) internal causes: in which case he may be not guilty by reason of insanity (**4.8**)

(ii) external causes: in which case he may be acquitted if he was not at fault (see automatism: **4.16**) or convicted if he was at fault (see intoxication **4.17**).

(iii) a mixture of both external and internal causes.

This chapter also explores the effect of intoxication on liability generally. Again, not really a defence, a person may be so incapacitated by drink or drugs that they do not form the necessary intent to justify conviction. Criminal offences have largely been designed with human wrongdoers in mind so finally in this chapter, we will look at the ways in which a company may or may not be convicted of criminal offences.

Childhood

4.2 A child under the age of 10 is *doli incapax* (ie incapable of committing a crime): see s 50 of the CYPA 1933. She may be the subject of care proceedings, but may not be prosecuted for a crime. From the age of 10 the child may be guilty. Until recently it was well established that until D reached the age of 14, P had to prove that the child not only had the *mens rea* for the relevant crime, but also that she knew that what she did was a wrong act and not merely an act of simple naughtiness or mischief. This requirement has been challenged in recent years, both in the courts and now by Parliament. The law was unsettled after the murder of a toddler by two 11-year-olds in 1993 shook the nation, resulting in a wave of popular emotion that something should be done to instil greater respect for the law amongst children. However, the HL upheld the *doli incapax* rule, reversing a DC attempt to abolish it:

> *C v DPP* (1996) D, aged 12, was seen with another boy using a crowbar to interfere with a motorcycle on a private driveway. When they saw the police, they ran away. D was convicted before the magistrates of interfering with a motor vehicle with the intention to commit theft or to take and drive away without consent, contrary to s 9(1) of the CAA 1981. DC: upheld D's conviction: the doctrine of *doli incapax* should no longer be regarded as part of the common law. HL: reversed the DC's decision. It is still the law that a child between the ages of 10 and 14 is presumed incapable of committing a crime unless there is clear evidence that he knew that what he did was seriously wrong.

The presumption was not merely window-dressing:

> *CC (A Minor) v DPP* (1996) D, aged 11 years and 11 months, at the time, and another boy, attacked a 12-year-old on his bicycle. D took a lock knife from his pocket and the other boy held it to V's throat. Before V was released, D said 'Cut his nose to make sure', referring to V bringing money to school for them the next day. Justices rejected a submission of no case to answer, finding that it was almost inconceivable that a boy of D's age would not know that it was seriously wrong to place a knife on someone's throat and demand money. DC (Mitchell J): quashed D's convictions for offences under ss 3 and 4 POA 1986. 'The tribunal of fact must avoid the trap of applying ... the 'presumption of normality'. That presumption is to this effect: any normal boy of his age in society, as it is today, must have known that what he was doing was seriously wrong. Such an approach as that reverses the relevant presumption of *doli incapax*'. Very little evidence was needed to rebut the presumption of *doli incapax*, but some evidence there had to be.

4.3 The police are today unlikely to prosecute a child unless they are confident that the child was truly 'criminal', and indeed there has been a vast increase in the last decade or so of police cautions (now reprimands and warnings). Why are children treated differently to adults? Partly because we do not blame them so much: a child may have acted intentionally or recklessly, but she may not have developed the ability to apply 'normal' moral standards. A child might pull the wings off a fly to see what will happen to it next, or stamp on a spider: is his behaviour as morally blameworthy as that of an adult who acts similarly? There are other, more pragmatic, reasons why children may be 'shielded' from the full force of the criminal law. 'Labelling theory' suggests that once a child is seen (and sees herself) as criminal, then she may become more criminal. Thus it is argued that criminal sanctions should be applied as a last resort.

4.4 However, the Government decided that the presumption should be abolished: 'to respond effectively to youth crime, we must stop making excuses for children who offend' (para 4.1 of the WP *No More Excuses* (Cm 3809)). Section 34 of the Crime and Disorder Act 1998 provides simply that:

> The rebuttable presumption of criminal law that a child aged 10 or over is incapable of committing an offence is hereby abolished.

Walker (1999) argues that this change does not abolish the presumption, but merely reverses the burden of proof: it may still be possible for a child to argue by way of defence that they did not know that what they were doing was wrong. Of course an adult who uses an under-age child to carry out their own crimes will be guilty of an offence themselves under the doctrine of innocent agency (see **6.5**). On the other hand, if you are attacked by a child, you may use reasonable force to resist that aggression even if the child is not convicted of a crime (see self- defence, **5.30**).

Mental disorder

4.5 When D's conduct is the result of mental disorder or mental illness, he may either be:

(i) unfit to plead

(ii) not guilty by reason of insanity

(iii) not guilty by reason of automatism

(iv) convicted of a more minor offence than that charged: thus if D is charged with murder, he may be convicted only of manslaughter if he is suffering from diminished responsibility by reason of some 'abnormality of mind' (see **8.9**).

(v) convicted of the offence charged, but the mental disorder may be taken into consideration at the sentencing stage.

Unfitness to plead

4.6 Very few people are found unfit to plead. This is presumably because severely mentally handicapped, ill or disordered people are diverted from the criminal justice system before they reach the stage of court proceedings. However, where the prosecution does initiate proceedings, D must be 'of sufficient intellect to comprehend the course of the proceedings in the trial so as to make a proper defence, to challenge a juror to whom he might wish to object and comprehend the details of the evidence'. This test was laid down by Alderson B in *Pritchard* (1836), where D was deaf and dumb. The test is not exactly up to date: defendants rarely get the chance to challenge jurors since the abolition of peremptory challenges in 1988, but the principle is clear: the accused must be able to plead, and to instruct his lawyers. He need not necessarily be capable of acting in his own best interests. Mackay (1995) argues that the test is too restrictive and should include a test of 'decisional incapacity' to cover, for example, the mentally disordered person who pleads guilty against the advice of their lawyer.

4.7 In practice where there is evidence that D is unfit to plead, the court first hears evidence on this issue. If he is fit to plead, then the trial proceeds. If he is not fit to plead, another jury then decides if D 'did the act or made the omission charged against him as the offence' (Criminal Procedure (Insanity and Unfitness to Plead) Act 1991 and *Antoine* (2000): see **2.3**). If the court is satisfied that he did what was alleged, then the court has a choice of disposals, including admission to hospital with or without a restriction order or an absolute discharge (see **4.8**). Until 1991, the law was extraordinarily harsh on those unfit to plead: indefinite committal to hospital was the only possible outcome. This now only applies in the case of murder, since the CP (IUP)A 1991 gave courts the discretion to choose from a wide variety of sentencing options. If D's condition improves, he may be remitted to court for trial: this appears to happen in about half of all cases.

Insanity

4.8 The rules on insanity derive from the celebrated case of *M'Naghten* (1843), who, in attempting to shoot the Home Secretary, had killed his Secretary. After M'Naghten's acquittal by a jury, the judges of the HL were asked to formulate rules for the guidance of juries. Despite some reluctance about answering hypothetical questions on which they had not heard argument, Tindal CJ did report that:

> … jurors ought to be told in all cases that every man is to be presumed to be sane, and to possess a sufficient degree of reason to be responsible for his crimes, until the contrary is proved to their satisfaction; and that to establish a defence on the ground of insanity, it must be clearly proved that, at the time of the committing of the act, the party accused was labouring under such a defect of reason, from disease of the mind, as not to know the nature and quality of the act he was doing; or, if he did know it, that he did not know he was doing what was wrong.

Thus D must be suffering from a defect of reason which causes him either not to know what he was doing, or not to know that what he was doing was wrong.

> *Windle* (1952) D was convicted of the murder of his suicidal wife. His defence had been that he was insane: he thought it was morally right to kill her. CCA: dismissed his appeal. Lord Goddard CJ: 'wrong' means contrary to law 'and does not have some vague meaning which may vary according to he opinion of different persons whether a particular act might or might not be justified'.

This definition is remarkably narrow – someone is only insane if he did not know that what he did is *legally* wrong. Should the test be a failure to realise that what he did was *morally* wrong? Does it also mean that a person who thinks that his act is morally wrong but not legally wrong, would be entitled to the defence of insanity?

4.9 Until the Criminal Procedure (Insanity and Unfitness to Plead) Act 1991, the court had no option but to impose a mandatory hospital order on someone found not guilty by reason of insanity, which of course made the defence very unattractive. Now if D is found to be not guilty by reason of insanity (except in murder cases, where a mandatory life sentence will be imposed), he may still be detained in a mental hospital, but the court has a variety of options: admission to hospital with or without a restriction order, a guardianship order, a supervision and treatment order, an absolute discharge. The burden is placed on D (on a balance of probabilities) to prove that he is insane (except that P may raise insanity if D pleads diminished responsibility to a murder charge). Given the consequences of an insanity verdict, it is perhaps odd that the burden to prove it lies on D: surely the defence raises important questions not only about D's own welfare but also about the welfare of the community and so either party (and the judge) should be able to raise it.

4.10 *Disease of the mind* To qualify for the defence of insanity, the accused must be suffering from a defect of reason caused by a disease of the mind. Curiously, this is a legal question for the judge, not a medical one.

> *Sullivan* (1984) D inflicted grievous bodily harm on V, a friend, during a minor epileptic seizure. When the trial judge ruled that his defence amounted to insanity, he changed his plea to guilty to assault occasioning actual bodily harm. HL: dismissed his appeal. Lord Diplock:
>
>> The nomenclature adopted by the medical profession may change from time to time ... But the meaning of the expression 'disease of the mind' as the cause of a 'defect of reason' remains unchanged for the purposes of the application of the M'Naghten Rules ... 'mind' in the M'Naghten Rules is used in the ordinary sense of the mental faculties of reason, memory and understanding. If the effect of a disease is to impair these faculties so severely as to have either of the consequences referred to in the latter part of the rules, it matters not whether the aetiology of the impairment is organic, as in epilepsy, or functional, as to whether the impairment itself is permanent or is transient and intermittent, provided that it subsisted at the time of the commission of the act.

Thus the HL held that a special verdict of not guilty by reason of insanity was correct where an epileptic fit brought about a temporary suspension of the mental faculties of reason, memory and understanding during which an offence was committed. Similarly, it has been held that both a person who commits an offence whilst sleep-walking (see *Burgess* (1991)) and one who suffers from arteriosclerosis – hardening of the arteries – (see *Kemp* (1957)) are rightly described as suffering from a disease of the mind.

71

This latter case is particularly odd given that arteriosclerosis is of physical rather than mental origin.

4.11 The rules have become particularly obtuse in relation to those suffering from diabetes. Since a disease of the mind is treated as something internal to D, if the cause of the disease is external, the defence does not apply. This distinction between internal and external causes results in an extraordinary distinction: if D is suffering from hyperglycaemia (high blood sugar level) caused by his failure to take insulin, then he is suffering from a disease of the mind. If he is suffering from hypoglycaemic (low blood sugar) caused by taking insulin but without appropriate food, he does not have a disease of the mind.

> *Quick* (1973) D, a diabetic and a nurse, was charged with a serious assault on a patient in his charge. He had taken his insulin, but had eaten no lunch. He had also been drinking alcohol. When the trial judge ruled that his diabetes was a 'defect of reason caused by a disease of the mind', he changed his plea to guilty. CA: quashed his conviction since his mental condition was caused not by his diabetes but by the use of insulin. The alleged malfunctioning of his mind had therefore been caused by an external factor and not by the disease. D's defence of automatism should have been left to the jury. The court could not say with the requisite degree of confidence that the jury would have convicted him and so his conviction had to be quashed as being unsatisfactory.

> *Hennessy* (1989) D, a diabetic in a hyperglycaemic state because he had not taken insulin for a few days, was convicted of taking and driving away a vehicle. CA: D's hyperglycaemia (excessive blood sugar) was caused by the diabetes when uncorrected by the administration of insulin and was rightly a disease of the mind. He was not therefore entitled to a defence of automatism.

In such cases, the culpability of the defendants is often similar: D's insulin balance has not been controlled for a period of time, often because of the 'pressures of life' upon them. Yet as the Ontario Court of Appeal said in the Canadian case of *Rabey* (1977), 'the ordinary stresses and disappointments of life which are the common lot of mankind do not constitute an external cause'. Should a diabetic be guilty of a crime when he fails to keep a reasonable control over his diabetes? However you answer that question, the label 'insanity' is hardly appropriate.

4.12 As *Hennessy* shows, the main impact of the M'Naghten Rules is to restrict other defences: automatism, for example. D cannot escape conviction by relying on the defence of automatism (which results in a complete acquittal) if she falls within the M'Naghten Rules. But many Ds choose to plead guilty to a crime rather than face the prospect of being found not guilty by reason of insanity:

> *Clarke* (1972) D was charged with theft from a supermarket. There was evidence that she had transferred goods from the wire basket in a supermarket into her shopping basket and then left without paying. Two doctors certified that she was suffering from mild depression and that this could cause absent-mindedness in which the patient might do things she would not normally do in periods of confusion and memory lapse. The trial judge held that this constituted evidence of insanity, and so D changed her plea to guilty. CA: quashed her conviction. Ackner J:
>
> > The M'Naghten Rules relate to accused persons who by reason of a disease of the mind are deprived of the power of reasoning. They do not apply and never have applied to those who retain the power of reasoning but who in moments of confusion or absent-mindedness fail to use their powers to the full.

4.13 *Proposals for reform* The insanity defence is rarely used for two main reasons. First, it is so narrow as to be seen as irrelevant. Secondly, there is sufficient stigma attached to the label that many wish to avoid it. If you are seriously mentally handicapped or ill, you will probably be unfit to plead. If you are not, you will be wary of the stigma and the possible penalty attached to the 'defence'. Many States in the USA have abolished the insanity defence. Rather as the acquittal of M'Naghten caused a furore in England in 1843, so did the acquittal of Hinckley for the attempted murder of the then President of the USA, Ronald Reagan, in 1982. The State of Idaho was first to abolish the defence, and others have followed suit. In these jurisdictions even the mentally ill and the insane may be prosecuted in the normal way. If a defendant has the necessary *mens rea*, then his mental condition becomes relevant only at the sentencing stage in much the same way that other social factors may be taken into account. If his 'craziness' means that he did not have the required *mens rea*, then he is not convicted. Under such a system, D may still be committed to a secure hospital under the provisions of the relevant civil law if he is perceived to be dangerous.

73

4.14 However if you prefer a solution that accepts that those who are not blameworthy should not be convicted of crimes, then there should be a defence of mental illness. The Butler Committee in 1975 recommended that the insanity defence should be replaced by a verdict of 'not guilty on evidence of mental disorder'. The DCC adopts the recommendations of the Butler Committee with some modifications. It provides both a defence of severe disorder (clause 35) and a qualified defence 'on evidence of disorder' (clause 36).

Clause 35 provides that

> (1) A mental disorder verdict shall be returned if the defendant is proved to have committed an offence but it is proved on the balance of probabilities (whether by the prosecution or by the defendant) that he was at the time suffering from severe mental illness or severe mental handicap.

> (2) Subsection (1) does not apply if the court or jury is satisfied beyond reasonable doubt that the offence was not attributable to the severe mental illness or severe mental handicap.

> (3) A court or jury shall not, for the purposes of a verdict under subsection (1), find that the defendant was suffering from severe mental illness or severe mental handicap unless two medical practitioners approved for the purposes of section 12 of the Mental Health Act 1983 as having special experience in the diagnosis or treatment of mental disorder have given evidence that he was so suffering.

'Severe mental illness' is defined in clause 34 as

> a mental illness which has one or more of the following characteristics—
> (a) lasting impairment of intellectual functions shown by failure of memory, orientation, comprehension and learning capacity;
> (b) lasting alteration of mood of such degree as to give rise to delusion appraisal of the defendant's situation, his past or his future, or that of others, or lack of any appraisal;
> (c) delusional beliefs, persecutory, jealous or grandiose;
> (d) abnormal perceptions associated with the delusional misinterpretation of events;
> (e) thinking so disordered as to prevent reasonable appraisal of the defendant's situation or reasonable communication with other;

'Severe mental handicap' is defined in the same clause as

a state of arrested or incomplete development of mind which includes severe impairment of intelligence and social functioning.

The main differences from the Butler Committee recommendations are that P or D would be able to raise the defence, and that the prosecution would be allowed to persuade the jury, if it can, that the offence was not attributable to the disorder. The Law Commission believe that this would 'improve the acceptability of the Butler Committee's generally admirable scheme' as a basis for legislation. Also controversial will be any attempt to define mental disorder: the area is a minefield for both doctors and lawyers.

4.15 Clause 36 would provide a separate defence that, where evidence of mental disorder causes a jury or court to doubt whether D acted with the required fault, they should be able to bring in a qualified defence. D would be 'not guilty on evidence of mental disorder'. Whereas the defence under clause 35 would apply whether or not the disorder negated D's *mens rea*, the defence under clause 36 would apply only to those whose *mens rea* was affected by the disorder. Meanwhile, the political mood seems to be becoming increasingly intolerant: the Home Office (1999) has proposed new civil powers which would allow the indefinite detention of 'dangerous' people with severe personality disorders, on the basis of the risk that they present rather than the crimes that they have committed.

Automatism

4.16 Clearly a person should not be guilty for acts committed as a result of an involuntary movement of their body. Normally they will not be guilty because they had no *mens rea*. If I hit you on the nose whilst sneezing, I am not guilty of assault since I was not subjectively reckless. However, it is more usual to say in these circumstances that D is not guilty because he did not do a voluntary act.

Hill v Baxter (1958) D was charged with dangerous driving, and claimed he had no recollection of what had happened. The magistrates dismissed the action against him. QBD: the magistrates came to the wrong decision in law. Lord Goddard CJ:

> ... there may be cases where the circumstances are such that the accused could not really be said to be driving at all. Suppose he had a stroke or a epileptic fit, both instances of what may properly be called acts of God; he might well be in the driver's seat even with his hands on the wheel, but in such a state of unconsciousness that he could not be said to be driving. A blow from a stone or an attack by a swarm of bees I think introduces some conception akin to *novus actus interveniens.*

But this case fell far short of that, and the defence of automatism was not applicable. Another, more recent, attempt to rely on the defence also failed:

> *A-G's Reference (No 2 of 1992)* (1993) D drove his lorry 700 yards along the hard shoulder of a motorway before crashing into a stationary van killing two people. D relied on expert evidence of a condition known as 'driving without awareness', a trance-like state induced by repetitive visual stimuli on flat featureless motorways. The judge left the defence of automatism to the jury, who acquitted D. CA: the defence of automatism should not have been left to the jury since automatism depends on a total destruction of voluntary control on D's part. 'Driving without awareness' involved only partial or reduced control.

Whether automatism negates the *actus reus* or the *mens rea* of an offence can be important: see **2.3** for a discussion of *Broome v Perkins* (1987) and whether a diabetic driver should have the defence of automatism. If automatism is related simply to the *mens rea*, D's recklessness may mean that he cannot rely on it. Remember that if the automatism is caused by insanity or intoxication, D will not be able to rely on it.

Intoxication

4.17 Many offenders have been drinking alcohol or taking drugs, or both. Are you less culpable if you have been drinking, because you didn't realise the extent of your criminality? Or are you more culpable, because society needs to stress that, on social policy grounds, you cannot hide behind your drunkenness in order to 'get away' with your crimes? English law reflects this dilemma by making a basic distinction between crimes of 'specific intent' and those of 'basic intent'. Crimes of specific intent are, generally speaking, those for which the required *mens rea* is intention. Here drunkenness may be used to show that D did not have the relevant intent. On the other hand, in crimes of basic intent (generally those for which the required *mens rea* is only recklessness or less) evidence of drunkenness actually supplies the necessary *mens rea*, and can never negate it.

> *DPP v Majewski* (1977) D spent a day taking a variety of drugs and drinking heavily. In the evening he was involved in a fight in a pub, and attacked both the landlord and the policeman who eventually arrested him. He was charged with assault occasioning actual bodily harm and with assaulting a police officer in the execution of his duty. His defence was that he was so intoxicated as to have no recollection at all of the events of the evening. CA and HL affirmed his convictions. Self-induced intoxication could not provide a defence to the offences charged.

4.18 There were seven separate speeches in the HL in *Majewski*, and it is not altogether clear where the line is to be drawn between those offences for which intoxication supplies evidence of *mens rea*, and those where evidence of intoxication may negate *mens rea*. However, it is clear that evidence of drunkenness may negate the required *mens rea* in crimes such as murder which are based on intention. If I am so drunk that I think you are a dartboard and I throw darts at you with the result that you die, I will not be guilty of murder as I did not intend to kill. I will nonetheless be guilty of manslaughter, a basic intent offence.

> *Metropolitan Police Comr v Caldwell* (1982) D quarrelled with the owner of a hotel. He got drunk and set fire to the hotel. He was convicted of arson, contrary to s 1(2) of the CDA 1971, despite his defence that he was so drunk that he never thought that he was endangering life. HL: upheld his conviction. Lord Diplock:
>
> > Reducing oneself by drink or drugs to a condition in which the restraints of reason and conscience are cast off was held to be a reckless course of conduct ...In the instant case, the fact that the respondent was unaware of the risk of endangering the lives of residents in the hotel owing to his self-induced intoxication would be no defence if that risk would have been obvious to him had he been sober.

The House in *Caldwell* seems to move the discussion from 'basic intent' to 'recklessness'. But is it right to convict people of an offence when their fault is more closely related to getting drunk, not to the crime that they actually commit? Is the recklessness (negligence?) involved in getting drunk as deserving of blame as the recklessness required for most crimes of basic intent? Before you can be convicted of an offence of assault occasioning actual bodily harm, for example, it has to be proved that you foresaw the risk that you might frighten someone (see **9.17**). D when drunk does not foresee the risk of the result which actually occurs. As Ashworth suggests, the rule is inconsistent with the principle of contemporaneity in that it bases D's conviction on the antecedent fault of voluntarily taking intoxicants (PCL, p 221).

4.19 The *Majewski* distinction leaves other inconsistencies. While it may not matter if the intoxicated have a possible defence to murder or intentional wounding, since they will still be guilty of a lesser offence (manslaughter or unlawful wounding), not all crimes of specific intent have a lesser basic intent offence beneath them. Thus, for example, if a drunk is charged with theft, he may not be guilty if he can show he was drunk and so did not intent to permanently deprive the owner of the goods. But there is no lesser offence of 'reckless stealing' with which he may be charged. The *Majewski* rule also means that drunkenness may lead to D's acquittal of a charge of attempt, whereas he would have been guilty had he successfully completed his attempt. Thus, whilst drunkenness is no defence to rape, it may be a defence to a charge of attempted rape.

4.20 It goes almost without saying (I hope) that if D gets drunk in order to give himself the courage to commit an offence, he has no defence (*A-G for Northern Ireland v Gallagher* (1963)). As Lord Denning said in that case:

> If a man, while sane and sober, forms an intention to kill and makes preparation for it ... and then gets himself drunk so as to give himself Dutch courage to do the killing, and while drunk carries out his intention, he cannot rely on this self-induced drunkenness as a defence to a charge of murder.

Such cases are in practice rare: perhaps because the very drunk are unlikely to carry out their plans successfully.

4.21   The rules of intoxication apply equally to alcohol and to drugs. If you deliberately take a drug which makes you do irresponsible (and criminal) things, you will be convicted. However, if the effect of the drug on you was unpredictable, you may have a defence:

> *Hardie* (1984) D took some of his ex-girlfriend's Valium to ease his misery at being asked to move out of her flat. He then started a fire in a wardrobe, and was in due course convicted of arson (and sentenced to 2 years' imprisonment). CA (Parker LJ): quashed his conviction.
>
>> If the jury came to the conclusion that as a result of the Valium, the appellant was, at the time unable to appreciate the risks to property and persons from his actions, they should consider whether the taking of the Valium was itself reckless.

Can this be reconciled with *Caldwell* recklessness (the required *mens rea* for arson)? The D in *Elliott v C* (see **3.25**) was guilty despite her 'inherent defects' which prevented her foreseeing risks, yet *Hardie* is acquitted when his inability to see a risk was caused by his voluntary (but non-reckless) taking of a drug. However, most commentators would say that the case to criticise is *Elliott.* The decision in *Hardie* has the merit of confirming at least some fault element in the *Majewski* rule. However, it also forces the courts, perhaps without the benefit of medical evidence, to decide whether taking a particular drug is 'dangerous' or 'non-dangerous'.

4.22   *Intoxication and mistake* Although a genuine mistake may relieve D of liability (see **5.24**), the courts have generally held that mistakes induced by drunkenness do not do so. Intoxicated people cannot rely on mistakes which they would not have made when sober. As Ashworth says, 'where the subjective rule for mistake clashes with the objective rules for intoxication, the latter takes priority' (PCL, p 220).

> *Woods* (1981) D and three others raped a girl when they were drunk. CA: upheld their convictions: self-induced intoxication is no defence to allegations of recklessness as to consent.

> *O'Grady* (1987) D and V, two drunk men, went to sleep in a large bed. D woke up to find his friend hitting him, so he fought back and eventually went back to sleep. In the morning he discovered that his friend was dead. He was charged with murder, but convicted of

manslaughter. CA (Lord Lane CJ): dismissed his appeal. 'A D is not entitled to rely, so far as self-defence is concerned, on a mistake of fact which has been induced by voluntary intoxication'.

4.23 But sometimes a statute is drafted so as to provide what looks like a wider defence. The CDA 1971, s 5(2) provides that D has a lawful excuse for causing criminal damage

> (a) if at the time of the act or acts alleged to constitute the offence he believed that the person or person whom he believed to be entitled to consent to the destruction of or damage to the property in question had so consented, or would have so consented to it if he or they had known of the destruction or damage and its circumstances; ...

This section has been interpreted so as to lead to the acquittal of those whose mistaken beliefs may be caused by their own drunkenness, particularly since s 5(3) states that

> For the purposes of this section it is immaterial whether a belief is justified or not if it is honestly held.

> *Jaggard v Dickinson* (1981) D, who had been drinking, mistook V's house for that of her friend, with whom she had planned to stay. Finding the house locked and no-one at home, she broke a window in order to get in. She was convicted of criminal damage. DC (Mustill J): quashed her conviction. The defence under the CDA 1971, s 5(2)(a) was still available although D was drunk.

The court is required by s 5(3) to focus on the existence of the belief, not its intellectual soundness; and a belief can be just as much honestly held if it is induced by intoxication, as if it stems from stupidity, forgetfulness or inattention.

4.24 The danger with this defence is that it suggests that if D sets fire to a hotel under the influence of LSD believing that he had the permission of the owner to burn it down (Glanville Williams' example at (1990) 140 NLJ 1564), he will be acquitted. Perhaps the answer is that the present law treats a mistaken belief brought about by intoxication in different ways according to whether it is categorised as negating an element of the offence or as forming part of a defence. Is this distinction appropriate, or indeed always possible to apply? The TA 1968, s 12(6) provides that a person does not commit an offence of taking a motor vehicle without authority

> by anything done in the belief that he has lawful authority to do it or that he would have the owner's consent if the owner knew of his doing it and the circumstances of it.

How would you categorise this?

In other statutes, it is made clear that mistaken beliefs induced by intoxication are no excuse. Section 6(5) POA 1986 provides that for the purposes of the offences in ss 1-5 of the POA (see chapter 12):

> a person whose awareness is impaired by intoxication shall be taken to be aware of that of which he would be aware if not intoxicated, unless he shows either that his intoxication was not self-induced or that it was caused solely by the taking or administration of a substance in the course of medical treatment.

4.25 *Proposals for reform* The Law Commission has looked at the question of drunken offenders several times. In the DCC they proposed simply to abolish the specific/basic intent distinction and to replace it with liability based on recklessness: D would be guilty of an offence which may be committed recklessly if he was intoxicated at the time. However, in 1993, the Law Commission produced a lengthy Consultation Paper (No 127) on *Intoxication and Criminal Liability*. This looked at six different proposals for reform, preferring one of the last two:

(i) option 5: abolish the *Majewski* approach without replacement. D's intoxication would be taken into account with any other relevant evidence in determining whether he had the mental element required for the offence. This is closer to the current Australian and New Zealand position (see the Australian case of *O'Connor* (1980)). The Canadian Supreme Court, too, stepped in this direction in *Daviault* (1994). Pointing out that 'the most vehement and cogent criticism' of the *Majewski* approach is that it substitutes proof of drunkenness for proof of the required mental element, the Supreme Court of Canada held that the mental element of voluntariness is a fundamental aspect of the crime which cannot be taken away by a judicially developed policy. Where D is incapable of forming the minimal intent required for a crime of general intent, he should have a defence akin to that of insanity or automatism.

(ii) option 6: abolish the *Majewski* approach and introduce a new offence of criminal intoxication. This offence would have been committed by a person who, while 'deliberately intoxicated' caused the harm proscribed by any of a number of specified offences (eg homicide, bodily harm, rape, criminal damage).

4.26 The final report (Law Com 229, published in 1995) was very much more cautious, recommending simply minimal changes which would make the law more coherent and easier to apply. In a major shift of opinion, the Law Commission concluded that the *Majewski* approach operated fairly, on the whole, and without undue difficulty. On the other hand, the Australian law was seen to create its own problems, relying on juries not to acquit unworthy drunks too readily. The Law Commission recommend that where the prosecution alleges any intention, purpose, knowledge, belief, fraud or dishonesty, evidence of intoxication should be taken into account in determining whether that allegation has been proved. For the purpose of any allegation of any other mental element of an offence (in particular, allegations of recklessness or awareness of risk) a voluntarily intoxicated defendant should be treated as having been aware of anything of which he would have been aware but for his intoxication. These proposals have the merit of dispensing with the need to distinguish between crimes of specific and of basic intent. The new rules, instead of applying to some offences but not to others, are so formulated as to be capable of applying in relation only to certain kinds of mental element.

4.27 *Involuntary intoxication* You might have thought that if your drink is 'laced' by someone else, ie you get drunk without realising it, that you might be excused the criminal offences that you then commit. This is not the case. Thus, you may be convicted of an offence under the RTA 1988, s 5 (driving, or being in charge, of a motor vehicle, with alcohol concentration above the prescribed limit), an offence of strict liability, even though you did not know your drinks had been laced (*A-G's Reference (No 1 of 1975)* (1975)). Even where P must prove recklessness or even intent, D may still be convicted:

Kingston (1995) D was invited to the flat of a man who intended to blackmail him. The blackmailer had already enticed a 15-year-old boy to the flat and had given him drugs which sent him to sleep. D then sexually abused the boy, and was photographed doing so. His defence was that his coffee had been drugged by the blackmailer, causing him to lose the inhibitions which normally controlled his paedophilic tendencies. CA: quashed his conviction: he was not guilty if, because of his intoxication, he forms an intention that he would not have formed if sober. HL: overruled CA, upholding D's conviction. Lord Mustill said that there is no principle of English law that if no blame was attached to the accused, he did not have the *mens rea* and therefore was not guilty.

4.28 Perhaps the main argument in favour of the HL's decision is that it prevents bogus claims. There is no easy line to draw between voluntary and involuntary intoxication: if I did not realise the strength of the gin and tonics that you give me, am I involuntarily or voluntarily intoxicated if I drink them? Doubtless the HL was influenced by the fact that D admitted to being a homosexual paedophile. But is this a reason for convicting him in this particular case? Should moral judgements such as this affect only the sentence, or also criminal liability? For another viewpoint, see Sullivan (1994) who argues that 'it is not a fair test of character to remove surreptitiously a person's inhibitions and confront him with a temptation he ordinarily seeks to avoid.' He argues for a character-based defence, to apply where D is in a state of unblameworthy disequilibrium and in that condition engages in untypical behaviour which is essentially the product of the exceptional circumstances prevailing at the time of the offence.

Corporate liability

4.29 These is something odd about including the liability of corporations in a chapter on incapacitating conditions, but then there is something odd about making companies liable for crimes. As it is, partnerships, unincorporated associations, the Crown and government agencies cannot be convicted of crimes. Most crimes seem to be addressed at human beings and not at corporate bodies, and the *mens rea* concepts in chapter 3 apply uncomfortably to companies. The difficulties go much further than simply *mens rea* questions: can a company 'act' or 'cause' something to happen? Yet companies do cause dreadful harms, and there are a number of ways the law has evolved in order to convict a company. Thus for many years the doctrine of vicarious liability (see **3.36**) has been used to convict companies of strict liability offences. A statute may also impose liability on a company specifically or by necessary implication. For example, if a statute penalises the occupier of premises, a company which is the occupier will be as guilty as any human occupier.

4.30 Sometimes a company is not merely vicariously liable, but is itself liable. The doctrine of identification means that the company itself is deemed to have *mens rea*. The law seeks to identify who is or are the 'brains' or controlling mind of the company, and then their acts can be attributed to the company, not because they are the servants of the company but because the law deems them to be the company. These principles apply more easily in the case of small companies than in the case of large ones:

> *Tesco Supermarkets v Nattrass* (1972) A pensioner complained to an inspector of weights and measures when he was unable to find a packet of washing powder at the advertised 'lower than normal' price. D, a company, was prosecuted under s 11 of the Trade Descriptions Act 1968, which provides that
>
>> If any person offering to supply any goods gives, by whatever means, any indication likely to be taken as an indication that the goods are being offered at a price less than that at which they are in fact being offered he shall ... be guilty of an offence.
>
> D argued that since the manager of the store had failed to check on whether there were enough boxes of soap powder, they had a defence under s 24(1) of the Act that the offence was due to the mistake of another person. The question was therefore whether the manager was 'another person'. DC: dismissed D's appeal, holding on a theory of delegation that the manager was an embodiment of the company. HL: allowed D's appeal. Here the board never delegated any part of their functions. They set up a chain of command, but they remained in control. The acts or omissions of shop managers were not acts of the company itself.

4.31 This is an extraordinarily narrow test. Not many people who work in Tesco could qualify as part of its 'controlling mind'. And is it not fair that since the 'profits of the crime' go to Tesco the company, so should

84

the penalty for breaking the criminal law? Or was the HL in effect saying that it did not approve of strict liability criminal offences? Wells points out that it was bizarre decision: the identification route to liability, which was developed as a means of finding corporations liable beyond the regulatory sphere, being exploited to allow the company to escape liability for a trading standards offence (see 1996 Archbold News Issue 1).

4.32 In recent years there has been great controversy surrounding the question of whether a company can be guilty of manslaughter.

> *P & O European Ferries (Dover) Ltd* (1990) A ferry, the *Herald of Free Enterprise*, sank in 1987 and 192 passengers died. The cause of the 'accident' was not only the negligence of a junior member of the ship's crew but also an irresponsible attitude to safety throughout D, the company which owned the ferry. D was indicted on four counts of manslaughter, but sought to have the indictment quashed. CA: where a corporation, through the controlling mind of one of its agents, does an act which fulfils the prerequisites of manslaughter, it is properly indictable for the crime of manslaughter.

The end of this particular story is that the trial judge directed the jury to return a not guilty verdict, in part because of the management's evidence that they had not been aware of the dangers. Charges against the junior staff were also dropped. The first company to be convicted of manslaughter in this country was OLL Ltd in December 1994, a small company whose cavalier attitude to safety caused the death of school children canoeists in Dorset.

4.33 Penalties for regulatory offences under such statutes as the Health and Safety at Work etc Act 1974 are being regularly increased, and at the same time the courts seem to be taking a firmer line in favour of corporate liability:

> *Tesco Stores Ltd v Brent London Borough Council* (1993) D was prosecuted with selling videos to under-age children. By way of defence, they argued that their controlling officers had no means of knowing the age of the purchasers, and the knowledge of the check-out assistant was irrelevant since she could not act as the company. CA: dismissed their appeal against conviction. Staughton LJ pointed out that it would be absurd to accept D's argument, since it would mean in effect that no large company could ever commit this offence.

British Steel plc (1995) D was prosecuted under s 3 of the HSAWA1974, which imposes a duty on employers to ensure, so far as is reasonably practicable, that others are not exposed to risk to their health and safety. D argued that because they had taken steps at a senior level to ensure safety, they should not be liable. CA: dismissed their appeal against conviction. Since all reasonable steps had not been taken at operating level, D was guilty. The Court commented on the inadequacy of a fine of £100 imposed where a man had died.

Gateways Foodmarkets (1997) V, the duty manager in a store, fell though a trap door in the lift control room and died. CA: upheld D's conviction under s 2 of the HSAWA 1974 (which imposes a duty on employers in relation to their own employees), and a fine of £10,000.

4.34   *Reform* One alternative would be to make companies subject to much stiffer punitive damages in civil courts. The Law Commission (in Law Com No 237) has also recommended an offence of corporate manslaughter:

(1) A corporation is guilty of corporate killing if-
(a) a management failure by the corporation is the cause or one of the causes of a person's death; and
(b) that failure constitutes conduct falling far below what can reasonably be expected of the corporation in the circumstances

Thus management failure would be a question of fact for the jury to determine: do you think it sounds a workable test, or unfairly vague?

4.35   Problems will remain in relation to imposing liability on companies. You can argue that the criminal law is right to concentrate on the criminal activities of individuals: people are much more frightened of the harm they may suffer on the street or in the home from a violent attacker than they are by the harm that may be caused by a big city fraud or a major pollution incident. We return to the topic in chapter 13.

Further reading

Butler Committee *Report of the Committee on Mentally Abnormal Offenders* (Cmnd 6244, 1975)

Clarkson, 'Kicking Corporate Bodies and Damning their Souls' (1996) 59 MLR 557

Fisse and Braithwaite, 'The Allocation of Responsibility for Corporate Crime: Individualism, Collectivism and Accountability' (1988) 11 Sydney LR 468

Gobert, 'Corporate Criminality: New Crimes for the Times' [1994] Crim LR 722

Home Office (1999) Managing Dangerous People with severe personality disorder (HMSO)

Horder, 'Pleading Voluntary Lack of Capacity' [1993] Camb LJ 298

Mackay *Mental Condition Defences in the Criminal Law* (1995)

Sullivan, 'Involuntary Intoxication and Beyond' [1994] Crim LR 272

Sullivan, 'The attribution of Culpability to Limited Companies' [1996] CLJ 515

Walker, 'The end of an old song?' [1999] NLJ 64

Wells *Corporations and Criminal Responsibility* (1993)

Self-test questions

1. Dee and Bee, both aged 13, are playing with a plastic gun. They point it at close range at a pensioner, Phil, and demand that he hands over his money. Phil is terrified and has a heart attack. He dies two days later. Dee and Bee maintain that they were only having fun and thought that Phil would know it was a game.

2. Dee believes that fairies live in the corner of the public park, and that they must never be disturbed. When she sees Phil, a gardener, stacking flower pots in the area where she believes the fairies live, she chases him away by throwing bricks at him. One grazes him on the arm as he flees.

3. Dee, a diabetic, is charged with dangerous driving. Her defence is that her doctor has been experimenting with a new regime of insulin treatment, and she was not sure whether in fact she had injected herself with the correct dose that morning. Medical evidence suggests that she might have been in a hypoglycaemic condition at the time the police stopped her.

4. David has sex with Violet without her consent. Is he criminally liable if he had been drinking heavily and thought she was consenting? Would your advice to him be different if he had been drinking orange juice which had been laced with neat lab alcohol by his so-called friends?

5. Should companies be capable of being convicted of crimes?

CHAPTER FIVE

General defences

SUMMARY
The chapter first explores the nature of a 'defence', and then key issues in relation to various defences:

Consent: There are few clear general principles on what D can consent to. If consent is available as a defence, so too is D's mistaken belief in consent.

Duress: Not available to some crimes (murder, attempted murder); also there is a lack of clarity about the degree of threats required.

Necessity: Not generally available as a justification, but it has crept in as an excuse as 'duress of circumstances'.

Mistake: Genuine (even if unreasonable) beliefs may excuse.

Self-defence and the prevention of crime: Common law defences and a statutory defence under s 3 CLA 1967 co-exist.

Introduction

5.1   In the last chapter we looked at various incapacitating conditions which act in some ways as defences: they explain why someone is not guilty of what otherwise looks like a crime. In this chapter we explore other ways in which D may escape liability. It is difficult to generalise about the nature of defences: sometimes a defence is seen simply as a way of showing that P has not proved all the elements of the crime. Glanville Williams suggested that all the elements of a crime are divisible into *actus reus* or *mens rea* and that the *actus reus* involves absence of defence (see **2.1**). Other writers prefer to argue that a crime is made up

89

of *actus reus*, *mens rea* and absence of defence. If a woman consents to sex, the man is not guilty of rape because an essential element of the crime (the absence of consent) is missing. Is the absence of consent an element in the offence or is the presence of consent a defence?

5.2 Can a clear distinction be drawn between the offence and the defence elements of a crime? Glanville Williams (1982) seemed to argue that there is no such clear distinction: he considered

> two draft statutes, each of which is intended to turn assault into a statutory offence. The first draft defines an assault as an intentional or reckless attack upon a person without his consent. Non-consent is then, presumably, a definitional element of the offence. The second draft defines assault as an intentional or reckless attack upon a person, but adds the proviso or qualification that the offence is not committed where the person attacked has consented. Consent now appears to be a matter of defence ... yet the difference between the two drafts is purely verbal, a matter of convenience in expression. Is there any reason why rules of substantive law should hinge upon a draftsman's convenience?

5.3 Campbell (1987) disagrees, suggesting that there is a clear conceptual difference: offence definitions delimit that against which the law always takes there to be prima facie reason, whereas defences set out conditions under which D is to be exonerated even though the prima facie reason against his conduct subsists. It would not make sense to say 'Sexual intercourse by a man with a woman is an offence. It is a defence to this offence that the woman was consenting'. Thus absence of consent to sex is part of the definition of the offence. There is no doubting that the law has traditionally adopted the distinction between offence and defences, and the student would be lost without it. Just be aware of the definitional difficulties. Ashworth prefers (in PCL) to talk of 'negative fault requirements' in order to point out that such matters are generally those that P does not have to disprove unless D raises them with some credibility.

5.4 The strong arguments in favour of codifying the criminal law (see 1.27) do not necessarily apply to defences. One should know in advance the limits of the criminal law, but not necessarily the outer limits of defences. The DCC therefore, and the Criminal Law Bill attached to the more recent Law Com Report No 218 preserve many existing common law rules and defences to maintain the flexibility within the operation of the law which is much valued. In this chapter, we will not examine all defences, but simply give examples of the most common. There are others: for example, new life was breathed into the defence of marital coercion (to be found in the CJA 1925, s 47) by the CA in *Shortland* (1996).

Justifications and excuses

5.5 Defences can be usefully subdivided into excuses and justifications (see JC Smith's readable and enjoyable 1989 Hamlyn Lectures). In essence, your behaviour may be said to be excused if you are not sufficiently at fault or culpable. An excuse can be seen as a 'concession to human frailty'. Such behaviour is not necessarily approved of, simply excused as not meriting punishment. On the other hand, your behaviour is justified if it was the most appropriate course of conduct in the circumstances. This distinction is important for two main reasons:

(i) it has legal consequences: for example, excusable conduct may be resisted by a person who is threatened by it, but justifiable conduct may not be resisted. Again, if D aids and abets a person who is merely excused liability, D may still be guilty of an offence; if D was aiding and abetting someone whose behaviour was justified, he too will not be guilty of an offence.

(ii) it may colour the way we think about the defence. The difference in the moral quality of excuses and justifications may help us devising improvements or reforms to the law. For a discussion of how the distinction can be useful when the law is in flux, see ATH Smith (1978) and Padfield (1992). Keep the distinction in mind: but remain conscious of the difficulties in maintaining the distinction in border-line cases.

Consent

5.6 Absence of consent is an essential element of many offences (and not a defence in the same strict sense as duress or self-defence, for example). In establishing a crime such as rape, P must exclude consent in order to establish the essential ingredients of the offence. There is no burden on D to raise the issue as there will be for the other defences. If you consent to sexual intercourse, then it is not rape; if I consent to you kissing me, then you have not assaulted me; if I agree to you destroying my property then you have not committed criminal damage or theft. But the law is more paternalistic than that: there are many things to which you are not permitted to consent: most obviously, death. If someone intentionally kills another, even though that other begs him to do it, the offence of murder (with its mandatory life sentence) is nonetheless committed. Whether or not euthanasia should be permitted is clearly a moral and political 'hot potato'. The issues were dramatically raised in *Airedale NHS Trust v Bland* (1993) which was discussed in the context of defining the difference between acts and omissions (**2.11**). *Bland* did not consent to his death: but might it be that the paternalistic attitude of the judiciary allowed them to decide that it was reasonable for the doctors to believe that, had he been able to, he would have consented? Do you think that the HL were correct to 'allow Bland to die'?

5.7 It is even more difficult to state the law with any certainty when it comes to non-fatal injuries. Assaults and woundings must be 'unlawful'. The unlawfulness stems in most cases from the lack of consent of the victim, but the courts have had great difficulty in establishing the line between those acts/omissions to which one may consent, and those to which one may not:

> *Donovan* (1934) D beat a 17-year-old consenting girl for his own sexual gratification. He was convicted of indecent and common assault. CCA: quashed the conviction because of a misdirection by the trial judge. Swift J stated *obiter* that if an act is unlawful in the sense of being in itself a criminal act, it is plain that it cannot be rendered lawful because the person to whose detriment it is done consents to it. No person can license another to commit a crime.

5.8 This rather circular advice proved of little help:

> *A-G's Reference(No 6 of 1980)* Two young men aged 18 and 17 quarrelled and agreed to settle their difference with a fight in the street. They were acquitted by the jury after the trial judge said that consent might be a defence if they had used only reasonable force. The issue of consent was referred for the opinion of the CA on a point of law under s 36 of the CJA 1972. CA (Lord Lane): held that consent was

not a defence as it was not in the public interest that people should cause each other actual bodily harm 'for no good reason'. He said that the public/private place distinction was immaterial: it was not a function of the criminal law of assault to stop public disturbances.

> Nothing which we have said is intended to cast doubt on the accepted legality of properly conducted games and sports, lawful chastisement or correction, reasonable surgical interference, dangerous exhibitions etc. These apparent exceptions can be justified as involving the exercise of a legal right, in the case of chastisement or correction, or as needed in the public interest, in the other cases.

5.9 Lord Lane gave no advice on when the 'public interest' might provide good reason for allowing people to consent to minor harms. He lists the usually accepted categories but these are not without problems. What is reasonable surgical interference? What is a lawfully conducted game? Why is boxing lawful, when the intent of the participants is to assault each other, and a lawful game can result in devastating injuries? Tattooing too is lawful (though it is unlawful to tattoo someone under the age of 18). Is the answer here to be found in the fact that where there is seen to be an effective system of regulatory control, whether created by a licensing regime, or by the standards or ethics of a profession, or by a species of self-regulation in which Parliament has trust, the activity may be safely left to be lawful? Tattoo parlours must be licensed by local authority environmental health departments, and tatooists must use sterilised needles. But there are of course many unlicensed tattooists: is this more an area for a public health campaign than for the criminal law? Many curious examples can be found in the case law:

> *Jones* (1986) Schoolboys aged 14 and 15 were tossed into the air by Ds, former school fellows, who had waited for them outside the school. One boy suffered a broken arm, the other a ruptured spleen. CA: quashed Ds' convictions for offences under s 20 of the OAPA 1861. A genuine belief, whether or not it was reasonably held, in consent to rough and undisciplined play could be a defence where there was no intention to commit an injury.

> *Aitken* (1992) RAF officers were convicted of inflicting grievous bodily harm contrary to s 20 of the OAPA 1861 after pouring white spirit over a drunk and sleeping colleague who was wearing a fire-resistant

flying suit, and then setting fire to it. He suffered 35% burns. Courts-Martial Appeal Court: quashed their convictions. Their mistaken belief in V's consent should have been left to the jury.

Brown (1994) A group of sado-masochist homosexuals inflicted pain on each other for pleasure. They pleaded guilty to offences under s 20 and s 47 of the OAPA 1861 after the trial judge ruled that consent could be no defence in these circumstances. HL (by a majority of 3 to 2): dismissed their appeals. Lords Templeman, Lowry and Jauncey were in the majority:

> In principle there is a difference between violence which is incidental and violence which is inflicted for the indulgence of cruelty. The violence of sado-masochistic encounters involves the indulgence of cruelty by sadists and the degradation of victims. Such violence is injurious to the participants and unpredictably dangerous. I am not prepared to invent a defence of consent for sado-masochistic encounters which breed and glorify cruelty and result in offences under ss 47 and 20 of the 1861 Act' (Lord Templeman).

Lords Mustill and Slynn (dissenting) concentrated on the issue of whether the public interest required the criminilisation of this behaviour and found no compelling reason for so doing.

Remember that this case was then taken to the ECHR but the complainants failed in their claim that their right to privacy had been infringed (see **1.24**). However, compare the case with

Wilson (1997) Evidence came from V's doctor that D, her husband, had branded his initials on V's buttocks with a hot knife, at her request. CA: quashed his conviction for an offence under the OAPA 1861, s 47. There was no aggressive intent, and there was no evidence that what he did was more dangerous than tattooing. It was not in the public interest that such consensual activity between husband and wife should result in a prosecution.

Emmett (1999) Evidence against D again came from V's doctor: 'high-risk' sexual activity had resulted on one occasion in haemorrhages to her eyes and bruising to her neck caused by asphyxiation, and on another in burns to her breast. CA: upheld D's conviction. Consent is no defence where the harm caused consists of more than transient or trivial injury.

Can these cases be reconciled? D's conviction in *Emmett* is upheld although he did not intend any injury. Does the case simply signify that the courts are tightening up on 'dodgy' domestic violence, even when consensual?

5.10 The law in relation to consent and sexual offences is difficult to set out clearly. It is of the essence of rape that the victim is not consenting, but the SOA 1976, s 1(2) provides that:

> It is hereby declared that if at a trial for a rape offence the jury has to consider whether a man believed that a woman or man was consenting to sexual intercourse, the presence or absence of reasonable grounds for such a belief is a matter to which the jury is to have regard, in conjunction with any other relevant matters, in considering whether he so believed.

This means that an unreasonable belief in her consent, if genuinely held, results in D's acquittal: should it? This is not as surprising as it may appear: juries will usually not believe that an unreasonable belief was genuinely held. As we shall see at **10.14**, there are two offences running alongside rape which allow for the conviction of those who obtain a woman's consent to sex by threats or fraud. Thus a man is not guilty of rape where his victim's 'consent' was obtained by fraud. However, fraud in any case only vitiates consent if it is a deception as to the nature of the act or as to the identity of the man: circumstances which one would have thought would be exceptionally rare.

> *Linekar* (1995) D had sex with a prostitute and left without paying. CA: quashed his conviction for rape. It was the absence of consent to sexual intercourse, rather than fraud, which constitutes the offence of rape. The reality of V's consent is not destroyed by D's pretence that he would pay her.

5.11 Neither a boy or a girl under the age of 16 can in law consent to indecent assault (see **10.16**). Although a mentally ill person may be deemed incapable of consenting, since a subjective belief in consent is enough, D may still be acquitted:

> *Kimber* (1983) D sexually assaulted a patient in a mental hospital. He was convicted of indecent assault under s14 of the SOA 1956. CA (Lawton LJ): dismissed his appeal. It is a good defence to show that D

95

honestly believed that she consented, though there were no grounds to believe it here. Recklessness was only proved if D did not believe that P was consenting or 'couldn't care less' ie he was indifferent to her wishes and feelings.

5.12 *Reform* Not surprisingly, the Law Commission has found an analysis of consent very tricky. They published a consultation paper on *Consent and Offences against the Person* in 1993 (Law Com CP 134), but instead of producing a report as a result of consultation (the usual process: see **1.28**), they felt compelled by the responses that they received to producing a fuller and longer consultation paper in 1995 on *Consent in the Criminal Law* (Law Com CP 139). In this, they provisionally propose that consent should not be a defence to those who intentionally or recklessly cause serious disabling injury, but that consent should be a defence to those who intentionally or recklessly cause other, less serious, injuries. Is it appropriate simply to draw a line at a certain level of injury, or is the issue more difficult than this? Roberts wrote a paper for the Law Commission on the philosophical foundations of the law on consent, which is included in an Appendix to Law Com CP No 139, and which concludes that those who advocate criminilisation from a paternalistic or moralistic perspective must overcome powerful and widely accepted liberal counter-arguments. 'The presumption in favour of individual autonomy places the burden of persuasion firmly on the shoulders of liberalism's opponents' (page 281).

Duress

5.13 If you commit a crime simply because you have been threatened with a dreadful consequence if you don't do it, you may have a defence. As we will see the 'standard' defence is duress, but this is narrowly construed. The courts are reluctant to acknowledge necessity as a defence (see **5.19**), and so a new 'hybrid' defence of duress of circumstances has evolved in the last 15 years. Duress is normally considered to be an excuse (see **5.4**), whereas its first cousin necessity is more properly a justification. But the courts are not consistent in their use of this terminology, and as we shall see, there are considerable overlaps between these three defences. Let us start with duress. Once D has introduced the defence, P has to prove beyond reasonable doubt that D was not acting under duress.

5.14 *Type of threat required* The threat must be of death or serious bodily harm, and is normally an imminent or immediate threat. A sliding scale of threats would perhaps be fairer, such that more minor threats might provide a defence to more minor offences, but would this create too much uncertainty?

Hudson and Taylor (1971) Ds gave false evidence in court because they were frightened by threats that they would be beaten up if they gave evidence against W. CA: quashed their convictions for perjury as the Recorder had been wrong to instruct the jury that the threats were not sufficiently present and immediate to constitute duress. CA: quashed their convictions. The Recorder should have left to the jury the question whether the threats had overborne Ds' will at the time when they gave evidence. Lord Parker CJ:

> It is essential to the defence of duress that the threat shall be effective at the moment when the crime is committed. The threat must be a 'present' threat in the sense that it is effective to neutralise the will of the accused at the time.

Valderama-Vega (1985) D was arrested with 2 kg of cocaine at Gatwick Airport. He was convicted of being knowingly concerned in the fraudulent evasion of the prohibition of the importation of a controlled drug despite his defence that he had received threats that his homosexuality would be exposed, as well as death threats to his family if he did not act as a courier. CA: dismissed his appeal. The defence of duress, which had been left fairly to the jury, should be available so long as it was reasonably possible to say that the threat of death or serious injury was a *sine qua non* of his decision to offend, though it need not be the only factor. The threats must be of death or serious injury whatever the offence.

Rodger and Rose (1998) D, life sentence prisoners, had become suicidal on learning that their tariffs had been substantially increased. CA: dismissed their appeals. Since the threat was not extraneous to the offender, a defence of duress was not available (see **5.22**).

Abdul-Hussain (1999) Fugitives from Iraq hijacked an aircraft from Sudan to Stansted, and were convicted under the Aviation Security Act 1982 after the trial judge ruled that a defence of necessity or duress of circumstances could not be left to the jury, since the threat was insufficiently close or immediate. CA (Rose LJ): allowed the appeals. The defence of duress should have been left to the jury: the imminent peril of death or serious injury to D or his dependants had to operate on his mind so as to overbear his will at the time he committed the act. The threat must be imminent, but need not be immediate. The Court stressed the need for legislation in this area.

> If Ann Frank had stolen a car to escape from Amsterdam and had been charged with theft, the tenets of English law would not, in our judgement, have denied her a defence of duress of circumstances, on the ground that she should have waited for the Gestapo's knock on the door.

5.15 In general, the test of duress is whether the threat was of such gravity that it might well have caused a reasonable man placed in the same position to act in the same way as D acted, and whether a sober person of reasonable firmness sharing D's characteristics would have responded to the threat as he did.

> *Bowen* (1996) D was convicted on five specimen counts of obtaining services by deception. He gave evidence that two men had threatened to petrol bomb him and his family if he did not do as instructed. Other witnesses gave evidence that he was a simple man (with an IQ of 68) who was abnormally suggestible and vulnerable. CA (Stuart-Smith LJ): dismissed his appeal. It was not necessary to direct the jury on D's low intelligence.
>
> > The mere fact that D is more pliable, vulnerable, timid or susceptible to threats than a normal person are not characteristics with which it is legitimate to invest the reasonable/ordinary person for the purpose of considering the objective test.
> >
> > Only if D belongs to a category of persons (probably based only on age or sex) who the jury may think less able to resist pressure than others should the judge comment on such characteristics.

Buchanan and Virgo (1999) assert that the *Bowen* test is unworkable: there are no recognised criteria for identifying a group whose ability to withstand threats is reduced.

5.16 The courts have wisely distinguished those cases where D has voluntarily put himself in a position where he would be likely to be subject to duress, in which case the defence is not available:

> *Sharp* (1987) D, a member of a gang which he knew used loaded firearms to carry out robberies, took part in a robbery in which a sub-postmaster was shot dead. D said that he had not wanted to participate in the robbery when he knew that firearms would be used but that he was threatened that his head would be blown off if he did not. CA (Lord Lane CJ):
>
> > where a person has voluntarily, and with knowledge of its nature, joined a criminal organisation or gang which he knew might bring pressure on him to commit an offence and was an active member when he was put under such pressure, he cannot avail himself of the defence of duress.

> *Shepherd* (1987) D's defence to charges of burglary was that the organiser had threatened him with violence if he dropped out. CA: quashed his convictions. Not every criminal conspiracy deprives its adherents of the defence of duress. It depends on the nature of the duress and whether D knew he was submitting himself to the risk of compulsion. Where there is evidence of duress, the jury should decide on the exact facts.

> *Baker and Ward* (1999) Ds, who were involved in supplying cannabis, failed to pay their suppliers, were provided with an imitation firearm and were told to carry out a robbery. They did not put themselves under police protection as they did not believe this would be effective. CA (Roch LJ): quashed their convictions and ordered a retrial. The jury should ask themselves first whether P had proved that D could have neutralised the threats by seeking the assistance of the police. If so, they had no defence. If not, they should then ask whether P had proved that Ds had voluntarily put themselves in a position where they were likely to be subjected to compulsion of the necessary kind to commit offences to obtain money by dealing in cannabis on the scale that they were doing and by incurring debts to their supplier of several thousands of pounds. If so, they had no defence. If not, the defence of duress was available.

5.17   Duress is not available as a defence to all offences.

Howe (1987) Ds confessed to taking part in the killing of Vs, but said that they acted through fear. HL: upheld their conviction for murder, overruling the decision in *DPP for Northern Ireland v Lynch* (1975), which had allowed the defence of duress to those who aid and abet murder. Lord Hailsham:

> I have known in my lifetime of too many acts of heroism by ordinary human beings of no more than ordinary fortitude to regard a law as either 'just or humane' which withdraws the protection of the criminal law from the innocent victim and casts the cloak of its protection upon the coward and the poltroon in the name of a 'concession to human frailty'.

This decision has been much criticised. JC Smith (1989) called it a 'blueprint for saintliness'. Milgate (1988) analyses seven reasons that can be found for overruling *Lynch*, but stands each one on its head. Thus, Lord Hailsham had suggested that since Parliament had not acted on the Law Commission's recommendation (in Law Comm No 83, 1977) that duress should be available in all cases of murder, it had clearly not accepted the report. Milgate points out that it is as easy to argue that since Parliament had not overruled *Lynch*, it should be taken to support it. As a result of *Howe*, we now may have a duty to be a hero. A taxi driver who delivers a bomb for a terrorist organisation because the gang are holding his family hostage has no defence: should he be allowed one? Certainly the law is now very inconsistent: where do we now draw the line between those offences for which duress is available and those where it is unavailable?

> *Gotts* (1992) D stabbed and seriously injured his mother, after his father had threatened to kill him if he did not do so. He was convicted of attempted murder after the trial judge ruled that his defence of duress could not be left to the jury. HL: dismissed the appeal. Lord Jauncey:
>
>> The reason why duress has for so long been stated not to be available as a defence to a murder charge is that the law regards the sanctity of human life and the protection thereof as of paramount importance.

Do you agree? It may be more appropriate for lawyers to talk of a 'right to life' (a legal/moral concept) and not the 'sanctity of human life' (a theological concept). Is the right to life an absolute right? Think again about the issues raised in *Bland* (**2.11; 5.6**).

5.18 What happens if D makes a mistake about the threat he is under? Duress seems to be only a defence if D reasonably believed in the facts which gave him good cause to fear: see *Graham* (**5.27**). If D reasonably believes there is a threat, it does not matter that there is in fact no threat: see *Cairns* (**5:22**).

Necessity

5.19 The status of necessity in English law remains unclear, largely because it is an area of common law where there is an absence of case law (though a statute may expressly or impliedly create a defence of necessity). One may argue that the dearth of case law suggests that necessity is not a defence; more convincing is the argument that necessity is so clearly a defence in some cases that no prosecutions are brought. Thus, if you break the speed limit to get a severely wounded person to hospital, or you burn down your neighbours shed simply to save a row of houses from fire, you may well not be prosecuted. The normal starting point in any discussion of necessity is *Dudley and Stephens*:

> *Dudley and Stephens* (1884) After a shipwreck, four men found themselves cast adrift in an open boat. After drifting for 20 days, and having not eaten for nine days and having been without water for seven days, two of the men agreed to kill the weakest, the cabin boy. Having done so, they fed on his flesh for four days, and were then picked up by a passing ship. They believed that if they did not feed on one of themselves, they would all have died of starvation. Lord Coleridge CJ upheld their conviction for murder, rejecting the defence of necessity.

5.20 It is unclear from Lord Coleridge's speech whether he was saying that it was not necessary in that case for Ds to kill the cabin boy, or whether there is simply no defence of necessity. The following cases may suggest that there is a general defence of necessity, except where expressly or impliedly excluded by statute.

> *Bourne* (1939) D, a well respected surgeon, carried out an abortion on a 14-year-old girl who had become pregnant as the result of a violent rape. He was prosecuted with unlawfully procuring a miscarriage. Macnaghten J, summing up to the jury, said they should

acquit if they believed that the doctor had acted in good faith for the purpose only of preserving the life of the girl. The doctor was acquitted.

Gillick v West Norfolk and Wisbech Area Health Authority (1986) In judicial review proceedings, P challenged the legality of a Department of Health memorandum which advised doctors that they would not be acting unlawfully if they prescribed contraceptives to girls under 16 without parental consent so long as they were acting in good faith to protect the girl against the harmful effects of sexual intercourse. HL: the memorandum was not unlawful. A girl under 16 does not merely by her age lack the capacity to consent. A doctor who in the exercise of his clinical judgement gave contraceptive advice and treatment to a girl under the age of 16 without her parents' consent does not commit an offence because the bona fide exercise by the doctor of his clinical judgement negated the *mens rea* which was an essential element of the offence

Re F (mental patient: sterilisation) (1990) The mother of a 36-year-old mentally handicapped woman issued a summons seeking a declaration that the sterilisation of her daughter would not be an unlawful act by reason only of the absence of the daughter's consent. HL: accepted that the sterilisation was in the woman's best interest, and granted a declaration. Conscious of the need for 'a measure to protect those from the insults of an unnecessary sterilisation' (Lord Griffiths), the House nonetheless accepted that 'a man who seizes another and forcibly drags him from the path of an oncoming vehicle, thereby saving him from injury or even death, commits no wrong' (Lord Goff).

5.21 The Law Commission has changed its mind several times about the need for a defence of necessity. More than 20 years ago, in Law Com WP No 55, they proposed a general defence of necessity, which should be available where D himself believes that his conduct is necessary to avoid some greater harm than that which he faces, and that the harm to be avoided must, judged objectively, be found to be out of all proportion to that actually caused by the defendant's conduct. However, in their 1977 Report ((Law Com No 83), they rejected this proposal, suggesting that such a defence was not required. The DCC includes a proposed defence of duress of circumstances (see **5.22** below) but not a justificatory choice-of-evil type defence.

Duress of circumstances

5.22   In the late 1980s a new defence appeared:

> *Willer* (1987) D's car was surrounded by a group of aggressive youths, and so he mounted the pavement and drove slowly out of a narrow alleyway. The Assistant Recorder refused to leave a defence of necessity to the jury and he was convicted of reckless driving. CA (Watkins LJ): quashed his conviction. The question whether D 'was wholly driven by force of circumstances into doing what he did and did not drive the car otherwise than under that form of compulsion' should have been left to the jury.

> *Conway* (1989) Fearing for the safety of his passenger, D drove recklessly to escape from people (who turned out to be plain clothes police officers) who he feared would make a fatal attack on his friend. No defence of necessity was left to the jury. CA (Wolf LJ): quashed D's conviction.

> > ... necessity can only be a defence to a charge of reckless driving where the facts establish 'duress of circumstances', as in *Willer* ie where D was constrained by circumstances to drive as he did to avoid death or serious bodily harm to himself or some other person ... 'Duress of circumstances' is available only if from an objective standpoint D can be said to be acting in order to avoid a threat of death or serious injury.

> *Martin* (1989) D's wife threatened suicide if he didn't drive her son to work, even though he was disqualified from driving. CA: quashed his conviction for driving whilst disqualified. Two questions should have been left to the jury: first, was D, or may he have been, impelled to act as he did because as a result of what he reasonably believed to be the situation, he had good reason to fear that otherwise death (including suicide) or serious physical injury would result? If so, may a sober person of reasonable firmness, sharing D's characteristics, have responded to that situation by acting as D did?

The defence is now regularly discussed in the case law: see *Abdul-Hussain* **(5:14)** and the following examples.

> *Rodger and Rose* (1998) Two life sentence prisoners escaped from Parkhurst Prison because they felt suicidal after the Home Secretary

significantly raised their tariffs (the minimum period they had to serve before their cases could be heard by the Parole Board). CA (Sir Patrick Russell): dismissed their appeals. They did not escape because of the Home Secretary's decision, but because of their own suicidal tendencies. The defences of 'duress by necessity or duress of circumstances' are not available unless the causative feature of the commission of the offence is extraneous to the offender:

> If allowed if could amount to a license to commit a crime dependant on the personal characteristics and vulnerability of the offender.

Cairns (2000) V spread-eagled himself onto D's windscreen. D, who was small and timid, did not know V and said he was intimidated by V's friend shouting from the roadside. He drove on, breaking when he got to a speed hump. V fell under the car and fractured his spine, which rendered him paraplegic. D was convicted under s 20 of the OAPA 1861 (see **9.8**). CA (Mansell LJ): quashed his conviction. Where D relies on the defence of necessity or duress of circumstances, it was sufficient for him to show that he acted because he reasonably perceived a threat of serious physical injury or death; he was not required to prove that the threat was actual or real.

5.23 The Law Commission seems to have accepted that this defence is an excuse, close to duress. The Criminal Law Bill in Law Com No 218 includes separate definitions of duress by threats; duress of circumstances; and justifiable use of force. By clause 36(2) various common law defences would be abrogated:

(a) the defence of duress, whether by threats or of circumstances;
(b) the defence of coercion of a wife by her husband;
(c) any defence available in respect of the use of force ...
but without prejudice to any distinct defence of necessity.

This seems to be a convenient way of side-stepping the problem: is or should the defence of necessity operate as a justificatory defence quite separately to the excusatory defence of duress?

Mistake

5.24 Some mistakes may mean that P fails to prove an essential element of the necessary guilty mind: intention or recklessness (see chapter 3).

For example, if I intentionally throw darts at you thinking you are a shop's dummy, I am not guilty of your murder if you die from the wounds I cause you. I did not intend to kill a person. However, we are here concerned with situations when a mistake may give rise to a distinct defence. Everyone is presumed to know the law: so only mistakes of fact may give rise to a defence. Why is this? Do we have a moral obligation to know the law? Husak and von Hirsch (1993) argue that ignorance of the law should normally be excused if D's legal mistake was a reasonable one in the circumstances, and that D's punishment should be mitigated if he did not know but should have known of the illegality of his conduct. However, it is not always easy to distinguish fact from law:

> *Gould* (1968) D was convicted of bigamy under s 57 of the OAPA 1861. At the time of the second marriage he honestly believed that his first marriage had been dissolved and he had reasonable grounds for this belief. In fact the marriage had not been dissolved and his first wife was still living. CA: quashed his conviction. An honest belief on reasonable grounds was a good defence to a charge of bigamy if the consequences of that belief being true would be that an offence had not been committed.

5.25 If knowledge of a surrounding circumstance is an ingredient of an offence then an honest mistake as to that circumstance may be a defence. This mistake need not be reasonable, as long as it is genuinely held.

> *DPP v Morgan* (1977) An RAF officer invited a group of colleagues to have sex with his wife, assuring them that she would be willing and that she might simulate reluctance for her own pleasure. They had sex with her while she kicked and screamed for the police, and then he had sex with her himself. HL: quashed their convictions for rape. The trial judge had been wrong to direct the jury that a belief in V's consent had to be reasonable:
>
> > Since honest belief clearly negatives intent, the reasonableness or otherwise of that belief can only be evidence for or against the view that the belief and therefore the intent was actually held' (Lord Hailsham).
>
> *Gladstone Williams* (1987) D punched V because he believed that V was beating up a third party, when in fact V was arresting the third party. CA (Lord Lane CJ): quashed his conviction.

The reasonableness or unreasonableness of D's belief is material to the question of whether the belief was held by D at all. If the belief was in fact held, its unreasonableness, so far as guilt or innocence is concerned, is neither here nor there.

Beckford v R (1988) D, a police officer, was at the scene where V, an armed man was terrorising his family. D shot V dead after he had given himself up and after he had been unarmed. D's defence was that he honestly believed that his life was in danger. The Jamaican CA upheld his conviction for murder on the ground that his belief that he was acting in self-defence had to be reasonable, and not just honestly held. PC (Lord Griffiths): quashed his conviction '... a man about to be attacked does not have to wait for his assailant to strike the first blow or fire the first shot; circumstances may justify a pre-emptive strike'.

These cases are cited in *B (a minor) v DPP* (2000) where, as we saw at **3.40**, the HL held that the offence under the Indecency with Children Act 1960 is not an offence of strict liability: P must prove that D knew that, or was reckless whether, the child was under 14.

5.26 Can one always distinguish a mistaken belief from the more culpable state of mind which may arise where D has no knowledge of the surrounding circumstances because he gave the matter no thought, or forgot it? Thus in rape can one distinguish mistake from reckless ignorance? At **10.10** we will consider whether the law should in rape acknowledge a duty to think arising from D's conduct. Should D be liable for his failure (omission) to think?

5.27 If D makes a mistake as to a defence, the mistake may have to be reasonable:

Graham (1982) D, a homosexual, lived in a *ménage à trois* with his wife and a man. D played a leading part in the killing of his wife, but said that he acted under duress, and that his behaviour was affected by the drink and drugs he had taken. CA (Lord Lane CJ): upheld his conviction for murder. There is an objective element in the defence of duress: the jury must determine whether the threat was one which the D in question could not reasonably have been expected to resist.

As a matter of public policy, it seems to us essential to limit the defence of duress by means of an objective criterion formulated in terms of reasonableness ...if a mistake is to excuse what would otherwise be criminal, the mistake must be a reasonable one.

5.28 Both the courts (see *DPP v Rogers* (1998)) and the Law Commission have resisted this development in the law, but it has been confirmed in *Abdul-Hussain* (1999): see **5.14**. In Law Com 218, the Law Commission say that there was 'almost no support' for the view that D's belief must be reasonable, and they recommend that reasonableness should be a matter of evidence only. Thus, the emphasis in their recommendation is on the actor's 'knowledge or belief'. Similarly, the courts do not always seem to follow *Graham*:

> *Scarlett* (1993) D, a publican, used excessive force to eject V, a drunken man, from his pub. V died, and D was convicted of manslaughter. CA: quashed his conviction. Provided that D 'believed that the circumstances called for the degree of force used, he was not to be convicted even if his belief was unreasonable'.

The CA has subsequently moved away from this position:

> *DPP v Armstrong-Braun* (1998) D, trying to protect great crested newts from building developments, obstructed V, who was using a mechanical digger on the site being developed. He was convicted of an assault under s 39 CJA 1988. CA: the force used by D when accused of battery in self-defence was to be assessed in an objective sense as to whether it was reasonably necessary in the circumstances as D subjectively believed them to be. There was no necessity for an additional test requiring a subjective approach to the question of proportionality of the response.

JC Smith (in [1999] Crim LR 128) comments 'the law was misstated, probably inadvertently, in *Scarlett* and it is best forgotten'.

5.29 The Law Commission use *Scarlett* (in Law Com No 218, page 3) to illustrate the need for a codification of the criminal law. Mr Scarlett spent five months in prison before the CA quashed his conviction, a conviction which happened, it could be said, just because everyone in the case had overlooked the requirement that the reasonableness of the force used must be judged in the circumstances as the accused believed them to be. But was this actually the law?

Self-defence and the prevention of crime

5.30   These offences are usually dealt with together since they are first cousins: self-defence (along with defence of property and defence of another) is a common law defence, whereas prevention of crime is to be found in the CLA 1967, s 3:

> (1) A person may use such force as is reasonable in the circumstances in the prevention of crime, or in effecting or assisting in the lawful arrest of offenders or suspected offenders or of persons unlawfully at large.

5.31   Both are normally seen as justificatory defences. A person may use such force as is reasonable in the circumstances for the purposes of self-defence, defence of property or of another, prevention of crime or lawful arrest. What is reasonable is a question of fact for the jury. D is judged on what is reasonable on the facts as he believed them to be (see *Beckford* at **5.25**).

> *A-G's Reference (No 2 of 1983)* (1984) D, of previously good character, made petrol bombs, intending to use them in the event of an attack on his shop by rioters in an area where serious rioting had occurred. CA: D had to satisfy the jury on a balance of probabilities that his object was to protect himself or his family or property against imminent apprehended attack and to so by means which he believed were no more than reasonably necessary to meet the force used by the attackers.

5.32   These are 'all or nothing' defences: why is there no half way house where excessive force is used, resulting in a partial reduction, rather as murder is reduced to manslaughter in cases of provocation (see **8.14**)?

> *Clegg* (1995) D, a British soldier based in Northern Ireland, was on night patrol. A car failed to stop at a checkpoint some way down the road, and sped passed D. Responding to a call to stop the car, D fired four shots at the car, and one killed the passenger. Scientific evidence suggested that the fatal shot was fired after the car had passed and was some 50 feet down the road. HL: upheld D's conviction for murder. Where a plea of self-defence to a charge of murder fails because the force used was excessive and unreasonable, D is guilty of murder not manslaughter.

Clegg was sentenced to a mandatory life sentence of murder, but despite this was released after a short time and returned to a post in the army. Perhaps better than a reform which would allow a reduction to manslaughter in such cases would be the abolition of the mandatory life sentence for murder. (In 1998 The Court of Appeal quashed Clegg's conviction and ordered a retrial on the grounds of fresh evidence.

5.33   *Unknown circumstances justifying force in self-defence*

> *Dadson* (1850) D shot and wounded a fleeing poacher. The degree of force was permissible if V was a felon: he was, but D did not know this. Pollock CB (in a five line judgement): D's conviction upheld as he was 'not justified in firing at the prosecutor'.

This case provides the starting point for a discussion of the principle that whenever D seeks to rely on a justification or excuse, he must have known or believed in those circumstances. Some writers would argue that the principle should be limited to excuses and not to justifications, but this argument takes us back to where we started in this chapter. Not everyone accepts that the distinction in English law is useful: JC Smith 'is not persuaded that the reception of the theory into English law is either practicable or desirable'.

Further reading

Buchanan and Virgo, 'Duress and Mental Abnormality' [1999] Crim LR 517

Campbell, 'Offence and Defence' in *Criminal Law and Justice* (ed Dennis (1987)

Husak and von Hirsch, 'Culpability and Mistake of Law' in *Action and Value in Criminal Law* (ed Shute, Gardner and Horder)(1993)

Milgate, 'Duress and the Criminal Law: Another Turn by the House of Lords' (1988) 47 CLJ 61

Padfield, 'Duress, Necessity and the Law Commission' [1992] Crim LR 778

Smith, 'On *Actus Reus* and *Mens Rea*', in *Reshaping the Criminal Law* (ed PR Glazebrook) (1978)

Smith *Justification and Excuse in the Criminal Law* (1989)

Glanville Williams, 'The Theory of Excuses' [1982] Crim LR 732

Self -test questions

1. Dee gives Phil a passionate kiss on the neck and an affectionate bite on the ear. The bite turns septic and Phil has to have a small part of his ear amputated. Discuss Dee's criminal liability if (i) Phil was consenting and (ii) he was not consenting.

2. Dee is arrested at Heathrow airport with a large quantity of heroin in her suitcase. Questioned by the police she admits knowing that she was bringing in a package which she suspected contained illegal materials of some sort, but the man who gave it to her told her to ask no questions or 'something bad would happen to her baby'.

3   Late at night Dee, an elderly lady, was attacked at night by a young man who she believed to be carrying a knife. She stabbed him in the face with her umbrella, permanently blinding him in the eye.

CHAPTER SIX

Accomplices

SUMMARY
A difficult area: an example of the courts acting flexibly, thereby creating uncertainties. What degree of involvement merits conviction? Flexible conduct requirements (aiding, abetting, counselling or procuring) + mens rea (an intention to encourage or assist + knowledge of 'the essential matters').

The extent of joint enterprise liability: D is guilty if he realises (without agreeing to such conduct being used) that X may kill or intentionally inflict serious injury, but nevertheless continues to participate with A in the venture: why?

Accomplice liability has been seen traditionally simply as 'derivative liability': other justifications may be more appropriate.

Important proposals for reform in Law Com CP No 131: assisting and encouraging crime: but what should the *mens rea* be?

Introduction

6.1 A person may be convicted of a substantive offence merely because he or she took part in a criminal activity with someone else. The Accessories and Abettors Act 1861 tidied up the procedure for indicting, trying and punishing all those who were parties to a crime (then principals in the first degree, accessories before the fact and so on). When the distinction between felonies and misdemeanours was abolished in 1967, the Act was amended. Section 8 now provides:

[W]hosoever shall aid, abet, counsel or procure the commission of any indictable offence, whether the same be an offence at common law or by virtue of any Act passed or to be passed, shall be liable to be tried, indicted, and punished as a principal offender.

Similarly s 44 of the Magistrates' Courts Act 1980 provides that a person convicted of aiding, abetting, counselling or procuring a summary offence is guilty of the like offence. Aiding and abetting is thus not a separate offence, but simply a means of convicting someone of the main offence. If A asks B to kill C, and B does so, both A and B will be convicted of murder.

6.2 Some crimes are defined such that they can only be carried out by two or more principals: see riot and affray, for example, (in chapter 12), but even here there may be secondary parties.

Jefferson (1994) Ds were involved in various disturbances in Bedford town centre following an English victory in the football World Cup in 1990. They were convicted of offences of riot and violent disorder. The prosecution's case was that their presence at various of the specific disturbances during the night was sufficient evidence that they aided and abetted the violence of the night. D argued that presence denoted an onlooker and not necessarily a participant. CA (Auld J): nothing in the POA 1986 excludes common law principles of aiding and abetting, and dismissed their appeals.

Unless Parliament specifically excludes the possibility, one can be a secondary party or accomplice to any offence, even an attempt:

Dunnington (1984) D stole a car in order to be the getaway driver for a failed robbery. CA (Beldam J): upheld his conviction for aiding and abetting an attempted robbery. Where a person does an act which would amount to aiding and abetting if the offence was completed, he may be convicted of the attempt.

Principals and accessories

6.3 In this chapter, the term 'principal' (rather than an alternative term perpetrator) and the term 'accomplice' (to deal with the accessory or secondary party who 'aids, abets, counsels or procures') are used. Although the law suggests that the accomplice may be charged as a principal, she will normally be charged as an accomplice in order to give her clearer details of what she is accused. The maximum penalty for the accomplice is normally the same as that for the principal, though there are exceptions. For example, the Road Traffic Offenders Act 1988, s 34(5) provides that, where disqualification is mandatory for the principal offence (in cases such as driving with excess alcohol), a person convicted of aiding and abetting such an offence is liable only to discretionary qualification.

6.4   Normally, the principal is the person who carries out the substantive crime, while the accomplice merely aids or abets. Sometimes both parties will be co-principals, for example where both Ds intend to kill and both stab V. Where one of two people is guilty of an offence, but P cannot prove which of the two did it, nor that there was any agreement between them, neither can be convicted:

> *Strudwick* (1993) M and her co-habitee S were jointly charged with the manslaughter of her child. CA: quashed S's conviction. His admission of some violence towards the child and his manifest lies were not sufficient evidence as to which of the Ds had struck the blows.

However, both will be guilty if one is the principal and the other the accessory, even if it is not known which was which, as long as it can be proved that both were either principal or accomplice:

> *Mohan v R* (1967) Ds both attacked V with cutlasses. It could not be proved who struck the fatal blow. PC: upheld their convictions for murder.

> *Russell and Russell* (1987) Ds, registered drug addicts in receipt of prescribed methadone, were convicted of the manslaughter of their daughter who died of a massive overdose of methadone. CA: dismissed their appeals. P had to prove simply that D aided, abetted, counselled or procured the commission of the crime by the other.

Thus both parties are guilty where it is proved that each must be liable either as principal or accessory.

6.5 *The innocent agent* Occasionally a person may be considered as the principal even when the *actus reus* was performed by another. This is where the main actor is in fact innocent: perhaps she is a child, or is unaware of the crime she has been set up to commit, or she has a defence. In Glanville Williams' words, 'the physical actor is treated as a puppet, so that the guilty actor who activates him to do the mischief becomes responsible not as an accessory but as a perpetrator acting through an innocent agent' (TCL, page 368).

> *Bourne* (1952) D was convicted of aiding and abetting his wife to commit buggery with a dog (and sentenced to eight years in prison). The evidence was that she had been terrorised into submission and had not consented. CA: upheld his conviction. The fact the wife had a defence did not mean that no offence had been committed, simply that she had no *mens rea*. Since D caused his wife to have connection with a dog, he was guilty.

> *Cogan and Leak* (1976) D compelled V, his wife, to have sex with C against her will. CA: quashed C's conviction since he believed she was consenting, but upheld D's conviction. The fact that C was acquitted did not affect the position that V had been raped.

6.6 *Actus reus* The conduct requirements are vague: Ashworth discusses 'the minimum conduct' needed before someone can be convicted as an accomplice (PCL, page 426). The 1861 statute uses the words 'aid, abet, counsel or procure', and even though the statute was probably only designed to provide a procedure and not a definition, the words seem to have taken on a life of their own. For many years, it was accepted that the particular words used in s 8 had no particular meaning. However, the position seemed to change in 1975:

> *A-G's Reference (No 1 of 1975)* (1975) D, who had laced someone's drinks knowing that he would be driving home shortly afterwards, was indicted for aiding and abetting driving with excess alcohol. CA (Widgery CJ): D should have been convicted.
>
> > ... if four words are employed here, 'aid, abet, counsel or procure', the probability is that there is a difference between each of those four words and the other three, because, if there were no such difference, then Parliament would be wasting its time in using four words where two or three would do ... To procure means to produce

by endeavour. You procure a thing by setting out to see that it happens, and taking the appropriate steps to produce that happening ... You cannot procure an offence unless there is a causal link between what you do and the commission of an offence.

6.7 In this case, Lord Widgery accepted the old pre-1861 distinction that if you were present at the substantive offence you were an aider or abettor, if you were absent you were a counsellor or procurer. However, you should not spend too much time trying to distinguish these words: once again the courts seem now to use them fairly indistinguishably. However, there may be an important distinction when one considers whether the accomplice has to communicate his objectives to the principal. Agreement is not always required: if D restrains the policeman who would have prevented P from committing the crime, without P being aware of this assistance, probably D is guilty of 'aiding' P. Smith and Hogan sum up the position thus (at p 128, 9th edn): '... the law probably is that:

(i) 'Procuring' implies causation but not consensus;

(ii) 'abetting and counselling' imply consensus but not causation;

(iii) 'aiding' requires actual assistance but neither consensus nor causation'.

6.8 As the Law Commission suggest, the distinction between aiding, abetting, counselling and procuring 'partakes of a considerable element of over-elaboration and indeed artificiality' (CP No 131, page 21). They therefore prefer to say that the physical element here consists either of encouragement or assistance (see **6.27**).

6.9 *Liability by mere presence* Can a person be convicted as an accomplice merely for watching? If so, this would suggest liability for a failure to act, for a mere omission (see **2.5**). There will be no problem establishing liability if the accomplice had a duty to act: if the tenant of my house deliberately leaves the door unlocked for the burglar, her failure to lock the door is in breach of her duty. Normally it is held that there must be an intention to encourage, and actual encouragement, but there is a fine line here. Does your presence at an animal rights demonstration mean that you are encouraging, and intending to encourage, offences of public disorder by others?

Coney (1882) D watched an illegal boxing match. CCCR (by a majority): mere voluntary presence did not necessarily render the audience guilty of aiding the illegal fight. Hawkins J: '... to constitute an aider and abettor some active steps must be taken by word, or action, with the intent to instigate the principal or principals'.

Clarkson (1971) Ds entered a room where soldiers were raping a woman. They watched and did nothing to stop the rape. CMAC: quashed their conviction for aiding and abetting rape. It is not enough that the presence of the accused has given encouragement: it must be proved that he intended to give encouragement.

6.10   The problem also arises where people are living together and may well know what their friends or partners are up to:

Bland (1987) D was charged with unlawful possession of controlled drugs because she lived with a man who she knew dealt in drugs. CA: quashed her conviction as there was no evidence of assistance, passive or active: there must be some positive encouragement.

6.11   As Ashworth points out, such cases illustrate 'a vivid conflict between the individuals' rights of privacy in their personal relationships and the social interest in suppressing serious crime' (PCL, p 432). The DCC would deal with the problem thus:

Clause 27(3): Assistance or encouragement includes assistance or encouragement arising from a failure by a person to take reasonable steps to exercise any authority or to discharge any duty he has to control the relevant acts of the principal in order to prevent the commission of the offence.

For Glanville Williams this is astonishingly wide: 'everyone who lets an offence happen shall be liable as though he had committed it himself' ((1990) Crim LR 780).

6.12   *Failure to exercise control* Failure to act may amount to participation where D has power to control the actions of others but fails to do so:

Du Cros v Lambourne (1907) D, the owner of a car, was sitting in the passenger seat while a friend drove at a dangerous speed. KBD: D was guilty of aiding and abetting dangerous driving since he allowed her to drive and did not interfere in any way. He failed to exercise his power to prevent the driving.

Tuck v Robson (1970) D, the licensee of pub, called 'time' at 11 pm and switched off the main lights; at 11.05 he called for glasses. No consumption of alcohol was allowed after 11.10, but when the police arrived at 11.23 some customers were still drinking up. D was convicted of aiding and abetting the consumption of alcoholic drinks after hours. DC (Lord Parker CJ): dismissed his appeal. D had the legal power to get customers to leave at closing time, and was guilty.

6.13   *Mens rea* D must intend to do acts of assistance and be aware of their ability to assist.

Blakely v DPP (1991) Ds laced P's drink with vodka, intending to inform him so that he would not be able to drive home and would have to stay the night. He left before they told him and was convicted of driving with excess alcohol (receiving an absolute discharge by way of sentence). Ds were convicted of procuring drunken driving. DC: quashed their conviction.

> While it might now be the law that advertent recklessness to the consequence of his deliberate act of assistance might suffice to convict some, if not all, of those accused of being an accessory before the fact, it was clear that inadvertent recklessness did not. It must, at least, be shown that the accused contemplated that his act would or might bring about or assist the commission of the principal offence: he must have been prepared nevertheless to do his own act, and he must have done that act intentionally ...In relation to those accused only of procuring and perhaps also those accused only of counselling and commanding, it might be ... that it was necessary to prove that the accused intended to bring about the principal offence.

6.14   D must know the essential matters which constitute the offence, but the line which shows exactly how much D must know to justify punishment has proved to be extremely difficult to draw. Clearly those who knowingly help others commit serious crimes should be guilty of an offence, but not those who do not really realise what is going on.

Bainbridge (1960) The cutting equipment used in a burglary was proved to have been bought by D six weeks earlier. He said he had bought it for a friend, but admitted that he was suspicious that the equipment was going to be used for an illegal purpose, but said he did not know that it was for burglary. He was convicted of being an accessory to office-breaking. CA (Lord Parker CJ): upheld D's conviction. While it was not enough merely to prove that D knew that some illegal venture was intended, it was not necessary to prove that he knew of the particular crime that was to be committed.

DPP for Northern Ireland v Maxwell (1978) D, a member of an illegal organisation in Northern Ireland, driving his own car, led a car to a remote country pub. He then left. The men in the second car, who D knew to be members of the organisation, then threw a bomb. D was convicted as an accomplice to doing an act with intent to cause an explosion. HL: dismissed his appeal. Lord Scarman: ' An accessory who leaves it to his principal to choose is liable, provides always the choice is made from the range of offences from which the accessory contemplates the choice will be made'.

6.15 *Possible defences to accomplice liability* It is not very clear whether there are specific defences available only to accomplices. The DCC suggests in clause 27 that three specific defences should be available to the accomplice:

(6) A person is not guilty of an offence as an accessory by reason of anything he does -
(a) with the purpose of preventing the commission of the offence; or
(b) with the purpose of avoiding or limiting any harmful consequences of the offence and without the purpose of furthering its commission; or
(c) because he believes that he is under an obligation to do it and without the purpose of furthering the commission of the offence.

6.16 These defences would appear to protect the accomplice from liability simply because of his worthy purpose or motive. Yet the normal rule, in line with the rules governing the liability of the principal (see **3.3**), is that a worthy motive will not excuse:

National Coal Board v Gamble (1959) D was the NCB, whose weigh bridge operator issued a ticket to a lorry driver certifying the lorry's weight. He told the lorry driver that he was nearly 4 tons overweight, but the lorry driver said that he would risk it. DC: upheld D's conviction for aiding and abetting the lorry driver's firm in the commission of the offence. Devlin J: *'mens rea* is a matter of intent only and does not depend on desire or motive'.

6.17 Despite this, examples of all three defences proposed in clause 27(6)can be found in the case law. First, the law enforcement defence:

Clarke (1985) D's defence to burglary was that he was there simply to assist the police. CA (Macpherson J): in exceptional cases an informer's conduct which was calculated and intended to frustrate the ultimate result of a crime could amount to a defence. It was for the jury to decide if a case fell within that exceptional and rare category.

6.18 Secondly, where D acts with the purpose of limiting harmful consequences:

Gillick v West Norfolk and Wisbech Area Health Authority (1986). A Department of Health memorandum stated that exceptionally contraceptive advice could be given to under 16s without parental consent. A mother sought a declaration that the memorandum was unlawful. HL: (by a majority 3-2) held that a doctor who supplies contraceptives to a girl under the age of 16, knowing that this will assist her boyfriend have unlawful sexual intercourse with a girl under the age of 16, is not an accomplice to the boy's offence. Lord Scarman: '… the bona fide exercise by a doctor of his clinical judgement must be a complete negation of *mens rea*'.

Look at the dissenting judgements of Lord Brandon and Lord Templeman: even if aiding the unlawful sexual intercourse is not the doctor's purpose or desire, if he knows it will result, does he not intend it (and see also **5.20**)?

6.19 The third possible defence is D's belief in his legal obligation. If I have been looking after your knife for you, and you ask for it back telling me that you intend to stick it into your mother (which you then do), do I (and should I) have a defence to aiding and abetting murder when I say that I believed that I had no option but to give you what was after all your own property? The answer in English law today is unclear.

Joint enterprise/common purpose

6.20   There is another way that people may be guilty of another's crime: where they embark on a joint criminal enterprise. If two or more people agree to carry out a common purpose or joint enterprise, the secondary party or accomplice may be liable for crimes committed in carrying out that purpose, even unforeseen consequences. It is not necessary for P to show that the accomplice intended the crime: it is enough that he should have foreseen the event as a real possibility. If the principal by mistake kills the wrong person or carries out the intended purpose by an unexpected method, then the accomplice is still liable. What happens if the principal intentionally deviates from the agreed course of conduct and goes beyond the common purpose?

Chan Wing-Siu (1985) Ds went to commit a robbery armed with knives, and one guarded V's wife while the others then killed V. PC (Sir Robin Cooke): upheld the convictions for murder of all Ds. A secondary party is criminally liable for acts by the primary offender of a type which the former foresees but does not necessarily intend. Liability

> turns on contemplation or, putting the same idea in other words, authorisation, which may be express but is more usually implied. It meets the case of a crime foreseen as a possible incident of the common unlawful enterprise. The criminal liability lies in participating in the venture with that foresight.

6.21   Liability turns on knowing that there was a possible risk that the principal might commit the offence. At that time there had been some suggestion that the accomplice should only be liable if he knew that the eventual outcome was 'probable' (see *Jubb and Rigby* (1984)), but the courts have preferred the 'possible' consequence test of *Chan Wing-Siu*: a test which required P to prove that D knew that the crime was a probable consequence was seen as unduly restrictive.

Slack (1989) Ds were two robbers, one of whom killed an elderly widow. They were both convicted of murder, although one said that although he knew his mate had a knife, he thought he would only use it to frighten people. CA (Lord Lane): dismissed D's appeal. For B to be guilty, he must be proved to have lent himself to a criminal enterprise involving the infliction, if necessary, of serious harm or death, or to have had an express or tacit understanding with A that such harm or death should, if necessary, be inflicted.

Hyde, Sussex and Collins (1991) Ds attack V outside a pub, and he died of a heavy kick to the head. Two Ds said there was no joint enterprise, and that the fatal blow was struck by the third. The third D said that there was no joint attack, and that he had not caused the blow. CA (Lord Lane CJ): dismissed their appeals.

If B realises (without agreeing to such conduct being used) that A may kill or intentionally inflict serious injury, but nevertheless continues to participate with A in the venture, that will amount to a sufficient mental element for B to be guilty of murder if A, with the requisite intent, kills in the course of the venture.

Powell and Daniels; English (1997) P, D and another went to buy cannabis from V, a small-time drug dealer. One of them shot V dead on his doorstep. P and D were convicted of murder as secondary parties, although it was not established who fired the shot. In the other case, E agreed with another man to attack V, a policeman with wooden posts. The other then produced a knife and stabbed V dead. HL: dismissed P and D's appeals; E's appeal was allowed. Lord Hutton:

> ... participation in a joint criminal enterprise with foresight or contemplation of an act as a possible incident of that enterprise is sufficient to impose criminal liability for that act carried out by another participant in the enterprise.

There will no longer be scope for argument over 'tacit agreements': the test is one of foresight. D must contemplate death

> ... as a possible incident of the joint venture, unless the risk was so remote that the jury take the view that the secondary party genuinely dismissed it as altogether negligible.

Lord Steyn and Lord Mustill examined the principles behind liability and exhorted Parliament to reform the law of homicide and the law of punishment for homicide. As Lord Mustill says, criminal law reform may not be a popular choice, 'but surely it is justice which counts'.

6.22 Thus it is the accomplice's foresight of what the principal might do that is important, not any actual agreement between them.

Hui Chi-ming (1992) X's girlfriend was being bullied to give him up. X and some friends (including D) then went to look for the bully. They selected the wrong man, and V, an innocent victim, was beaten with lead pipe. He died of his injuries. P alleged the pipe was wielded by X; no witness saw D speak to anyone or strike a blow at the scene of the crime. Four of the group were indicted for murder: X was convicted by the jury of manslaughter, and two of the others changed their pleas to guilty to manslaughter; one was discharged on the direction of the judge. Three months later, D and one remaining member of the group were indicted for murder. The other pleaded guilty to manslaughter, but D refused to do so. He was tried and convicted of murder (and sentenced to death). PC (Lord Lowry): dismissed his appeal. D had sufficient *mens rea* 'if he had foreseen that the principal might commit [an act of murder] as part of the joint venture and had participated in it with that foresight'.

This case appears very harsh: D whose role was minimal was convicted of murder, whilst the principal was convicted only of manslaughter (and the jury did not know this last fact as evidence of the principal's earlier conviction was deemed inadmissible).

6.23   Nor does it matter whether or not D is present at the scene of the crime:

Rook (1993) Three men agreed to kill a taxi-driver's wife for £20,000. D took a leading part in planning the murder, but said he did not plan to go through with it. He believed, wrongly, that if he did not turn up at the scene of the crime, his colleagues would not go ahead without him. However, they did. CA (Lloyd LJ): upheld D's conviction for murder. It was no defence for a secondary party to say that he did not intend the victim to be killed if he contemplated or foresaw the killing as a real or serious risk. His absence on the day of the murder did not amount to unequivocal communication of his withdrawal from the agreement to murder.

6.24   What happens if the principal commits a different and less serious offence than that agreed?

Howe (1987) Ds confessed to taking part in the killing of Vs, but said that they acted through fear. HL: upheld their conviction for murder.

The case withdrew the defence of duress from those accused of aiding and abetting murder (see **5.17**) but it is also important as the House overruled the decision in *Richards* (1974), which had held that the accomplice who was not present at the scene could not be convicted of a more serious crime than the actual perpetrator.

Thus, where a person procures or incites another to commit murder, but that other person is convicted only of manslaughter, the incitor/procurer may still be convicted of murder.

6.25   As we saw in **6.5**, even where the principal is not convicted of any offence, the accomplice may still be where he acted as an innocent agent. Where D procures the *actus reus* of an offence, this may itself constitute that offence:

> *Millward* (1994) D instructed his employee to tow a trailer behind a tractor on a main road. Due to a defective hitch mechanism, the trailer became detached and killed someone in another car. The employee was acquitted of causing death by reckless driving, but D was convicted of procuring the offence. CA: dismissed his appeal. The *actus reus* had been taking the vehicle on the road in a defective condition. D could procure the *actus reus* of an offence irrespective of whether or not the principal offender had the necessary *mens rea*.

As JC Smith points out (at [1994] Crim LR 529), this case breaks new ground, and marks a move away from the traditional idea that accomplice liability is a form of derivative liability.

6.26   *Derivative liability* The traditional justification for accomplice liability is simply that D's liability derives from that of the principal. JC Smith (1997) distinguishes basic accessory liability (D is liable for the commission by P of crime X which D intentionally assists or encourages P to commit) from parasitic accessory liability (D is liable not because he intentionally assisted or encouraged P, but merely because he foresaw that P would commit crime X). Yet this causes many problems: why should someone be guilty just because someone else is? Kadish (1985) prefers to say that liability is 'dependent', rather than derivative (see **6.27**). If liability is derivative, the decision in *Howe* (see **6.24**) is curious. However, perhaps *Howe* says little more than that those who aid and abet criminals should not get away with it. An alternative route to liability would be to extend the doctrine of innocent agency. If you send a child into the house to steal for you, you are guilty as a principal acting through an innocent agent. Thus in *Cogan and Leak* (**6.5**) it could be argued that the husband should have been guilty not of being an accomplice, but as the principal. Or that someone who secretly laces someone's soft drinks with alcohol, should be guilty of drunken driving as a principal, not as an accomplice. There may be linguistic complaints that Leak did not rape his wife, or that the drink spiker couldn't even drive, but does this matter? Another theory to justify liability might base liability on what the accomplice set out to do. Thus J C Smith justifies accomplice liability in murder cases by emphasising the difference between recklessness whether death be caused (which is sufficient for manslaughter but not murder) and recklessness whether murder be committed. The accomplice's recklessness must extend to the principal's *mens rea* for murder (on which see **8.5**).

6.27 *Reform* Law Commission CP No 131 (1993) proposed that the present division between aiding and abetting and incitement (see **7.27**) should be abandoned and that all the matters addressed by 'those two institutions' should be replaced by a single set of rules. They start from first principles, identifying the conflicting demands of, on the one hand, the need to provide an efficient and clearly-defined means of controlling those who involve themselves in the commission of crime by others; and, on the other hand, the need to formulate such rules in terms that do not impede or threaten legitimate social activities. They adopt Kadish's analysis:

> Two kinds of action render the secondary party liable for the criminal actions of the primary party: intentionally influencing the decision of the primary party to commit a crime, and intentionally helping the principal actor commit the crime, where the helping actions themselves constitute no part of the actions prohibited by the definition of the crime (at (1985) 73 California LR 342).

Kadish explains (at page 405) that these are the only two forms of affecting the conduct of the perpetrator which are consistent with the notion of the perpetrator having freely chosen to act as he did. The Law Commission suggest the abolition of the current rules on complicity, by extending the law of inchoate offences (see the chapter 7) and by creating two new offences: assisting crime and encouraging crime. The proposal on 'encouraging crime' is discussed in chapter 7; for the moment we will consider only the proposal to introduce a new crime of assisting crime.

6.28 *Assisting crime* The Law Commission propose that:

(1) A person commits the offence of assisting crime if he

(a) knows or believes that another ('the principal') is doing or causing to be done, or will do or cause to be done, acts that do or will involve the commission of an offence by the principal; and

(b) knows or believes that the principal, in so acting, does or will do so with the fault required for the offence in question; and

(c) does any act that he knows or believes assists or will assist the principal in committing that offence.

(2) Assistance includes giving the principal advice as to commit the offence, or as to how to avoid detection or apprehension before or during the commission of the offence.

(3) A person does not assist the commission of an offence for the purposes of this section if all that he does is to fail to prevent or impede the commission of that offence.

(4) 'Offence' in sub-paragraphs (a)-(c) of sub-section (1) above means the breach of a specified prohibition laid down by statute or the common law; but, provided the defendant knows or believes sufficient facts to show that such a breach is taking place or will take place, he need not know the time, place or other details of the offence.

(5) A person also commits an offence under this section if he knows or believes that the principal intends to commit one of a number of offences and does any act that he knows or believes will assist the principal in committing whichever of those offences the principal in fact intends.

6.29 *Mens rea of the proposed offence* The Law Commission emphasised that they had not reached a final decision as to how the *mens rea* of the offence should be expressed. They suggest two possible formulations (the first of which is included in the proposal included above):

- that the assister knows or believes that the principal crime is being or will be committed; or

- that the assister's purpose is that the principal crime should be committed.

6.30 The Law Commission's uncertainty arises from their concern that the ambit of the criminal law should not be too wide. If the offence would be committed whether or not the principal offence occurs, only requiring knowledge or belief is perhaps too wide. The reach of the criminal law is spread too far if it brings within it those who have not committed a substantive crime themselves and who, while prepared to assist those who do commit such crimes, do so not to promote those crimes but for other motives. For example, if a generous host believes that her guest is going to drive home in his car, but continues to ply him with drink to an extent which puts him over the statutory limit, should she be guilty of a crime if in the event he does not drive home, and she never wanted him to anyhow? Or should someone who sells oxy-acetylene cutting equipment, believing that the purchaser intends to use it to commit a burglary, but whose personal interest is only in his own profit, be guilty of an offence where the purchaser does not commit the burglary, either because he is arrested at the scene of the crime, or because he thinks better of it, or because he never intended to do so? The 'knowledge or belief' test also raises the *Gillick* problem (see **6.18**): we have already considered whether a doctor who prescribes contraceptives to a 15-year-old in order to minimise the risk of pregnancy should be guilty of an offence. One of the attractions of the 'purpose' definition is that it excludes the need for such vague defences as 'limiting harmful consequences'.

6.31 However, if the mental element is limited to purpose, this excludes those who may well be seen to be culpable: the regular supplier of goods or of transport who knows that they are to be used for criminal purpose, but is merely interested in making a profit on the sale; or suppliers, such as the supplier of oxy-acetylene equipment mentioned above, who may well positively prefer the completed crime not to take place, so long as they obtain payment, since that may make their part in the affair less likely to be detected. Is there a mid-way between purpose and belief? For example, if a test of intention was adopted, the courts might well evolve a *Nedrick*-type (see **3.10**) test of intent: 'If the jury are satisfied that at the material time D recognised that his act would be virtually certain to assist the principal, then that is a fact from which they may find it easy to infer that he intended to assist the principal, even though he may not have had any desire to achieve that result'. In cases where a consequence is foreseen as virtually certain, then intention may be inferred. This test would provide a narrower test of culpability than that of mere knowledge or belief, but would not be exclusive as the purpose test.

6.32 *Actus reus of the proposal* The definition of assistance is said to include giving advice, such as advice on how to avoid detection, but to exclude a simple failure to prevent an offence from occurring. Should the *de minimis* principle apply in order to include only substantial or material assistance? Given that the police and CPS have a discretion not to prosecute, is it necessary to try to develop a definition to exclude minimal help? Should it be possible to commit the crime by an omission? At present a publican who does not expel customers who are drinking after hours, or the owner of a car who sits in the passenger seat while another drives it recklessly, is guilty of a crime (see **6.12**). Is it right to place the obligations of law enforcement on such people?

Concealing offences

6.33 It is worth noting that a person who helps a person after the main crime may be guilty, not simply as an accomplice, but of themselves committing a substantive offence. A person who knowing or believing that another person is guilty of an arrestable offence, does 'any act with intent to impede his apprehension or prosecution' is guilty of an offence under the CLA 1967, s 4. Similarly, anyone who accepts money (or other bargain) in return for withholding information about an arrestable offence will be guilty of an offence under the CLA 1967, s 5. A person who lies in court under oath may be guilty of the serious offence of perjury, and someone who intentionally interferes with the due administration of justice in court may be guilty of a criminal contempt of court.

Further reading

Giles, 'Complicity: the problems of joint enterprise' [1990] Crim LR 383

Kadish, 'Complicity, Cause and Blame: A Study in the Interpretation of Doctrine' (1985) 73 California LR 324

Law Commission *Assisting and Encouraging Crime* (Consultation Paper No 131, 1993)

Smith, JC, 'Criminal Liability of Accessories: Law and Reform' (1997) LQR 453

Smith, KJM, *A Modern Treatise on the Law of Criminal Complicity* (1991)

Smith, 'Secondary participation in crime – can we do without it?' (1994) 144 NLJ 679

Self-test qustions

1. Discuss the liability of the participants in the following events:
    (i) Dee and Acka agree to beat up Phil in order to teach him a lesson for his own brutish behaviour in the past. Unknown to Acka, however, Dee has decided to kill Phil if she gets the chance. When they find Phil, Acka knocks him to the ground, and Dee kills Phil with a knife that Acka did not know that Dee was carrying.
    (ii) Dee invites Phil to a party. Although she knows that he plans to drive home, she plies him with wine all evening. When he says he ought not to have any more she laughingly assures him that the police never stop people in her area. He eventually drives home, is stopped by the police and is subsequently convicted of drunken driving.
    (iii) Dee, Bee and Fee decide to burgle an old lady's house. Bee remains outside to be a look out, but soon gets bored and goes off to the pub. When Dee and Fee find a box of jewellery, Dee decides to kill Phyllis, the old lady, so that she can't give any information on the burglars to the police. Fee looks on without attempting to stop Dee, who stabs Phyllis with a bread knife she finds in the kitchen. Phyllis dies.

2. Do you think that the Law Commission's proposals in Consultation Paper 131 represent an improvement in the current law on secondary liability?

CHAPTER SEVEN

Inchoate offences

SUMMARY

Attempt: Since the CAA 1981, liability for attempts is purely statutory. D must perform a 'more than merely preparatory' act with the intention that the crime be committed. Is this definition too vague, leaving too much to the jury?

Conspiracy: This is now governed by the CLA 1977, but common law offences survive uncomfortably alongside. There must be an agreement to commit the crime; but much debate concerning the mental element: see *Anderson*; *Siracusa*.

Incitement: This is still largely governed by the common law; D must have encouraged another to commit a crime, with the intention that the crime be committed.

Problems:

(i) inconsistencies (eg in relation to those crimes which would be impossible to complete) and overlaps between the three offences.

(ii) it is difficult to prosecute those who help others commit crimes: see Spencer's proposed offence of 'facilitation', and Law Commission's CP No 131, *Assisting and Encouraging Crime*.

Introduction

7.1 The criminal law needs to be able to punish those who fail to complete their crimes, but how far back should liability extend? Merely having the idea that you might rob a bank is surely too far removed from the completed offence to justify punishment. The inchoate offences cover various areas where English law penalises offences which have not been completed. The *Oxford Reference Dictionary* defines inchoate as 'just begun or undeveloped'. The crime proper has just begun. How far must D have gone before he becomes guilty of an offence? Ashworth (PCL, page 484-7) points out that many offences are really inchoate in nature: possession offences, or those defined in terms of doing an act 'with intent to …' (eg burglary or perjury). However, only the three inchoate offences of incitement, conspiracy and attempt are discussed here. These offences overlap and produce numerous inconsistencies. J C Smith (1986), commenting on *Sirat* (1985, see **7.32**), stated that 'the law is hopelessly muddled and irrational'. A simple example is that most incitements are in practice attempted conspiracies, but the offence of attempted conspiracy was abolished by s 1(4) of the CAA 1981. Similarly, an incitement to incite is a crime, despite the fact that any inciter is likely to want to succeed and an incitement to conspire is no longer a crime. Figure 2 seeks to explain these curiosities.

Figure 4[2]

	To attempt	To conspire	To incite	To aid, abet, counsel, procure
An attempt	Inept	**Abolished** s 1(4)(a) CAA 1981	**Offence** *Cromack* (1978)	**No offence** s1(4)(b) CAA 1981
A conspiracy	Inept	Inept	**Offence** *Hollinshead* (1985)	**No offence** *Hollinshead* (1985)
An incitement	Inept Save where D knows cannot get beyond attempt	**Abolished** s 5(7) CLA 1977 (but would be restored by DCC)	**Offence** *Sirat* (1985)	**No offence** *Bodin and Bodin* (1979)
Aid, abet, counsel, procure	**Offence** *Dunnington* (1984)	**Offence**	**Offence**	**No offence**

2   Adapted from a chart created by Graham Virgo, whose permission to reproduce it is gratefully acknowledged.

130

7.2   What harm is the law seeking to prevent in the case of inchoate offences, that which would have been done had D been successful, or the potential harm which D (or other Ds) might commit if the law did not seek to deter unsuccessful criminals? The law in this area illustrates the tension which exists in criminal law between harm-based liability and intention-based liability. Ashworth (1987), at page 7, lays down these tensions clearly:

> Those of us who accept both the proposition that intentions are more important than outcomes in determining criminal liability and the proposition that the reach of the criminal law should be kept to the minimum have a great deal more thinking to do.

Another tension is created by the courts' struggle to adapt unsuitable offences in order to convict those who are in reality simply guilty of 'trying to help others commit a crime'. To remedy this, in 1987 JR Spencer proposed a new offence of facilitation. This proposal has been developed by the Law Com CP No 131, Assisting and Encouraging Crime (see **6.27**; **7.33**).

7.3   *Jurisdictional issues* The common law position is that where there has been an agreement to carry out a crime abroad, the agreement even if made in England cannot be enforced unless the implementation of the agreement would necessarily have involved the commission of an offence in England. However, widespread concern that there should be more international co-operation in law enforcement has led to two statutory amendments in this area. First, the CJA 1993, s 5 makes it an offence in certain circumstances to conspire, attempt or incite offences of dishonesty and blackmail even where the substantive offence would not itself be triable in this country. More recently, the Sexual Offences (Conspiracy and Incitement) Act 1996 makes it an offence to conspire to commit certain sexual acts abroad against children.

Attempt

7.4   This is perhaps the most straight-forward of the inchoate offences, since it is closest to the completed offence. Ashworth (PCL, page 461) distinguishes completed attempts (you have done everything you set out to do: fired the gun, or smuggled the goods you think are drugs into the country) from incomplete attempts (you are arrested before you fire the gun or before you enter the bank that you plan to rob), since it is easier to justify punishing the former than the later. However, English law punishes both. Common law attempt was replaced by a statutory offence in the CAA 1981:

> s 1(1) If, with intent to commit an offence to which this section applies, a person does an act which is more than merely preparatory to the commission of the offence, he is guilty of attempting to commit the offence ...

> (2) A person may be guilty of attempting to commit an offence to which this section applies even though the facts are such that the commission of the offence is impossible.

> (3) In any case where-
> (a) apart from this subsection a person's intention would not be regarded as having amounted to an intent to commit an offence: but
> (b) if the facts of the case had been as he believed them to be, his intention would be so regarded, then, for the purposes of subsection (1) above, he shall be regarded as having had an intent to commit that offence.

7.5 *Actus reus* D must have carried out acts 'more than merely preparatory' to the commission of the offence. What does this mean? First, the word 'act' suggests that an omission cannot constitute an attempt. Would it not be an attempted murder if a mother deliberately withheld food from her child intending the child to die? More careful drafting might have avoided this problem which has not yet been faced by the courts. The DCC would define the word 'act' in this context to include 'an omission only where the offence intended is capable of being committed by an omission' (see clause 49(3)).

7.6 Secondly, the test for when an act is 'more than merely preparatory' is not explained. Section 4(3) of the CAA leaves the jury with a wide, largely uncontrolled, discretion:

> Where, in proceedings against a person for the offence under section 1 above, there is evidence sufficient in law to support a finding that he did an act falling within subsection (1) of that section, the question whether or not his act fell within that subsection is a question of fact.

The old common law tests were more restrictive: for example, the *Eagleton* (1855) test was that D must have done the last act towards the

132

commission of the offence proper. Other tests included whether D had 'burnt his boats' or 'crossed the Rubicon'. Clearly a balance needs to be struck between the social interest in preventing harm at an early stage, and, at the same time, upholding individual liberties. The police need to be able to arrest, for example, the bank robber outside the bank and not only once he has taken aim and fired at the cashier. Yet if he is arrested too soon we will not necessarily know whether he really intended to rob the bank. Consider whether you think that the three cases discussed below draw the line appropriately:

Boyle and Boyle (1986) Ds damaged a door with a view to breaking in and burgling. CA: upheld their conviction for attempted burglary, holding that whatever test was applied they were clearly guilty. [However, under the pre-1981 law it seems unlikely that they would have been guilty: they had not 'burnt their boats' or 'crossed the Rubicon'].

Gullefer (1990) D distracted dogs in a greyhound race hoping that a 'no-race' would be declared and that he would get his £18 bet back. CA (Lord Taylor CJ): quashed his conviction for attempted theft: when he jumped on to the track he was not attempting to steal £18, but was still at the stage of preparation. 'It seems to us that the words of the Act of 1981 seek to steer a mid-way course' ie the statute provided a compromise between a preparatory act and the last act before the commission of the substantive crime.

Jones (1990) D bought a gun, shortened the barrel, got into the back of V's car, and pointed the gun at him. The gun was loaded, but the safety catch had not been removed. CA (Lord Taylor CJ): upheld D's conviction for attempted murder. Courts should look at the natural meaning of the words of the section and should not attempt to adapt old common law tests.

7.7 Should so much discretion be left to the jury? KJM Smith (1991) argues, for example, that *Gullefer* and *Jones* offer the lower courts inadequate guidance. Nearly thirty years ago, Glazebrook went further, suggesting in a challenging article (1969) that it was neither necessary nor desirable to have a law of attempted crime at all. Thus he argued that since the key issue in rape should not be whether D succeeded in penetrating his victim, but whether he assaulted her with sexual intent, the crime should be redefined to emphasise this. However, this argument falls foul of the 'fair labelling' principle (**1.2**): people understand that rape means non-consensual sex. To widen the definition would be inappropriate. There are also evidential dangers in a taking too subjective a position, since guilty intent should not start to overshadow guilty conduct. We do not necessarily want to punish those who have criminal thoughts, but do not carry them out. This uncertainty perhaps explains s 4(3), which gives such a wide role to the jury.

7.8 *Mens rea* D must intend to complete the crime. The criminal law is not so wide as to impose liability on those who merely take risks, nearly committing crimes. Intention here does not necessarily mean purpose. James L J's statement in *Mohan* (1976; see **3.8**), that what is needed is proof of 'a decision to bring about [the offence], no matter whether the accused desired that consequence of his act or not', was applied in *Pearman* (1985), where the CA held that the word 'intent' in s 1 has the same meaning as at common law.

> *Walker and Hayles* (1989) Having threatened to kill V, Ds dropped him from a third floor balcony. CA upheld their conviction for attempted murder. Lloyd L J confirmed that normally there is no need in attempt for a direction on inferred intention.

7.9 What if the substantive crime involves *mens rea* both in relation to the prohibited act and in relation to the circumstances surrounding the act? One view is that the section requires intent with regard to every element of the offence. However, this is clearly not the current position:

> *Khan* (1990) D was convicted of attempted rape, after the judge summed up to the jury that recklessness as to the woman's consent was sufficient to constitute the offence. CA (Russell L J): dismissed his appeal.

>> The intent of the defendant is precisely the same in rape and in attempted rape and the *mens rea* is identical, namely an intention to have intercourse plus a knowledge of, or recklessness as to, the woman's absence of consent.

This reasoning also presumably applies to other offences such as burglary, or obtaining by deception. Thus to be convicted of an attempted obtaining by deception, D must intend to obtain, but recklessness as to whether the representation is false should be enough. In *Khan*, the CA

134

drew a distinction between consequences (which must be intended) and circumstances (which need not be). But the distinction is not really clear: the consequence of rape could be defined as sex with a woman who is not consenting. Why is consent merely a circumstance? (See Glanville Williams(1991)). The reasoning in *Khan* was extended in:

> *A-G's Reference (No 3 of 1992)* (1994) Ds threw a petrol bomb, which smashed into a wall, towards Vs. No-one was hurt. The question referred to the CA was whether a D could be convicted of attempting to commit aggravated criminal damage, contrary to s 1(2) CDA (see **12.6**), when he was merely being reckless as to whether life was endangered. CA (Schiemann J): it was enough for the Crown to establish a specific intent to cause damage by fire and that D was reckless as to whether life would be endangered.

This decision has been criticised for leading in the direction of a general law of reckless attempts, which is not what the law does or should provide for. What of the offence of having sexual intercourse with a girl under the age of 16 (see **10.15**): should a man be guilty of an attempt at this offence when he fails to have sex, and in any case believed the girl to be 16? Or take another strict liability offence: a pub landlord is guilty of an offence if he sells alcohol to the drunk (see **3.39**): if a drunk fails to pay, and the landlord thinks he is not drunk, should he be guilty of an attempt to sell alcohol to the drunk?

7.10 *Impossibility* There are numerous reasons why a crime might fail. You might fail to kill me because you are a bad shot, or because you are using a useless gun, or because I am already dead. Whether or not you should be guilty of attempted murder in these cases is subject to enormous debate, best explored through two cases:

> *Anderton v Ryan* (1985) D admitted to the police that she believed that she was handling a stolen video player, although there was no evidence that it was in fact stolen. HL (by 4-1; note Lord Edmund Davies' dissent): quashed her conviction for attempting to handle stolen goods. Lord Bridge distinguished the person who acts 'in a criminal way with a specific intent to commit a particular crime which he erroneously believes to be, but which is not, in fact, possible', who is guilty under s 1(3), from the person who does objectively innocent acts where 'the action is throughout innocent and the actor has done

everything he intended to do'. This latter person, the House concluded, is not guilty.

Glanville Williams (1986) wrote a 50-page diatribe against the decision, which explored the criticisms of it shared by many academics. He summarises his analysis as an

> account of how the judges invented a rule based upon conceptual misunderstanding; of their determination to use the English language so strangely that they spoke what by normal criteria would be termed untruths; of their invincible ignorance of the mess they made of the law; and of their immobility on the subject, carried to the extent of subverting an Act of Parliament designed to put them straight.

7.11 It was perhaps not surprising that the HL soon caved in in the face of such an onslaught:

> *Shivpuri* (1987) D, who admitted to customs officers that he thought he was smuggling illegal drugs, was convicted of attempting to be knowingly concerned in dealing with a controlled drug, namely heroin, although it was proved that the material he was smuggling was in fact harmless. HL, expressly overruling their decision in *Anderton v Ryan*, upheld his conviction. Lord Bridge acknowledged his gratitude to Glanville Williams, saying that he was unable to extract from his own speech in *Anderton v Ryan*, or from that of Lord Roskill, a clear and coherent principle.

The HL is normally reluctant to overrule their previous decisions, given 'the especial need for certainty as to the criminal law' (*Practice Note (Judicial Precedent)* [1966] 3 All ER 77; but see also *Howe* [1987] discussed **5.17**). Were they right to do so here, or has the law now gone too far in punishing impossible attempts? It can be argued that *Shivpuri* represents subjectivism gone mad: if you take your own umbrella from my house, believing that it is mine, you are now guilty of attempted theft. Are you being charged with attempted theft of my umbrella (I don't have one: so clearly nonsense) or attempted theft of your own umbrella (also clearly nonsense)? Society needs protection from would-be drug smugglers such as *Shivpuri*, but the case raises both pragmatic and moral questions. Is it necessary to imprison such a person for a number of years for a crime he failed to commit? The fact that he was caught by customs officers may serve as a greater deterrent than any court sentence: he now knows that customs officers do catch people, and that if he is caught again, he will be sent to prison. Is it just to imprison someone for their mistaken belief? The law is close to punishing thought crime. If *Shivpuri* had denied all knowledge of any drugs to the customs officers, he could not have been convicted of any crime.

7.12 Another problem arises where people use impossible means. If you attempt to kill your enemy by sticking pins into a wax model of her, should you be guilty of attempted murder? French law would say no, since there is no 'real' connection between the act done and that sought to be achieved. The answer to the problem is unclear in English law. One answer is to say that the police have a discretion not to prosecute those who they deem to be harmless. And at least the HL has abolished the need to distinguish different categories of impossibility: see **7.31** for a discussion of how this is still necessary in the case of impossible incitements.

Conspiracy

7.13 Why is it necessary to have a law of conspiracy? Once the parties have gone far enough, all conspirators can be charged as accomplices to an attempt (see **6.2**). However, D may still be charged with a conspiracy even if the substantive offence has been completed: the conspiracy may be easier to prove, and the rules of evidence more relaxed. Thus following the decision of the HL in *Preddy* (1996), that those who commit mortgage frauds cannot be guilty of theft or obtaining property by deception in that they do not intend to deprive the owner of the cheque permanently of it (see **11.36**), prosecutors may fall back again on conspiracy to defraud as an alternative route to conviction. Ashworth (PCL pages 471-7) discusses the 'double-life' of conspiracy, partly as an inchoate offence and partly as a quasi-substantive offence. Thus while the rationale for inchoate offences, including conspiracy, is often early prevention of crime, prosecutors may choose to prosecute someone for conspiracy simply because this is seen as a fuller and better description of their criminal course of conduct.

7.14 Common law conspiracies were largely abolished by s 5(1) of the CLA 1977. A common law conspiracy was wider than simply an agreement to commit a crime, including such offences as conspiracy to defraud, corrupt public morals or outrage public decency. Unfortunately, largely due to the uncertainties surrounding fraud at that time, the Act did not abolish these, which has created many subsequent problems: we return to this at **7.22**.

7.15 *Statutory conspiracy* The CLA 1977, s 1 provides:

(1) Subject to the following provisions of this part of this Act, if a person agrees with any other person or persons that a course of conduct shall be pursued which, if the agreement is carried out in accordance with their intentions, either -
(a) will necessarily amount to or involve the commission of any offence or offences by one or more parties to the agreement, or
(b) would do so but for the existence of facts which render the commission of the offence or any offences impossible,
he is guilty of conspiracy to commit the offence or offences in question
...

(2) Where liability for any offence may be incurred without knowledge on the part of the person committing it of any particular fact or circumstance necessary for the commission of the offence, a person shall nevertheless not be guilty of conspiracy to commit that offence by virtue of subsection (1) above unless he and at least one other party to the agreement intend or know that the fact or circumstance shall or will exist at the time when the conduct constituting the offence is to take place.

7.16 *Actus reus* There must be an agreement, which may involve minimal or no conduct, between at least two people. Unlike in many other countries (France, USA, for example), there is no need for some act in pursuance of the agreement; the agreement itself is deemed sufficiently culpable to come within the criminal law. As O'Connor LJ said in *Siracusa* (1989), 'the essence of the crime of conspiracy is the agreement'. Other conspirators need not be identified, nor need all the parties know about each other. A person who conspires only with a child under ten does not commit a conspiracy, nor do a husband and wife who conspire only with each other.

7.17 The use of the word 'necessarily' in s 1(1)(a) might suggest that a conditional agreement might not amount to a conspiracy. However, if two burglars agree to kill if they get caught, then this conditional agreement constitutes conspiracy to murder:

> *Jackson* (1985) D agreed to shoot V, their friend, in the leg if he was convicted of burglary, as they believed he would then get a more lenient sentence. CA: upheld their conviction for conspiracy to pervert the course of justice.

Ashworth calls the word 'necessarily' in the section an 'unduly concrete term' (PCL, at page 478), and the enactment of cl 48 of the DCC would avoid its use:

> (1) A person is guilty of conspiracy to commit an offence or offences if—
> (a) he agrees with another or others that an act or acts shall be done which, if done, will involve the commission of the offence or offences by one or more of the parties to the agreement; and
> (b) he and at least one other party to the agreement intend that the offence or offences shall be committed.

7.18 *Mens rea* According to s 1, D must intend that the crime be carried out, but this has caused difficulties:

> *Anderson* (1986) D agreed to supply diamond cutting wire to help a prisoner escape. He did it for money, with no intention to help the prisoner escape, indeed he thought that the plan was doomed to failure. HL: upheld his conviction for conspiracy to effect the escape. Lord Bridge:
>
> > The necessary *mens rea* of the crime is, in my opinion, established if, and only if, it is shown that the accused when he entered into the agreement, intended to play some part in the agreed course of conduct in furtherance of the criminal purpose which the agreed course of conduct was intended to achieve. Nothing less will suffice; nothing more is required.

If A asks B, who agrees, to kill C, then A and B should be guilty of conspiracy but does Lord Bridge's definition cause a difficulty where A does not agree to play some part in the agreed course of conduct? In *Anderson*, D did not really intend to help the prisoner escape but he surely merited punishment. This case was one of those raised by Spencer (1987) when he proposed a new offence of facilitation. It would seem that Anderson's culpability lay in his knowingly helping other criminals, rather than in his role in the possible escape. O'Connor L J in *Siracusa* (1989) tried to unravel the confusion:

> We think it obvious that Lord Bridge cannot have been intending that the organiser of a crime who recruited others to carry it out would not himself be guilty of conspiracy unless it be proved that he intended to play some active part himself thereafter ... Consent, that is the agreement or adherence to the agreement, can be inferred if it is proved that he knew what was going on and the intention to participate in the furtherance of the criminal purpose is also established by his failure to stop the unlawful activity.

7.19 It would perhaps have been more logical if Anderson had been charged with aiding and abetting a conspiracy. What of the person who is taking part in order to help the police? At **3.3**, we discussed the distinction between intent and motive: a good motive does not necessarily negate *mens rea*:

> *Yip Chiu-cheung v R* (1995) D was charged with conspiring with a US drugs enforcement officer who had agreed to act as his courier. D argued there was no conspiracy since the officer did not have the *mens rea* for the offence, since his motive was simply to entrap D. PC (Lord Griffiths): the officer did intend to commit the crime: 'the fact that ... the authorities would not prosecute the undercover agent does not mean that he did not intend to commit the crime'. D was therefore rightly convicted of conspiracy.

7.20 Section 1(2) also provides that the conspirator will not be guilty of an offence unless he 'intends or knows' certain facts: would 'believes' be clearer in this context?

7.21 *Impossibility* At common law the fact that the substantive crime was impossible could be a defence:

> *DPP v Nock* (1978) Ds agreed to produce cocaine from a specific powder which in fact could never yield cocaine. HL: quashed their conviction for conspiracy. Impossibility was a defence.

However, now re-read s 1(1)(b) (inserted by s 5 of the CAA 1981), which makes it clear that impossibility is no longer a defence to a statutory conspiracy. Today statutory conspiracies to do impossible things will be treated in the same way as attempts to do impossible things (see **7.11**)

7.22 *Common law conspiracies today*   Confusion over the status of common law conspiracies continues. The CLA 1977, s 5 provides that

(1) Subject to the following provisions of this section, the offence of conspiracy at common law is hereby abolished.

(2) Subsection (1) above shall not affect the offence of conspiracy at common law so far as relates to conspiracy to defraud.

(3) Subsection (1) above shall not affect the offence of conspiracy at common law if and in so far as it may be committed by entering into an agreement to engage in conduct which -
(a) tends to corrupt public morals or outrages public decency; but
(b) would not amount to or involve the commission of an offence if carried out by a single person otherwise than in pursuance of an agreement ...

7.23   *Conspiracy to defraud* If the parties agree to commit an offence under the Theft Acts, for example, a statutory conspiracy may be charged. But the prosecution may instead charge D with a common law conspiracy. The HLs' decision in *Ayres* (1984), that the common law and the statutory offence were mutually exclusive, resulted in many Ds having their convictions quashed simply because they had been wrongly charged with the common law offence. Two years later, the CLRC was therefore asked to review the restriction on the use of a charge of conspiracy to defraud in the light of *Ayres*, and to consider whether these restrictions could be removed without causing injustice. Their Report (18th Report, 1986), which is a model of clarity and good essay-writing style, concluded that the simplest solution to the problem was also the most satisfactory: the full ambit of conspiracy to defraud should be restored. This was achieved in the CJA 1987, s 12.

7.24   For there to be a common law conspiracy to defraud, D must be dishonest. Yet his motive need not be to commit economic loss:

Wai Yu-tsang v R (1992) D, the chief accountant of a bank, was convicted of conspiring with others to defraud the bank and its existing and potential shareholders, creditors and depositors. He said that he had concealed the dishonouring of certain cheques in the bank's accounts on the managing director's instructions and in order to prevent a further run on the bank. He believed he was acting in the bank's best interests. PC (Lord Goff): upheld his conviction. It is enough that the conspirators have dishonestly agreed to bring about a state of affairs which they realise will or may deceive V into so acting, or failing to act, that he will suffer an economic loss or his economic interests will be put at risk. The mere fact that D did not wish his victim to suffer harm will not itself prevent the agreement from constituting a conspiracy to defraud.

7.25 *Conspiracy to corrupt public morals or outrage public decency*

Shaw v DPP (1962) D published a Ladies' Directory, offering the names, addresses and telephone numbers of prostitutes. His intent was to help prostitutes ply their trade after the SOA 1959 had made it more difficult for them to solicit on the street (see **10.20**). HL: upheld his conviction for conspiring to corrupt public morals. A conspiracy to corrupt public morals was a common law offence and there was evidence fit to be left to the jury.

> There is in [the] court a residual power, where no statute has yet intervened to supersede the common law, to superintend those offences which are prejudicial to the public welfare (Viscount Simonds).

Knuller v DPP (1973) Ds all took part in the publication of a magazine which included advertisements by homosexuals for partners. HL: upheld their conviction for conspiring to corrupt public morals, relying on *Shaw*. Parliament alone would be the proper authority to overrule such an authority.

Is s 5(3) of the CAA 1981, which preserves common law conspiracies to corrupt public morals or outrage public decency, really necessary? Cases such as *Gibson* (1990; **1.22**) have confirmed that the offence of outraging public decency still exits, and therefore a conspiracy to outrage public decency can be charged as a statutory conspiracy. What behaviour could be left open for the common law conspiracy?

7.26 *Common law conspiracy and impossibility* The decision in *DPP v Nock* (1978), that impossibility could be a defence to (common law) conspiracy, has survived the insertion of s 1(1)(b) into the CLA 1977 by the CAA 1981 (see **7.21**) since this section applies only to statutory conspiracies.

Incitement

7.27 Incitement is still governed by the common law, although there are some specific statutory offences of incitement such as OAPA 1861, s 4 (incitement to murder) and CLA 1977, s 54 (incitement to commit incest). If the offence is tried on indictment, the sentence is at the discretion of the judge. An incitement to commit a summary offence or one triable either way is punishable to the same extent as the completed offence (MCA 1980, s 45(3) and s 32(1)(b)).

7.28 *Actus reus* D must have encouraged or persuaded someone to commit an offence. If that other person commits the crime, then D is liable for that crime as an accessory (see chapter 6). If D communicates his encouragement, the incitement is complete, even if it has no influence: the incitement need have no effect. There must be an element of persuasion or encouragement: just offering to supply someone with equipment for a burglary which they already intend to commit would not constitute incitement.

> *Most* (1881) D wrote an article in a newspaper advocating the assassination of the crowned heads of Europe. QBD: upheld his conviction. An endeavour to persuade or to encourage is nevertheless an endeavour to persuade or an encouragement even if D did not personally address those people whom his encouragement reaches.

However, the incitement must come to the attention of the incitee. If the encouragement (eg in the form of a letter) is intercepted, then D is probably guilty only of attempted incitement.

7.29 *Mens rea* D must intend that the crime be committed, and must know the circumstances of the act which make it an offence. The person incited need not have the *mens rea*, but D must believe that they would.

> *Invicta Plastics Ltd v Clare* (1976) D, a company, advertised in magazines a device which would give car drivers advance warning of a police radar speed trap. QBD: upheld their conviction for inciting others to

use unlicensed apparatus for wireless telegraphy contrary to the Wireless Telegraphy Act 1949, s 1(1).

Ds were not charged with incitement to speed since it would be difficult to prove this, and were simply charged with inciting people to have a radio without a license. As Spencer (1987) points out, this is an artificial decision, stretching the ambit of incitement to include incitements to people in general too far.

7.30   *Impossibility* If D knows that the person incited does not have the *mens rea* for the full offence, this person will be an innocent agent and D will be the principal offender if the full offence is committed (see **6.5**). If the act incited would not constitute a crime, there will be no incitement: see *Taaffe* (1984) at **3.14**. Where the person incited is the person protected by the criminal offence in question, then D cannot be guilty since the victim would not be committing an offence:

> *Whitehouse* (1977) D's daughter aged 15 refused to have sex with him. CA (Scarman L J): allowed his appeal against his conviction for incitement to commit incest. Had he had sex with her, he would have committed incest, but she no crime. Therefore he could not be guilty of incitement to commit incest.

As a result of this case, a new offence was introduced by s 54 of the CLA 1977: it is now an offence for a man to invite a girl aged under 16 who is his daughter, grand-daughter, or sister to have sex with him. But the general principle of *Whitehouse* remains good: at common law, the incitor is not liable if the person incited cannot commit the crime in question.

7.31   If the incitement encourages someone to commit a crime using inadequate means, D's liability depends on whether D knew that the means were inadequate. If the crime is impossible whatever means are used, D will not be guilty of incitement.

> *Fitzmaurice* (1983) D was asked by his father to find someone to rob a woman on her way to the bank. In fact, the robbery was a fiction invented by the father who hoped to create a situation in which he could claim a reward. CA (Neil L J): upheld D's conviction of incitement to commit robbery. The element of persuasion was satisfied by a

'suggestion, proposal or request accompanied by an implied promise of reward'. The old common law decision on conspiracy, *DPP v Nock* (1978) (see **7.21**) applies to incitement, and impossibility could render an incitement lawful. Here, however, the future robbery was possible, so D was rightly convicted.

Thus impossibility may be a defence to incitement: it is important to assess the possibility at the time of the incitement, not at the time of the further offence. The Law Commission proposed in the DCC, cl 50, to bring all the inchoate offences into line, by reversing *Fitzmaurice*. If this were enacted, impossibility would no longer be a defence to any inchoate offence.

7.32 *Incitement to commit other inchoate offences* Section 5(7) of the CLA 1977 abolished the offence of incitement to conspire, yet the offence of incitement to incite still seems to exist.

Sirat (1985) D incited B or someone else to commit grievous bodily harm on W. CA (Parker LJ): quashed his conviction for incitement to cause grievous bodily harm, as it was unclear whether he had been convicted of incitement to conspire or incitement to incite.

> It may appear to be absurd that, where a person is inciting actual agreement to be made for the commission of a crime, he should be guilty of no offence, but that where he does not seek actual agreement but mere encouragement he should be guilty. This, however, is not necessarily absurd, for there may well be circumstances where there is no question of an agreement being sought but where the particular form of incitement is more effective than any form of agreement.

Can you think of any examples to illustrate Parker LJ's point, or do you agree with JC Smith that the law is hopelessly muddled (see **7.1**)? Logically it would seem that any incitement to attempt to commit an offence must necessarily be an incitement to commit that offence, though as Figure 1 points out there may be an offence of incitement to attempt where D knows that the incitee cannot progress beyond the attempt.

7.33 *Proposals for reform: encouraging crime* The crime of incitement punishes actions far removed from the completed offence, and has been stretched in extraordinary ways to compensate for the limitations of the law on accessory liability. We looked at **6.28** at the Law Commission's proposals in Consultation Paper No 131 for a new offence of assisting crime. In the same document they proposed a new offence of encouraging crime. This crime, the Law Commission suggest, would take over from the current offence of incitement and the 'abetting' and 'counselling' part of complicity liability (and presumably the 'procurement' element). Their formulation is that:

(1) A person commits the offence of encouraging crime if he
  (a) solicits, commands or encourages another ('the principal') to do or cause to be done an act or acts which, if done, will involve the commission of an offence by the principal; and
  (b) intends that that act or those acts should be done by the principal; and
  (c) knows or believes that the principal, in so acting, will do so with the fault required for the offence in question.

(2) The solicitation, command or encouragement must be brought to the attention of the principal, but it is irrelevant to the person's guilt whether or not the principal reacts to or is influenced by the solicitation, command or encouragement.

(3) The defendant need not know the identity of the principal, nor have any particular principal or group of principals in mind, provided that he intends his communication to be acted on by any person to whose attention it comes.

(4) 'Offence' in sub-paragraphs (a) and (c) of sub-section (1) above means the breach of a specified prohibition laid down by statute or the common law; but for the purposes of this section the defendant may solicit, command or encourage the commission of such an offence without intending that it should be committed at a specified time or place.

7.34 The offence of encouragement would therefore cover cases both where D's acts are designed to instigate the commission of the offence by the perpetrator, and cases where he is merely supporting him in a decision which he has already made. Is an act of encouragement something significantly stronger than Kadish's 'influencing' actions, on which the Law Commission's proposals are modelled (see **6.27**)? A spectator at an illegal fight or concert may encourage the perpetrators, but he probably does not influence them. Should she be criminally liable? The Law Commission conclude that where such people do intend to encourage the criminal activities of others, then this offence should extend to them.

7.35 The Law Commission suggest that the act of encouragement should have to be brought to the attention of the perpetrator, though no proof of influence would be required. D need not know the identity of the perpetrator. The *mens rea* would be an intent that the offence encouraged be committed. This, they say, is less controversial than in the case of assisting (see **6.30**): if D's conduct actually assisted the commission of the offence, then there are, as we have seen, strong arguments both for and against imposing criminal sanctions even though the giving of such assistance was not D's purpose. Where D's conduct doesn't assist, but simply emboldens the perpetrator, the Law Commission conclude that it would extend the law too far to make D's conduct itself criminal, unless she intended it to have that effect. However, this is a strange argument which can work two ways: the offence of encouragement may sometimes be less serious, sometimes more serious than the offence of assistance. This is recognised by the Law Commission when they recommend that the maximum penalty for both crimes should be the same as for the principal offence. For similar reasons, there is also a strong argument for saying that the same test should apply in relation to the mental element for both offences.

7.36 There can be little doubt that the law discussed in the last two chapters is in need of urgent reform. When that reform comes must remain a question of some doubt: the Law Commission's proposals have yet to be finalised, yet alone brought before Parliament.

References and further reading

Ashworth, 'Defining criminal offences without harm', in Smith, P (ed) *Criminal Law Essays* (1987)

Glazebrook, 'Should we have a law of attempted crime?' (1969) 85 LQR 27

Law Commission. Consultation Paper No 131 (1993)

Smith, 'Proximity in Attempt: Lord Lane's "midway course"' [1991] Crim LR 576

Smith (1986) Crim LR 245

Spencer, 'Trying to help another commit a crime', in Smith, P (ed) *Criminal Law Essays* (1987)

Williams, 'The Lords and impossible attempts, or *quis custodiet ipsos custodes*'? (1986) 45 CLJ 33

Williams, 'Wrong turning on the law of attempt' (1991) Crim LR 416

Self-test questions

1. In the pub one night, Dee tells Andy the barman that she wishes Phil was dead. She then telephones Phil and threatens to kill him within the next month. She writes to Bob offering him £5,000 to kill Phil and posts the letter. Bob receives the letter and agrees to kill Phil. He finds him apparently asleep in the park and shoots him at close range through the head. Unknown to either Dee or Bob, Phil had already been dead for three hours at the time he was shot. Explore all the possible inchoate offences to be found in this sorry tale.

2. Dee tells Bob that she would like him to blackmail Phil for her and that if he is not prepared to help, she would like him to find someone else who is prepared to do so.

3. Dee decides to rob a bank. She tells Fee her plans and asks for her help, saying that they can then share the proceeds. Fee tells her that she will help, but in fact, Fee tells the police of the plan. Dee is arrested the next day.

CHAPTER EIGHT

Homicide

SUMMARY

Murder: Intentional killing. The main problems lie in defining and inferring intent.

Voluntary manslaughter: Specific defences under the HA 1957, each of which cause difficulties in interpretation:
s 2: Diminished responsibility: extremely vague test of abnormality of mind.
s 3: Provocation: 'sudden loss of control' + a reasonable man test.
s 4: Suicide pact: is this necessary since the Suicide Act 1961 legalised suicide?

Involuntary manslaughter: the overlap between 'constructive manslaughter' (D does an intentional, unlawful and dangerous act which causes death); reckless manslaughter and the recently re-emerged gross negligence manslaughter needs to be explored. Causation issues.

Proposals for reform: in particular, Law Com Report No 237: Legislating the Criminal Code: Involuntary Manslaughter.

8.1　Homicide is the word used to describe any unlawful killing of a human being. The most common homicide offences in English law are murder and manslaughter, but there are others: for example, infanticide, child destruction, causing death by dangerous driving. The difference between murder and manslaughter is vital since anyone convicted of murder is subject to a mandatory life sentence of imprisonment (until 1965 the death penalty was imposed for murder). Even though it is rare for a mandatory life sentence prisoner to serve the rest of his or her life in prison, the system for release gives wide discretionary powers to the

Home Secretary. The Home Secretary may insist that a prisoner's release remains unacceptable (as in the case of Myra Hindley, convicted in 1966: see *R v Secretary of State for the Home Department, ex p Hindley* (2000)). On the other hand, in the case of those convicted of manslaughter, the sentencing judge may impose any sentence. Where the judge deems the convicted person to be a danger to the public and decides to impose a life sentence for manslaughter, the Parole Board decides when and whether to release the prisoner, and the Home Secretary is bound by their recommendation to release.

8.2 The arguments concerning the various elements of the law of murder and manslaughter in England are often clouded by the knowledge that there is a mandatory life sentence for all murderers. If you were starting from scratch, or if the mandatory life sentence were abolished, would you distinguish between varying degrees of culpable homicide? There is a world of difference between the person who deliberately kills someone in cold blood, and the person who causes death by his gross negligence. Despite the sentencing differences, there are good arguments based on fair labelling (see 1.2) that the more heinous killings should be distinguished from other, less culpable killings. If we accept that there should be different categories of culpable homicide, does English law draw the line in appropriate places? It is astonishing that the borderlines between murder and manslaughter, and between manslaughter and no criminal liability remain so unclear. Confusion may also be created by the terminology: many of the terms used (voluntary and involuntary manslaughter, malice aforethought) have little meaning in ordinary modern English. The need for an updated law is evident.

Murder

8.3 *Actus reus* The *actus reus* of both murder and manslaughter is the killing of a person. Thus, any act which shortens life may amount to murder. Students should re-read **2.14** etc, where the problems of causation were explored: for example, it is important to remember that the *de minimis* rule means that D's act must be the substantial cause of the victim's death. A recent problem has surrounded the interpretation of a person: any child born alive is a person, but a foetus is not.

A-G's Reference (No 3 of 1994) (1998) D stabbed his girlfriend who he knew to be pregnant. The girlfriend recovered, but V, her baby, was born prematurely as a result of the wound and died after 120 days. The trial judge held that D could not be convicted of murder or manslaughter and ordered D's acquittal. HL: D was rightly acquitted of murder: malice could not be transferred twice (see **3.33**). A foetus can not be treated as part of the mother but as a unique organism. Murder could not be committed where unlawful injury was deliberately inflicted on the mother where the child was subsequently born alive and enjoyed an existence independent of its mother before it died, even though the injuries inflicted in utero contributed substantially to the death. However, liability for manslaughter could be established: see **8.32**. Lord Mustill announces towards the beginning of his speech that

> … the law of homicide is permeated by anomaly, fiction, misnomer and obsolete reasoning.

This speech is well worth reading as a thorough, and highly critical, review of the historical development of the offence.

8.4   *Year and a day rule* Until 1996, D's conduct had to cause death within a year and a day. This rule made good sense in days gone by when any longer period could have raised questions about whether it really was D's act which caused V's death. However, the rule came under increasing criticism, especially as modern medicine and life-support machines meant that a murderer could avoid liability simply because of lengthy medical attempts to save someone's life. In 1995 both the House of Commons' Select Committee on Home Affairs and the Law Commission produced papers recommending the abolition of the rule, and this Parliament did in the Murder (Abolition of the Year and a Day Rule) Act 1996. The Act does provide a safeguard against prosecutions long after the event: the consent of the Attorney-General is needed for proceedings against a person for a 'fatal offence' if either the injury alleged to have caused the death was sustained more than three years before the death occurred, or the person to be prosecuted has previously been convicted of an offence committed in circumstances alleged to be connected with the death.

8.5   *Mens rea* The *mens rea* of murder is 'malice aforethought'. Perhaps surprisingly, this has long been interpreted not only to include an intention to kill, but also an intention to cause grievous bodily harm.

The meaning of intention was discussed at **3.2**. After s 1 of the HA 1957 had abolished constructive malice, there was some doubt as to whether in future an intention merely to cause grievous bodily harm would be enough to constitute murder, but the following case removed all doubt:

> *Vickers* (1957) D broke into the cellar of a shop with intent to steal. When disturbed by V, a woman of 73, he kicked and punched her. She died of the injuries she sustained. CCA: upheld D's murder conviction. Section 1 did not abolish implied malice ie the implication of malice aforethought from a voluntary act inflicting grievous bodily harm and causing death.

8.6 In practical terms this decision is useful: it is often difficult to prove that D intended to kill, but if he shows such disregard for human life that he beats someone up sufficiently badly to kill them, most people would be happy to say he is a murderer. But it does raise a question of principle: if D merely intends grievous bodily harm and V happens unfortunately to die, is this not more appropriately described as manslaughter? Merely doing an act with the knowledge that it is highly probable that death or serious bodily harm will result is not enough to constitute the *mens rea* of murder. However, if the jury accepts that D had such knowledge, it is open to them to infer that he had the required intent: see the discussion of *Moloney*; *Hancock and Shankland*; *Nedrick* at **3.9, 3.10**. Lord Mustill said in *A-G's Reference (No 3 of 1994)* (1998) (see **8.3**) that the grievous bodily harm rule

> is an outcropping of old law from which the surrounding strata of rationalisations have weathered away. It survives but exemplifies no principle which can be applied to a new situation.

8.7 *Possible reform* Clause 54 of the DCC proposes that:

> (1) A person is guilty of murder if he causes the death of another -
> (a) intending to cause death
> (b) intending to cause serious personal harm and being aware that he may cause death,
> unless section 56 (diminished responsibility), 58 (provocation), 59 (use of excessive force) or 64 (infanticide) applies.

This proposal would modify the present law in various respects. First, an intention to cause serious personal harm would only constitute a sufficient fault for murder if D was also aware that he might cause death. This will rarely pose an evidential problem in practice and may be a useful narrowing of the definition. Secondly, the definition of intention in the DCC is wider than that presently used in the definition of murder (see **3.10**). Under *Nedrick* the jury may infer intent if they believe that D knew that death was virtually certain to result from his act. Under the DCC (clause 18(b)(i)), as we saw at **3.11**, D intends to kill if he is aware that it will occur in the normal course of events. Does this accord with your understanding of the word? Finally, it is worth noting that the DCC talks of 'causing death': this is wide enough to include deaths caused by omissions (see **2.7**).

Voluntary manslaughter

8.8   The Homicide Act 1957 introduced three partial defences to murder. Thus where a person intentionally kills someone but whilst under diminished responsibility, or acting under provocation or in furtherance of a suicide pact, they may only be convicted of manslaughter. Thus 'voluntary manslaughter' would be murder but for the existence of the defence.

Diminished responsibility

8.9   HA 1957, s 2 provides:

(1) Where a person kills or is a party to a killing of another, he shall not be convicted of murder if he was suffering from such abnormality of mind (whether arising from a condition of arrested or retarded development of mind or any inherent causes or induced by disease or injury) as substantially impaired his mental responsibility for his acts and omissions in doing or being a party to the killing.

(2) On a charge of murder, it shall be for the defence to prove that the person charged is by virtue of this section not liable to be convicted of murder.

(3) A person who but for this section would be liable, whether as principal or as accessory, to be convicted of murder shall be liable instead to be convicted of manslaughter.

(4) The fact that one party to a killing is by virtue of this section not liable to be convicted of murder shall not affect the question whether the killing amounted to murder in the case of any other party to it.

8.10 This definition is remarkably loose: what is an abnormality of mind which substantially impairs mental responsibility? Clearly, if D is insane within the meaning of the *M'Naghten Rules* (see **4.8**), then she will be acquitted. But here we are dealing with someone who is sufficiently 'sane' to merit a conviction for manslaughter.

> *Byrne* (1960) D, a sexual psychopath, strangled V, a young woman at a hostel. CCA: allowed his appeal against his conviction for murder, substituting a manslaughter conviction (it is worth noting that despite this, his sentence of life imprisonment was upheld). Lord Parker CJ suggested that 'abnormality of mind' includes 'the mind's activities in all its aspects ... a state of mind so different from that of ordinary human beings that a reasonable man would term it abnormal'.

> *Ahluwalia* (1992) D entered into an arranged marriage and suffered years of violent and abusive behaviour by V, her husband. He threatened to kill her and taunted her about his affair with another woman. One night, after he threatened to beat her, she set fire to his bedroom while he slept. He died and she was convicted of murder. CA (Lord Taylor CJ): as a result of fresh medical evidence the conviction was unsafe and a retrial was ordered. At the retrial, P accepted a plea of guilty by reason of diminished responsibility. (See **8.16** for more on this case.)

8.11 Griew (1988) argued that s 2 is so badly worded that it can be made to work and to work better than its framers intended. The fact that s 2 encourages role confusion between judge, jury and psychiatrists is both its main advantage and its main disadvantage. It may sometimes work well in practice as a means of avoiding a mandatory life sentence for those who juries decide do not deserve it. But does the section hand power to juries, or to the psychiatrists whose evidence they receive? The Lane Committee (1989), in arguing against a mandatory life sentence for murder, concluded that the medical profession stretch s 2 out of motives of humanity.

8.12 *Diminished responsibility and intoxication* Where D has taken drugs or alcohol, the jury must disregard this unless alcoholism can be proved

154

as a form of mental abnormality. Asking a jury to ignore causes of abnormality which fall outside s 2 can give them a pretty impossible task:

Atkinson (1985) D, aged 18, stole alcohol and drank it with friends. They then burgled a house and were disturbed by V, the 77-year-old occupant. D punched and beat her, with the result that she died of a fractured skull. There was medical evidence that he had grossly arrested or retarded development of mind, and that alcohol had also played a part in the events. CA: dismissed the appeal, accepting JC Smith's comment at [1984] Crim LR 553 that the two questions for the jury, in logical sequence, should be: 'Have the defence satisfied you on a balance of probabilities – that if the D had not taken drink – (i) he would have killed as he in fact did? And (ii) that he could have been under diminished responsibility when he did so'.

Tandy (1989) D, an alcoholic, strangled her 11-year-old daughter after discovering that the girl was suffering sexual abuse at the hands of D's boyfriend. D had that day drunk most of a bottle of vodka. CA (Watkins LJ): upheld her conviction for murder. Faced with a conflict of medical evidence on whether alcoholism is a disease of the mind and whether D's drinking was 'voluntary' or not, Watkins LJ decided that the real question was whether her abnormality of mind was a direct result of her alcoholism or a result of the fact that she was drunk on vodka. Where D had simply not resisted the impulse to drink, she could not rely on the defence of diminished responsibility.

This case illustrates many of the difficulties in this area. By dismissing her appeal, the CA was upholding the mandatory life sentence on Mrs Tandy (who shortly afterwards committed suicide in prison). Do you think that such a D can ever prove that taking the first drink was involuntary?

8.13 *Reform* Clause 56 of the DCC in large measure adopts the recommended changes of the CLRC's 14th Report. It would maintain the separation between diminished responsibility and the effects of intoxication:

(1) A person who, but for this section, would be guilty of murder is not guilty of murder if, at the time of his act, he is suffering from such mental abnormality as is a substantial enough reason to reduce his offence to manslaughter.

(2) In this section 'mental abnormality' means mental illness, arrested or incomplete development of mind, psychopathic disorder, and any other disorder or disability of mind, except intoxication.

(3) Where a person suffering from mental abnormality is also intoxicated, this section applies only where it would apply if he were not intoxicated.

One difference with the present law is that D would only have to raise evidence of diminished responsibility, and not prove it on a balance of probabilities. This would bring the defence in line with provocation (see below). It also uses slightly clearer medical terms, though whether even this formulation would adequately separate out the medical from the moral issues involved remains to be seen.

Provocation

8.14   HA 1957, s 3 provides a second partial defence, which reduces murder to manslaughter:

Where on a charge of murder there is evidence on which the jury can find that the person charged was provoked (whether by things done or by things said or by both together) to lose his self-control, the question whether the provocation was enough to make a reasonable man do as he did shall be left to be determined by the jury; and in determining that question the jury shall take into account everything both done and said according to the effect which, in their opinion, it would have on the reasonable man.

As Ashworth (1976) pointed out, this definition involves a subjective element (was D provoked to lose his self-control?) and two objective elements (would the reasonable man have been provoked? would the reasonable man have responded to the extent that D reacted?).

8.15   *The subjective element* D must be able to show he lost his self-control. At first sight this may seem a curious defence: if the criminal law is excusing loss of self-control, is it legitimising violent responses? Any words or acts (whether or not the victim's) may constitute provocation, and they need not themselves be unlawful:

Doughty (1986) D killed V, his two-week-old baby. The trial judge refused to leave a defence of provocation by the baby's crying to jury. CA (Stocker LJ): Section 3 should have been left to jury as there was a causal link between the crying and D's act. The Court therefore substituted a conviction for manslaughter (and a sentence of five years' imprisonment).

8.16   The issue has been particularly controversial in the case of women who kill their violent husbands. The case of *Ahluwalia* (1992) was raised at **8.10** above in relation to diminished responsibility. On the defence of provocation, Lord Taylor CJ said:

> The phrase 'sudden and temporary loss of self-control' encapsulates an essential ingredient of the defence of provocation in a clear and readily understandable phrase. It serves to underline that the defence is concerned with the actions of an individual who is not, at the moment when he or she acts violently, master of his or her own mind. ... it is open to the judge when deciding whether there is any evidence of provocation to be left to the jury and open to the jury when considering such evidence, to take account of the interval between the provocative conduct and the reaction of the D to it ... in some cases, such an interval may wholly undermine the defence of provocation; that, however, depends entirely on the facts of the individual case and is not a principle of law.

Thornton (1992 and 1996) D married V in August 1988, knowing him to be a heavy drinker and a possessive man. She suffered significant violence in the home. In June 1989 she told a work colleague that she would kill him. Later that month, after a series of rows, she went to the kitchen to calm down. There she sharpened a carving knife and made to stab V, expecting him to ward off the blows. Instead he was fatally stabbed in the stomach. At the trial, D relied on diminished responsibility, but the trial judge put the defence of provocation before the jury, explaining that it required some sudden loss of control. The CA originally (1992) dismissed the appeal:

> It is within the experience of each member of the court that in cases of domestic violence which culminate in the death of a partner there is frequently evidence given of provocative acts committed by the deceased in the past, for it is in that context that the jury have to consider the accused's reaction. In every such case the question for the jury is whether at the moment the fatal blow was struck the

accused had been deprived for that moment of the self-control which previously he or she had been able to exercise (per Beldam LJ).

However, the case was referred back to the CA in 1995 and in *Thornton (No 2)* the Court ordered a retrial. The LCJ recognised that 'sudden loss of control' may be triggered by even a minor incident.

8.17 This decision goes some way towards acknowledging what has irritated many commentators in recent years: that provocation is a stereotypically 'male' defence in that it is a typically male reaction to 'flip' in anger. It is a defence evolved over the centuries in cases where people retaliated in outrage or in loss of self-control (see Horder, 1992). Women are more likely to 'burn' slowly inside, and then perhaps reach breaking point. Without a sudden loss of control, they fall outside the defence. This leads some people to argue that the defence should be widened to include 'slow burn' reactions as well 'sudden loss of self-control'; others argue that the defence should simply be abolished (see Padfield (1996)).

8.18 *The objective elements* These too cause many problems: if a reasonable person would have done as D, then why is he convicted of any crime? And who is the reasonable man?

> *Camplin* (1978) D, a 15-year-old, killed V, a middle-aged man who had buggered him and mocked him. He was convicted of murder. CA: substituted manslaughter by reason of provocation. HL: dismissed Crown's appeal. Lord Diplock: The judge should explain to the jury that the reasonable man is a person having the power of self-control to be expected of an ordinary person of the sex and age of the accused, but in other respects sharing such of the accused's characteristics as they think would affect the gravity of the provocation to him.

8.19 This test has been difficult to apply in practice. What are relevant characteristics?

> *Newell* (1980) D, a chronic alcoholic, killed his friend who made derogatory remarks about his ex-girlfriend. The trial judge suggested that the jury should ask itself whether 'a sober man would, in relation to that drunken observation, batter his friend over the head with a nearby 2 lb ashtray?' CA: Lord Lane LJ: refused leave to appeal against

his conviction for murder. The jury should not be invited to take chronic alcoholism into account on the question of provocation since relevant characteristics must have a sufficient degree of permanence to make it part of individual's character and personality. More importantly, there must be some real connection between the nature of the provocation and the particular characteristic of D by which it is sought to modify the reasonable man test.

8.20 Thus temporary characteristics are not relevant, but where does one draw the line? Does religion, or a suicidal tendency, 'have a sufficient degree of permanence' to make it a part of the individual's character? The HL in *Morhall* (1996) held that an addiction to glue sniffing was a relevant characteristic, as it was of particular relevance. The CA had decided the other way, largely it would seem because an addiction to solvent abuse was not consistent with the concept of a reasonable man. What do you think? In *Thornton (No 2)* (1996, see **8.16**), Lord Taylor CJ held that, depending on the medical evidence, 'battered wife syndrome' may affect D's personality so as to constitute a relevant and significant characteristic.

8.21 A key question is whether a characteristic is relevant only if it affects the gravity of the provocation (except where the characteristic is age or gender), or whether any characteristic which affects D's ability to exercise self-control should be considered:

Luc Thiet Thuan v R (1997) D was alleged to have killed V, his ex-girlfriend, and relied on both provocation and diminished responsibility. Despite evidence of brain damage which could make it difficult for D to control his impulses, the trial judge when summing up to the jury on provocation did not refer to the brain damage. D was convicted of murder. The PC (by a majority) upheld the conviction. D's mental infirmity which reduced his powers of self-control was not a relevant characteristic. The test of provocation was an objective one, and D's individual peculiarities were not relevant. Lord Steyn (dissenting) relied on *Ahluwalia* and *Thornton (No 2)*, decisions which he described as 'a logical extension of *Camplin*'. But even more important than the promptings of legal logic, he said, are the dictates of justice.

Campbell (1997) D killed a hitchhiker in a long drawn out and frenzied attack, after she had hit him to avoid his sexual advances. He was convicted in 1985, but in 1996 the CA ordered a retrial on the grounds that fresh medical evidence on the effects of epilepsy should be left to the jury when considering a defence of diminished responsibility. The LCJ gave some comments on what the trial judge should say to a jury on the subject of provocation:

> There is compelling force in the construction which the majority [of the Privy Council in *Luc Thiet Thuan*] have put on a section which makes reference to the reasonable man and gives no express warrant for elaborating or qualifying that concept. We are, however, conscious that the body of Court of Appeal authority which is in doubt represents a judicial response, born of everyday experience in criminal trials up and down the country, to what fairness seems to require. If the concept of the reasonable man expressed in section 3 were accepted without any qualification, successful pleas of provocation would be rare indeed, since it is not altogether easy to imagine circumstances in which a reasonable man would strike a fatal blow with the necessary mental intention, whatever the provocation. It is in recognition of human frailty that the scope of the defence of provocation has, to a very limited extent, been enlarged.

8.22   Ashworth argued (at (1976) CLJ 292, at page 300) that 'the proper distinction ... is that individual peculiarities which bear on the gravity of the provocation should be taken into account, whereas individual peculiarities bearing on the accused's level of self-control should not'. Thus, to benefit from the defence, D must prove that the provocation was related to the relevant trait. This inevitably leads juries to have to make fine distinctions: a characteristic such as post-natal depression or personality disorder may well have to be taken into account in answering the subjective question, but ignored when it comes to the objective test.

> *Smith* (2000) D, suffering from severe depression, stabbed V, his friend, fatally during an argument about some tools that D alleged that V had stolen. He was convicted of murder. CA: (Potts J): D's severe depression was a relevant characteristic which the jury should have been taken into account. HL [decision expected soon].

8.23   *Provocation and other defences* D's advisers are often in something of a quandary. If they raise a defence of self-defence, for example, which would result in an acquittal, it will be difficult for them to argue at the same time that D was provoked. The two defences run counter to each other. In such a case, the judge should himself put the defence of provocation to the jury:

Johnson (1989) D had behaved unpleasantly at a night-club. As he walked away, V poured beer over him and pinned him to wall. A woman also abused him and pulled his hair. D stabbed V to death with a flick-knife. His defence at trial was self-defence, and the trial judge refused to leave provocation to the jury since self-induced provocation could not constitute a defence. CA: allowed his appeal, substituting a conviction for manslaughter. If there is some evidence of provocation, the defence must be left to the jury.

8.24 *Mistake and provocation* An honest but mistaken belief in the existence of facts which, had they existed, would have provoked a reasonable person will be a defence: *Brown* (1776). This mistake need not be a reasonable one. For a discussion of the effect of mistakes generally, see **5.24**.

Suicide pacts

8.25 HA 1957, s 4 provides that

(1) It shall be manslaughter, and shall not be murder, for a person acting in pursuance of a suicide pact between him and another to kill the other or to be a party to the other being killed by a third person.

(2) Where it is shown that a person charged with the murder of another killed the other or was a party to his being killed, it shall be for the defence to prove that the person charged was acting in pursuance of a suicide pact between him and the other.

(3) For the purposes of this section 'suicide pact' means a common agreement between two or more persons having for its object the death of all of them, whether or not each is to take his own life, but nothing done by a person who enters into a suicide pact shall be treated as done by him in pursuance of the pact unless it is done while he has the settled intention of dying in pursuance of the pact.

8.26 Suicide itself ceased to be a crime in the Suicide Act 1961, but s 2 makes clear that a person who aids, abets, counsels or procures the suicide of another or an attempt by another to commit suicide, shall be liable on conviction on indictment to 14 years' imprisonment.

> *McShane* (1977) D encouraged her mother to commit suicide so that she could inherit her money. She was convicted of attempting to counsel or procure her mother's suicide, contrary to the Suicide Act 1961, s 2 and with attempting to cause to be taken by her mother a destructive or noxious thing so as to endanger life, contrary to the OAPA 1861, s 23. CA: Orr LJ dismissed her appeal. The Court went so far as to say that no consent can render a dangerous act innocent, but that statement is too broad (see **5.6**).

8.27 The DCC suggests that killing in pursuance of a suicide pact should not be manslaughter, but a particular offence which they designate 'suicide pact killing', (see clause 62), punishable with a maximum of seven years' imprisonment. This is as well as the offence of complicity in suicide, which reproduces the effect of the Suicide Act 1961, s 2. Are both really necessary?

Involuntary manslaughter

8.28 Those guilty of manslaughter by reason of diminished responsibility or provocation intended to kill. We now turn to those who did not intend to kill: involuntary means simply that they did not have an intent to kill. In recent years it has generally been accepted that someone may be convicted of involuntary manslaughter by two very different routes: constructive manslaughter and reckless/gross negligence manslaughter. Very often P may find that the facts justify following either route, but the overlap is by no means total. However, these categories are by no means clear cut, and this area of the law is riddled with confusion. This is another depressing area of the criminal law, one in desperate need of a statutory overhaul.

Constructive manslaughter

8.29 Where D causes death by an intentional unlawful and dangerous act, she is guilty of manslaughter. The act must be unlawful in itself: driving a car negligently is therefore probably not sufficient. In this context the courts have held that there must be an act: failure to act would appear to be insufficient:

> *Lowe* (1973) D, of low intelligence, suggested to his partner that she should take their baby to the doctor. Despite saying that she had done so, she did not, as she was frightened that the baby would be taken into care by the local authority. The baby died of dehydration. CA: whilst D could be convicted of wilful neglect contrary to s 1(1) of the CYPA 1933, his conviction for manslaughter was quashed:
>
> > We think that there is a clear distinction between an act of omission and an act of commission likely to cause harm. … if I strike a child in a manner likely to cause harm it is right that, if the child dies, I may be charged with manslaughter. If however, I omit to do something with the result that it suffers injury to health which results in its death, we think that a charge of manslaughter should not be the inevitable consequence, even if the omission is deliberate (per Phillimore LJ).

8.30 This distinction between acts and omissions is surely untenable (see also **2.6**). In any case, a father has a duty to care for his child. It was also an unnecessary decision. If the court had simply decided that D's omission was not unlawful, then he would have been acquitted without the court having to exaggerate the distinction between acts and omissions. An example of an act which was held not to be unlawful is found in:

> *Jennings* (1990) D, who had been drinking heavily, had armed himself with a sheaf knife to protect himself from X, who he believed was looking for him. His brother was killed trying to restrain him. He was convicted of constructive manslaughter after the trial judge had advised the jury that he had no defence except on the question whether a bystander would have realised that some injury was inevitable from the unlawful act being committed by D. CA (Lord Lane CJ): allowed the appeal. A knife is not an offensive weapon per se. Therefore walking down a walk way with a knife in hand is not an unlawful act which could have constituted the 'unlawful act' for this purpose.

8.31 Whether or not an act is dangerous depends on whether it is likely to do physical harm:

> *Church* (1966) D was taunted by V about his impotence. He knocked her out, panicked and dumped her body in a river, where she

163

drowned. He was convicted of manslaughter. CCA (Edmund Davies LJ): applying *Meli v R* (see **2.9**), the series of acts which culminated in her death were sufficient to constitute manslaughter.

> The unlawful act must be such as all sober and reasonable people would inevitably recognise must subject the other person to, at least, the risk of some harm resulting therefrom, albeit not serious harm.

DPP v Newbury (1977) Three teenage Ds dropped a paving stone on to a passing train. It landed on the cab, and killed the guard. The point of law certified to be of general public importance was 'Can a D be properly convicted of manslaughter, when his mind was not affected by drink or drugs, if he did not foresee that his act might cause harm to another?'. HL: upheld their convictions for manslaughter. Lord Salmon affirmed the objective test that it is not necessary to prove that D knew that the act was unlawful or dangerous, merely whether sober and reasonable people would realise its danger.

Dawson (1985) Three men held up the attendant at a petrol station in order to rob him. Shortly afterwards he died of a heart attack. The trial judge told that the jury that it was sufficient to convict them of manslaughter that the unlawful act was likely to cause emotional disturbance. CA (Watkins LJ) quashed their convictions: the harm referred to in *Church* must be physical harm. (See also **2.15** for discussion of this case).

Goodfellow (1986) D wished to be rehoused so he set fire to his council house. This caused the death of his wife, his girlfriend and his child. He was convicted of both manslaughter and arson. CA (Lord Lane CJ): upheld his conviction (and a sentence of six years' imprisonment). There is no requirement that the act be directed at V. The questions for the jury were: (i) was the act intentional? (ii) was it unlawful? (iii) was it an act which any reasonable person would realise was bound to subject some other human being to the risk of physical harm, albeit not necessarily serious harm? (iv) was that act the cause of death?

Ball (1989) D stored live and blank cartridges together, but thought he was firing a blank at V. CA: upheld his conviction for manslaughter. In manslaughter arising from an unlawful and dangerous act, D's state of mind is only relevant to establish (a) that the act was committed intentionally, and (b) that it was an unlawful act. Once (a) and (b) were established, the question whether the act was dangerous was to be judged not by D's appreciation, but by that of the sober and reasonable man. At this stage, D's intention, foresight or knowledge are irrelevant.

8.32   Why is it that someone should be guilty of manslaughter simply because they intentionally did another unlawful and dangerous act? As well as posing theoretical problems, constructive manslaughter is also difficult to prove in that P must prove that D acted both unlawfully and dangerously.

A-G's Reference (No 3 of 1994) (1998) D stabbed his girlfriend who he knew to be pregnant. The girlfriend recovered, but V, her baby, was born prematurely as a result of the wound and died after 120 days. The trial judge held that D could not be convicted of murder or manslaughter and ordered D's acquittal. HL: D was rightly acquitted of murder (see **3.33**; **8.3**). However, since D intended to stab the mother and that was an unlawful and dangerous act, it followed that the requisite mens rea was established and although the child was a foetus at the time, on public policy grounds she was to be regarded as coming within that mens rea when she was a living person. Lord Hope:

> it is clear from the authorities that, although D must be proved to have intended to do what he did, it is not necessary to prove that he knew that his act was likely to injure the person who died as a result of it.

Most proposals for reform in this area in recent years have suggested that this category of manslaughter is no longer necessary (see **8.37**).

Reckless/gross negligence manslaughter

8.33   For many years it was accepted that someone whose 'gross negligence' caused death was guilty of manslaughter:

Bateman (1925) CCA (Lord Hewart):

... the facts must be such that, in the opinion of the jury, the negligence of the accused went beyond a mere matter of compensation between subjects and showed such disregard for the life and safety of others as to amount to a crime against the State and conduct deserving of punishment.

Andrews v DPP (1937) Lord Atkin:

simple lack of care as will constitute civil liability is insufficient ... Probably of all the epithets that can be applied 'reckless' most nearly covers the case ... but it is probably not all-embracing, for 'reckless' suggests an indifference to risk, whereas the accused may have appreciated the risk and intended to avoid it and yet shown such a high degree of negligence in the means adopted to avoid as would justify a conviction.

8.34 Increasing concern about the interpretation of gross negligence led the courts to accept that the concept of 'recklessness' as developed by the HL in *Metropolitan Police Comr v Caldwell* (1982) and *Lawrence* (1982) (see **3.22**) might be a better way of expressing the degree of culpability necessary to justify a conviction for manslaughter:

Seymour (1983) After an argument with his girlfriend, there was an accident between D's lorry and her car. He proceeded to crush his girlfriend between the two vehicles. He was convicted of manslaughter (and sentenced to five years' imprisonment). HL: dismissed his appeal. Lord Roskill held that the new test of recklessness developed in *Caldwell* and *Lawrence* should be applied throughout the criminal law.

It is appropriate also to point out that in order to constitute the offence of manslaughter the risk of death being caused by the manner of D's driving must be very high.

Kong Cheuk Kwan v R (1985) Two hydrofoils collided on a clear sunny day. Two passengers were killed, and D, who was in command of one of the hydrofoils, was convicted of manslaughter. PC (Lord Roskill): allowed the appeal. Lord Roskill confirmed that it was no longer useful to refer to negligence or to the *Bateman* test:

the model direction suggested in *Lawrence*, and held in *Seymour* to be equally applicable in cases of motor manslaughter, requires first, proof that the vehicle was in fact being driven in such a manner as to create an obvious and serious risk of causing physical injury to another and second, that D so drove either without having given any thought to the possibility of there being such a risk or having recognised that there was such a risk nevertheless took it.

8.35 By 1989, it seemed that the problems were fast disappearing: Lord Lane CJ was able in *Goodfellow* (see **8.31** above) to point out that D in that case could equally well have been convicted of reckless manslaughter. He laid down one simple test which should be laid before the jury:

> Has the accused acted in such a way as to create an obvious and serious risk of causing physical harm and, having recognised that there was some risk involved, had gone on to take it.

8.36 However, in an about turn, the HL now seems to have rejected the application of *Caldwell /Lawrence* to manslaughter, returning to the older test of gross negligence:

> *Adomako* (1995) D, an anaesthetist, failed to notice that the tube from a ventilator had become disconnected during an operation and the patient died. HL (Lord Mackay): rejected D's appeal against his conviction for manslaughter.

> > [t]he ordinary principles of the law of negligence apply to ascertain whether or not the D has been in breach of a duty of care towards the victim who has died. If such a breach of duty is established the next question is whether that breach of duty caused the death of the victim. If so, the jury must go on to consider whether that breach of duty should be characterised as gross negligence and therefore as a crime. This will depend on the seriousness of the breach of duty ... in all the circumstances in which the D was placed. The jury will have to consider whether the extent to which the D's conduct departed from the proper standard of care incumbent upon him involving as it must have done a risk of death ..., was such that it should be judged criminal.

Lord Mackay does not rule out the use of the word 'reckless' in directions to juries. He appears keen that the definition should not be too precise:

> the essence of the matter, which is supremely a jury question, is whether having regard to the risk of death involved, the conduct of

the defendant is so bad in all the circumstances as to amount in their judgement to a criminal act or omission.

However, the end result it is that is today extraordinarily difficult to define the law with any certainty. The Law Commission (in Law Com No 237) says this about Lord Mackay's test:

> The first problem ... is that it is circular: the jury must be directed to convict D of a crime if they think his conduct was 'criminal'. In effect, this leaves a question of law to the jury, and, because juries do not give reasons for their decisions, it is impossible to tell what criteria will be applied in an individual case ...Other problems arise out of the Lord Chancellor's use of the terminology of 'duty of care' and 'negligence', and his linkage of the civil and criminal law in his speech. The meanings of these words are not entirely clear in a criminal law context ... (para 3.9/3.10).

8.37 *Reform* Clause 55 of the DCC included an offence of reckless manslaughter and this remained the recommendation of Law Com No 237 of 1996. Their draft Bill included a clause which provided:

> (1) A person who by his conduct causes the death of another is guilty of reckless killing if-
> (a) he is aware of a risk that his conduct will cause death or serious injury; and
> (b) it is unreasonable for him to take that risk having regard to the circumstances as he knows or believes them to be.

This offence would clearly be based on a test of subjective recklessness. The Law Commission recommended the abolition of unlawful act manslaughter in its present form, but also recommended an offence of killing by gross carelessness:

> (1) A person who by his conduct causes the death of another is guilty of killing by gross carelessness if -
> (a) a risk that his conduct will cause death or serious injury would be obvious to a reasonable person in his position;
> (b) he is capable of appreciating that risk at the material time; and
> (c) either-
>   (i) his conduct falls far below what can reasonably be expected of him in the circumstances; or
>   (ii) he intends by his conduct to cause some injury or is aware of, and unreasonably takes, the risk that it may do so.

They give the example of a climbing instructor who takes a group of inexperienced climbers out with inadequate equipment in bad weather. Would it be easy for a jury to apply the test of whether D's conduct fell *far* below what could reasonably be expected of him? Do you think this additional offence is necessary?

8.38 In May 2000, the Home Office (2000) published its proposals for reform. It accepts the Law Commission's proposals in respect of the offences of reckless killing and killing by gross carelessness, but proposes a third offence of manslaughter, where the intention was only to cause some injury and the resulting death was unforeseeable. The question here is whether people should be punished for what they could not have foreseen, what the Law Commission call the 'lottery effect'. For the Law Commission's, and the Government's, recommendations on 'corporate killing' see **4.34**.

Causing death by dangerous driving

8.39 In 1956 Parliament introduced a new offence of causing death by reckless driving, largely it seems because juries were reluctant to convict bad drivers of manslaughter. Reckless driving was replaced by dangerous driving by the RTA 1988, s 1:

> A person who causes the death of another person by driving a
> mechanically propelled vehicle dangerously on a road or other public
> place is guilty of an offence.

Dangerous driving is defined in s 2A of the Act objectively: a person is to be regarded as driving dangerously if (a) the way he drives falls far below what would be expected of a competent and careful driver, and (b) it would be obvious to a competent and careful driver that driving in that way would be dangerous. This avoids the problems discussed above in relation to the meaning of 'recklessness' in manslaughter. The maximum sentence is 10 years' imprisonment and/or a fine. Of course, in a particularly serious case of death caused by dangerous driving, P may still charge D with manslaughter, which brings with it the possibility of a much higher sentence.

Offences against the foetus

8.40 Child destruction is an offence defined in s 1 of the Infant Life (Preservation) Act 1929:

(1) ...any person who, with intent to destroy the life of a child capable of being born alive, by any wilful act causes a child to die before it has an existence independent of its mother, shall be guilty of an offence ...

(2) For the purposes of this Act, evidence that a woman had at any material time been pregnant for a period of 28 weeks or more shall be prima facie proof that she was at that time pregnant of a child capable of being born alive.

8.41 Despite the statutory presumption that a foetus over 28 weeks old is capable of being born alive, P may still attempt to prove that a younger foetus was capable of being born alive:

C v S (1988) A civil case in which a man sought an injunction to prevent the abortion of a foetus between 18 and 21 weeks' old. CA (Sir John Donaldson MR): If the foetus had reached the normal stage of development, it would be incapable of ever breathing, and so it was not capable of being born alive. There was therefore no need to decide whether the putative father had a right to be heard, and the mother could obtain an abortion.

Rance v Mid-Downs Health Authority (1991) Another civil case where a mother unsuccessfully sued for damages for the hospital authority's negligence in not picking up the abnormalities in her foetus, seen on a scan when the foetus was 26 weeks' old. The mother, who would have had the foetus aborted, had now given up her career to care for her severely handicapped child. DC (Brooke J): A foetus of 26 or 27 weeks' gestation, who could breathe unaided for a short period, was capable of being born alive. Therefore the mother's claim that she lost the right to an abortion failed.

8.42 An alternative offence is abortion, contrary to the OAPA 1861, s 58:

Every woman, being with child, who, with intent to procure her own miscarriage, shall unlawfully administer to herself any poison or other noxious thing, or shall unlawfully use any instrument or other means whatsoever with the like intent, and whosoever, with intent to procure the miscarriage of any woman, whether she be or be not with child, shall unlawfully administer to her or cause to be taken by her any poison or other noxious thing, or shall unlawfully use any instrument or other means whatsoever with the like intent, shall be guilty [of an offence].

This carries a maximum penalty of life imprisonment.

8.43 However, since the Abortion Act 1967 was passed, certain abortions have been lawful. Significant changes were introduced by the Human Fertilisation and Embryology Act 1990, such that the AA 1967, s 1 now reads:

> A person shall not be guilty of an offence under the law relating to abortion when a pregnancy is terminated by a registered medical practitioner if two registered practitioners are of the opinion, formed in good faith -
> (a) that the pregnancy has not exceeded its 24th week and that the continuance of the pregnancy would involve risk, greater than if the pregnancy was terminated, of injury to the physical or mental health of the pregnant woman or any existing children of her family; or
> (b) that the termination is necessary to prevent grave permanent injury to the physical or mental health of the pregnant woman; or
> (c) that the continuance of the pregnancy would involve risk to the life of the pregnant woman, greater than if the pregnancy were terminated; or
> (d) that there is a substantial risk that if the child were born it would suffer from such physical or mental abnormalities as to be seriously handicapped.

Thus a pregnancy may be terminated lawfully up to 24 weeks if the continuance of the pregnancy would involve risk, greater than if the pregnancy was terminated, of injury to the physical or mental health of the pregnant woman or any existing children of her family. Abortions may be lawful for a longer period of time to prevent grave injury to the mother.

Infanticide

8.44 Introduced in 1922, this offence is now governed by IA 1938, s 1:

(1) Where a woman by any wilful act or omission causes the death of her child being a child under the age of 12 months, but at the time of the act or omission the balance of her mind was disturbed by reason of her not having fully recovered from the effect of giving birth to the child or by reason of the effect of lactation consequent upon the birth of the child, then, notwithstanding that the circumstances were that but for this Act the offence would have amounted to murder, she shall be guilty of [an offence], to wit of infanticide, and may for such offence be dealt with and punished as if she had been guilty of the offence of manslaughter of the child.

8.45 There is little justification for this offence, especially not drafted as it is, except that it avoids the mandatory life sentence for murder. It is in effect a defence to murder: a mother who kills her baby will be guilty only of manslaughter. The CLRC (1980) suggested widening it to include situations where the woman's mind is disturbed 'by reason of circumstances' consequent upon the birth, in order to include the social and financial stresses that may follow the birth of a child. Women who kill their children seem often not to be blamed as severely as are men: in *Sainsbury* (1989) the CA looked at the statistics which showed that in the 59 cases of infanticide dealt with between 1979 and 1988, not one had resulted in a custodial sentence. There had been 52 probation/supervision orders, and six hospital orders, one of which was restricted.

Mercy killings/euthanasia

8.46 English law has not yet developed a defence or partial defence on these grounds. Controversy surrounds the issue: in Holland, assisted deaths may be permitted. In this country, too, of course, doctors often assist a dying patient to die by increasing the doses of pain-relieving drugs which also accelerate death, but the courts seem to have accepted the doctrine of 'double effect': as long as the doctor intends to relieve pain, the courts are not concerned that he also knowingly hastens death. But a doctor (or loving friend) who helps someone to die remains liable to a mandatory life sentence for murder. A 'slippery slope' of uncertainty has been created by the courts' decisions in such cases as *Bland* (see **2.11**). Is this an area which is best left vague, or should Parliament legislate to clarify the boundaries of what is and what is not legal?

Further reading

Ashworth, 'The Doctrine of Provocation' (1976) CLJ 292

Ashworth, 'Reforming the Law of Murder' [1990] Crim LR 75

Griew, 'The Future of Diminished Responsibility' [1988] Crim LR 75

Home Office, 'Reforming the Law of Involuntary Manslaughter: The Government's Proposals' (2000)

Horder *Provocation and Responsibility* (Clarendon Press, 1992)

Committee on the Penalty for Homicide (Lane Committee) *Report* (Prison Reform Trust, 1993)

Law Commission *Legislating the Code: Involuntary Manslaughter* (1996; Law Com No 237)

Padfield, 'Manslaughter: the dilemma facing the law reformer' (1995) 59 JCL 291

Padfield, 'Why does provocation diminish culpability?' (1996) 55 CLJ 420

Williams 'The mens rea of murder – leave it alone' (1989) LQR 387

Self-test questions

1. Dee decides to punish Phil for breaking off their relationship. She tampers with the clutch and accelerator in his car hoping to make the car unusable. However, the car starts normally but the clutch suddenly gives out when he is doing 65 mph on a busy motor way. Phil is killed in the resulting crash. Discuss Dee's liability.

2. In the course of an argument, Phil shouts at Dee that she is excessively ugly. She picks up a beer glass and smashes it into his face and neck. He suffers severe bleeding, and is taken to hospital. He is given an overdose of painkillers by Florence, an inexperienced nurse, and dies. Discuss the liability of Dee and Florence.

3. Dee, suffering from post-natal depression, after the birth of her second child, suffocates to death her three-year-old son. She tells the police that she believed she had the best interest of the boy in mind, since he was severely handicapped and she couldn't believe that he faced a happy future.

CHAPTER NINE

Crimes of non-fatal violence

SUMMARY
Still governed by the piecemeal OAPA 1861, these offences contain many inconsistencies:
s 18: wounding or *causing* grievous bodily harm with intent
s 20: reckless *infliction* of grievous bodily harm or wounding
s 47: reckless assault *occasioning* actual bodily harm
assault and battery now governed by s 39 CJA 1988

Particular problems:
(i) *actus reus*: the use of the different words (causes, inflicts, assaults) makes it very difficult to interpret the offences as a hierarchical ladder;
(ii) *mens rea*: recklessness is subjectively applied, but the debate continues as to the extent of the harm that D must risk. *Parmenter/Savage*.

Many proposals for reform: note in particular the DCC (1989) followed by Law Com No 218 (1993): *Legislating the Criminal Code: Offences against the Person and General Principles*.

Introduction

9.1 Confusion in this area arises largely because the source of the majority of offences of violence remains an 1861 statute, which was never intended to be a neat codification but merely a consolidation of earlier statutes. It is worth reading the whole statute: although many offences are rarely charged, it is a fascinating source of information on how far language (and society) have shifted in the last 150 years (including offences such as placing wood etc. on a railway with intent to endanger passengers; obstructing a clergyman or other Minister in discharge of his duties; making gunpowder to commit offences). In this chapter, we concentrate only on a few of the major offences. As Lord Mustill said in *Mandair* (1995; see **9.4**) the unsystematic language of the 1861 Act is a constant source of difficulty. Codifying this area has been a major concern of the Law Commission in recent years. Once they realised that they were unlikely to succeed in getting the DCC (see **1.27**) passed though Parliament in one dose, they concentrated on this area as being most in need of reform. In this chapter we will look in parallel at the law as it is, and the proposals for reform. If you accept that there should be some attempt to grade different offences of violence, on what would you base these gradations? If your emphasis is on the degree of harm, would it be the harm actually caused or the harm threatened or the harm intended? Look again at **1.8** before starting this chapter.

Grievous bodily harm with intent (intentional serious violence)

9.2　The most serious non-fatal offence of violence is that specified in s 18 of the OAPA:

> Whosoever shall unlawfully and maliciously by any means whatsoever wound or cause any grievous bodily harm to any person with intent to do some grievous bodily harm to any person, or with intent to resist or prevent the lawful apprehension or detainer of any person, shall be guilty of [an offence], and being convicted thereof shall be liable to [imprisonment] for life.

9.3　Immediately one is struck by the out-moded language. What is meant by wounding or causing serious bodily harm? 'If the skin is broken, and there was a bleeding, that is a wound' (per Lord Lyndhurst CB in *Moriarty v Brooks* (1834)). Thus even a minor cut may be a wound. Yet this is the most serious offence of violence. Wounding is included in the definition for historical reasons: a hundred years ago a minor wound was more likely to lead to serious consequences than it might today. The courts have gone a small way towards limiting the scope of the definition:

> *C (a minor) v Eisenhower* (1984) V was hit by an air-gun pellet near his eye, which caused blood vessels in his eye to rupture. D was convicted of an offence (under s 20: see **9.8**). CA: quashed his conviction:

'wound' means a breaking of the whole skin: the rupture of internal blood vessels in the eye was insufficient to constitute wounding.

The DCC and Law Com No 218 omit any reference to wounding: a serious wound would constitute serious injury, and a minor wound would constitute injury.

9.4   *Cause* Another key word in s 18 of the OAPA 1861 is 'cause', which has a wider meaning than the word 'inflict' used in s 20 (see **9.8**). Someone may cause a result in many ways beyond inflicting it. I cause you injury if I fail to warn you of a danger I have created: do I thereby 'inflict' injury on you? I cause you injury if I leave a bucket balanced on the door which falls on your head when you push open the door: do I 'inflict' your injuries? In the OAPA 1861, the more serious the offence, the wider the definition of the *actus reus*. This has caused particular problems where D is charged with an offence under s 18, but the jury wish to bring in a lesser verdict, under s 20, since by s 6(3) of the CJA 1967 the jury may only bring a verdict of guilty to a lesser offence than that charged if the allegations on the indictment 'amount to or include (expressly or by necessary implication)' an allegation of another offence. There have been many difficult appeals, the most recent controversy surrounding *Mandair*:

> *Mandair* (1995) D was alleged to have thrown sulphuric acid in the face of V, his wife, when in a bad temper. His defence was that he was nowhere near the scene of the accident when the acid somehow splashed into V's face. D was charged with causing grievous bodily harm with intent, contrary to s 18 of the OAPA 1861. Since there was doubt as to whether he intended to inflict the serious injury suffered by V, the trial judge left to the jury the option of returning the lesser verdict of 'causing grievous bodily harm, contrary to s 20'. CA: quashed his conviction on the ground that 'causing grievous bodily harm' was an offence unknown to law, but the HL restored his conviction. Lord Mackay (delivering the main speech) held that although it is better, where it is proposed that the jury should consider an alternative verdict on a lesser count, to add a new count to the indictment, an oral direction could suffice. Here it was clear that the jury's verdict of 'causing grievous bodily harm contrary to s 20' could only mean causing grievous bodily harm contrary to s 20 in that what D did consisted of inflicting grievous bodily harm on another person. Lord Mustill dissented on this last point, stating that the case was

'concerned not with a mere technicality but rather with the important principle that a defendant can be punished for a statutory offence only if he has been properly convicted of that offence'.

9.5 Whilst the decision of the majority of the HL in *Mandair* may be satisfactory in the result, it is equally unsatisfactory that the HL has needed to deal with such questions. This case alone shows the importance of updating the OAPA.

9.6 *Mens rea* An offence under s 18 involves proof of one of the ulterior intents specified: an intent to wound, to do grievous bodily harm or to resist or to prevent the lawful arrest of any person. For the appropriate meaning of the word intend, see **3.13**. If D's sole intent is to resist arrest, it seems odd to convict him of an offence subject to a maximum of life imprisonment. Don't forget that the inclusion of the word 'unlawful' in both s 18 and s 20 (below) should remind you that there may be defences available to D which make his act lawful (see **5.6** on consent).

9.7 *Reform* Clause 2 of the draft CLB in Law Com No 218 provides:

(1) A person is guilty of an offence if he intentionally causes serious injury to another
(2) An offence under this section is committed notwithstanding that the injury occurs outside England and Wales if the act causing injury is done in England and Wales.

The Law Commission explain their 'general policy' grounds for clause 2(2) by way of an example: if someone in London posts a letter bomb to Paris that causes serious injury when it is opened there, English courts should have jurisdiction. The provision may become more important as the courts come to recognise injury caused by telephone calls: see *Ireland* (1998) at **9.16**.

Inflicting grievous bodily harm or wounding (reckless serious violence)

9.8 Next down the ladder of seriousness is s 20 of the OAPA 1861:

Whosoever shall unlawfully and maliciously wound or inflict any grievous bodily harm upon any other person, either with or without any weapon or instrument, shall be guilty of [an offence], and being convicted thereof shall be liable to [imprisonment for not more than five years].

Again, the wording of this section has led to many difficulties. First, the word 'inflicting' grievous bodily harm. There has long been an argument as to whether indirect actions can constitute an infliction, or whether a direct 'assault' was needed. Compare the approach taken by two nineteenth century courts:

Martin (1881) D extinguished the lights of the Theatre Royal in Leeds and bolted the door. In the resulting panic, several people were injured. He was convicted of an offence under s 20 OAPA 1861. CCCR (Lord Coleridge CJ): in a very brief judgement, dismissed the appeal. D was not legally represented, and the LCJ made it very clear that he had no time for the appeal, holding that D did inflict grievous bodily harm on those injured in the panic.

Clarence (1888) D, knowing that he had gonorrhoea had sexual intercourse with his wife, and infected her. He was convicted of offences under both s 20 and s 47 of the OAPA 1861. CCCR (composed of 13 judges who reached a majority decision 9-4) allowed his appeal under both sections. Whilst it is difficult, because of the number of judgements (all very brief!), to identify the ratio decidendi of this decision, Wills J seems to sum it up well: where there was no assault, there was no infliction of harm.

9.9   This last case, unsatisfactory as it seems to be, continues to cause problems. The actus reus of assault is normally construed to mean the victim is caused fear (see **9.23**). Is it right to say that where someone was not assaulted (ie if they consented to the act in question because D lied to them, or perhaps if they did not know that it was happening at all), there could be no offence under s 20 of the OAPA 1861? There have been numerous appeals, often on the grounds that a jury brought in a lesser verdict than that charged, and sometimes on the basis of incorrect wording. However, as we saw in **9.4** the HL has now decided in *Mandair* that these 'technical' problems can safely be ignored. Even before that, the HL in *Metropolitan Police Comr v Wilson* (1984) (see **9.18**) had decided that there can be an infliction of grievous bodily harm without an assault being committed, but the reasoning of the House was not clear. Common sense, of course, suggests that someone who causes/

179

inflicts grievous bodily harm should be guilty whether or not the victim is frightened. Perhaps the difficulties have now been resolved:

> *Ireland; Burstow* (1998) I made repeated silent phone calls at night to three women who suffered psychiatric illness, and appealed against his conviction for offences under OAPA 1861, s 47 (see **9.16**). B conducted an eight-month campaign of harassment against one woman, which included silent and abusive phone calls and sending her a menacing note. D was convicted of inflicting grievous bodily harm, contrary to s 20. HL: dismissed both appeals. The words 'bodily harm' were capable of covering recognised psychiatric illnesses. An offence of inflicting grievous bodily harm could be committed even though no physical violence was applied directly or indirectly to the body of the victim. Lord Steyn:
>
> > The criminal law has moved on in the light of a developing understanding of the link between the body and psychiatric injury. In my judgement *Clarence* no longer assists.

9.10 *Mens rea* This has proved equally problematic. D must have acted maliciously. It has long been accepted that this means that D must have acted recklessly, but reckless as to what: about whether some harm was caused or whether grievous bodily harm was caused? And must he himself have been aware of the risk that he was taking?

> *Mowatt* (1968) D or his mate stole £5 from V's pocket. When V seized him, D hit out, allegedly in self-defence. D punched V, pulled him up from the ground and continued to punch him until he was nearly unconscious. He was charged with robbery and under s 18 of the OAPA. He was convicted of larceny (abolished in 1968, and replaced by theft: see **11.2**) and under s 20. CA (Diplock LJ): dismissed his appeal. In an offence charged under s 18, the word 'maliciously' adds nothing to the definition of the offence. Within s 20, the word has the meaning applied in *Cunningham* (1957) (see **3.18**): D must foresee some physical harm, though not necessarily harm of the gravity charged. It would generally not be necessary to give juries specific guidance on the meaning of the word reckless.

9.11 Is this test fair? Why should D be liable for the consequences of his act unless he foresaw a consequence falling into the same legal category as that which actually occurred? Glanville Williams argues that this test 'distorts the accepted meaning of statutory malice' (TCL, page 190) and believes that D should only be guilty if he foresaw the *actus reus* of the offence charged, not that of a lesser offence. The issue has continued to confuse:

> *Sullivan* (1981) D, who had been drinking, drove his car down a narrow road, mounting the pavement in order to frighten pedestrians, one of whom was badly injured. Charged with offences under ss 18 and 20, he was convicted of an offence under s 20. CA (Lord Lane LJ): before a person can be convicted of an offence under s 20 it must be proved that he was aware that the probable consequences of his voluntary act would be to cause some injury to his victim – an intention to frighten is not enough.

9.12   This case marked what Glanville Williams called a minor success for the subjective approach, but the introduction of an objective test of recklessness for some offences after *Caldwell* led to increased confusion. There was some suggestion that an objective test of recklessness might apply to this offence (see *DPP v K* (1990)) but this decision was overruled in *Spratt* (1991).

9.13   In the summer of 1990 two other cases (*Savage* and *Parmenter*) reached the CA on the question of what D must be aware that he is risking before he can be guilty under s 20, but the courts gave varying results. The issue was resolved (for the time being) by the HL in

> *Savage; DPP v Parmenter* (1992) S threw beer over another woman in a busy pub. The glass slipped from her hand, and V suffered cuts. She was convicted of an offence under s 20 (but the CA substituted a conviction under s 47). In a separate case, P injured his three-month-old son, but said that his inexperience with babies meant that he did not realise that what he was doing would hurt the baby. He was convicted of an offence under s 20 (but the CA quashed his conviction). HL (Lord Ackner): While acknowledging that Glanville Williams and JC Smith in their textbooks and in articles and commentaries argue that a person should not be criminally liable for consequences of his conduct unless he foresaw a consequence falling into the same legal category as that set out in the indictment, such a general principle runs contrary to the decision in *Roberts* (1971)(see **9.17** below), which in Lord Ackner's opinion was correct:

... it is quite unnecessary that the accused should either have intended or have foreseen that his unlawful act might cause physical harm of the gravity described in s 20 ... it is enough that he should have foreseen that some physical harm to some person, albeit of a minor character, might result.

9.14 *Reform* In Law Com No 218, the Law Commission recommends simply that 'a person is guilty of an offence if he recklessly causes serious injury to another'. This involves a test in terms of awareness of risk of injury of the type that occurred. See **9.34**.

Assault occasioning actual bodily harm (causing some injury)

9.15 The next offence in the hierarchy (and again one that can be tried in either the MC or CC) is found in s 47 of the OAPA:

Whosoever shall be convicted of any assault occasioning actual bodily harm shall be liable ... to [imprisonment for five years].

The maximum penalty for this offence is the same as that under s 20. In reality however, the sentences imposed are likely to be much lower than for offences under s 20.

9.16 What constitutes actual bodily harm?

Miller (1954) D was charged with raping V, his wife, and with actual bodily harm. V had filed for divorce, but the hearing had been adjourned for D to attend. Lynskey J (the trial judge; there was no appeal) stated that actual bodily harm includes 'any hurt or injury calculated to interfere with the health or comfort' of the victim. This included hysterical and nervous conditions. Since a divorce petition has no effect in law, he could not, as the law then was, be guilty of rape (but see now *R v R* (1992; **10.12**). He was guilty of an offence of actual bodily harm.

Chan-Fook (1994) D aggressively questioned V, whom he suspected of stealing his fiancee's engagement ring. D then dragged V to a second floor room, and locked him in. V, fearing that D would return, escaped through a window and was injured when he fell to the ground. D was convicted of an offence under s 47 on the basis of the psychological harm that V had suffered. CA (Hobhouse LJ): quashed his conviction. The phrase 'actual bodily harm' may include psychiatric injury, but it does not include mere emotions such as fear or distress nor panic nor does it include, as such, states of mind that are not themselves evidence of some identifiable clinical condition. Here there was no evidence to be left to the jury in support of allegations of any psychiatric injury.

Ireland (1998) (see **9.9**) D made repeated silent phone calls to women who suffered psychiatric harm as a result. He was convicted of offences under s 47. HL: dismissed his appeal. A silent telephone call can constitute an assault occasioning actual bodily harm: V may fear the *possibility* of immediate personal violence.

9.17 The *mens rea* of actual bodily harm is again a test of subjective recklessness:

Roberts (1971) D assaulted V, a passenger in his car, by trying to take her coat off. In fear, she jumped out of the car, and was injured. CA (Stephenson LJ): the *mens rea* of actual bodily harm was the *mens rea* of assault only. Once that was satisfied, there was simply an objective test of whether D's action had caused the injury ie whether it was the natural consequence of the assault.

Thus since an intention to frighten is enough, Glanville Williams argues that 'at the most, the crime becomes one of half *mens rea*' (TCL, page 192). As we will see at **9.34**, the Law Commission would change this.

9.18 *Can a person tried for an offence under s20 be convicted of an offence under s 47?* This is a particular problem because of the unclear wording of the OAPA. Clearly s 47 was not designed simply as a lesser version of s 20. Yet it would be a procedural headache if D could only be convicted of an offence under s 47 if it had been specified on the indictment. The difficulty is that the word inflict in s 20 does not necessarily imply an assault, but an assault is clearly necessary for a conviction under s 47. Section 6(3) of the CLA 1967 makes clear that where a person is tried on indictment for any offence except treason or murder, and the jury finds him not guilty of the offence charged, the jury may find him guilty of another offence where 'the allegations in the indictment amount to or include (expressly or by implication)' an allegation of the other offence. The HL faced this problem head on in

> *Metropolitan Police Comr v Wilson; Jenkins* (1984) W had been charged with an offence under s 20, but was convicted under s 47; J had been charged with burglary, but was convicted under s 47. HL (Lord Roskill only): Applying s 6(3), a conviction under s 47 was possible. 'Inflict' does not imply assault, but it is narrower than 'cause' because it includes only the direct application of force. The House followed the Australian case of *Salisbury* (1976) in deciding that there can be an infliction of grievous bodily harm without an assault, but that a conviction under s 47 was possible if the facts were sufficient to prove an assault. This can only be determined on examination of the facts of each particular case at the time of trial. Lord Roskill noted the danger that D might be convicted of a charge not fully investigated at trial, but said that it was up to the trial judge to guard against this.

9.19 Whilst this may make good practical sense, it again highlights the difficulties involved in trying to make a neat ladder of offences out of a statute which was not so designed (see also the discussion of *Mandair* (1995) at **9.4** above).

Common assault and battery

9.20 Section 39 of the CJA 1988 replaced s 42 of the OAPA 1861:

> Common assault and battery shall be summary offences and a person guilty of either of them shall be liable to a fine not exceeding level 5 on the standard scale, to imprisonment for a term not exceeding six months, or to both.

The difficulties here are often created by the sloppy use (even by the judiciary) of the two terms assault and battery.

9.21 *Battery* A battery involves the direct application of force, such as punching, spitting or merely touching. It is often said that the touching must be both unlawful and hostile. In *Wilson v Pringle* (1987), a civil case in which one schoolboy sued another for injuries caused when they were mucking around in the corridor at school, the CA held that the element of hostility in a battery must be a question of fact. However, in *Re F (mental patient: sterilisation)* (1989; **5.20**) Lord Goff doubted whether there was a requirement that the touching be hostile. It is yet another example of an unhelpful and out-date word clouding the interpretation of the criminal law.

9.22 The *mens rea* of battery is an intention to apply unlawful force, or subjective recklessness as to whether such force will be supplied.

> *Venna* (1976) D was involved in a fight in the street, and kicked V, a police officer, whose hand was fractured. He was convicted of actual bodily harm and threatening behaviour. CA (James LJ): dismissed his appeal. The element of *mens rea* in battery is satisfied by proof that D either intentionally or recklessly applied force to the person of another.

It is hardly surprising that the CA rejected the argument that battery could only be committed intentionally; otherwise it would be easier to prove the more serious offence of s 20 than the offence of battery.

9.23 *Assault* A common assault (sometimes known as a psychic, as opposed to a physical, assault), on the other hand, is the intentional or reckless causing of an apprehension of immediate unlawful personal violence (ie a battery). The essence of the offence is that the victim fears the direct application of force: no touching is necessary. Even though it must be fear of immediate violence, someone may apprehend the application of force through a closed window (*Smith v Chief Superintendent of Woking Police Station* (1983).

9.24 *Can words alone constitute an assault?* Words coupled with actions clearly constitute an assault. It would be odd if it were impossible to assault someone in a dark alley at night, or impossible to assault a blind person. Yet there are uncertainties here: largely perhaps because there are few prosecutions for such minor offences. Words alone can negative an assault:

> *Turbervell v Savage* (1669) P put his hand on his sword and said, 'If it were not assize-time, I would not take such language from you'. KBD: held that there was no assault. P's declaration was that he would not assault him, and it requires both the intention and the act to make an assault.

Since *Ireland* (1998; **9.9**; **9.16**) it has been clear that even silent telephone calls may constitute an assault.

9.25 Even modern statutes cause their fair share of confusion: it has been held that to charge assault and battery contrary to s 39 in the same count is bad for duplicity (*DPP v Taylor* (1992)). Nor can a person charged with an offence under s 47 be convicted of the summary offence of common assault unless it was specified as a separate count on the indictment (*Mearns* (1991)). As was pointed out in **1.13**, the work of a criminal law practitioner is often more complicated by procedural and evidential issues rather than by questions of substantive law.

9.26 *Reform* Clause 6 of Law Com No 218 states that:

(1) A person is guilty of the offence of assault if-
(a) he intentionally or recklessly applies force to or causes an impact on the body of another -
  (i) without the consent of the other, or
  (ii) where the act is intended or likely to cause injury, with or without the consent of the other; or
(b) he intentionally or recklessly, without the consent of the other, causes the other to believe that any such force or impact is imminent.

(2) No such offence is committed if the force or impact, not being intended or likely to cause injury, is in the circumstances such as is generally acceptable in the ordinary conduct of daily life and the defendant does not know or believe that it is in fact unacceptable to the other person.

This would abolish battery as a separate offence. Both modes of assault are therefore expressed in the same offence. But are both actually necessary? Since most assaults (in the clause 6(1)(b) sense) will be attempted assaults (in the clause 6(1)(a) sense), do we still need an offence of assault (in the clause 6(1)(b) sense)? The answer to this may depend on whether the proposed offence is triable only summarily since generally it is not an offence to attempt to commit an offence which is triable only summarily (s 1(4) CAA 1981: see **7.4**).

Threats

9.27 An assault has to involve fear of immediate force. The law does not protect against future threats. The only form of non-immediate threat that is an offence at present is provided by s 16 of the OAPA 1861 (as substituted in Sch 12 to the Criminal Law Act 1977):

> A person who without lawful excuse makes to another a threat, intending that that other would fear it would be carried out, to kill that other or a third person shall be guilty of an offence and liable on conviction on indictment to imprisonment for a term not exceeding 10 years.

It is the person to whom the threat is made who must be frightened that it will be carried out:

> *Tait* (1990) D made threats to a five-month pregnant woman stating 'I will come back and get your baby', by which she understood him to mean to kill her unborn baby. CA (Mustill LJ): quashed his conviction. A threat to kill a foetus by bringing about a miscarriage does not constitute an offence under s 16. The foetus was not 'another person' distinct from its mother.

9.28 Most people would suggest that Tait's behaviour should be a criminal offence. But which? Perhaps he could have been prosecuted under s 5 of the Public Order Act 1986, but we shall critically examine the use of this statute in cases of domestic violence at **12.12**. Another solution would be to widen the existing offence to include threats other than those to kill. The DCC, which generally set out to enact current law, proposed a significant change in this area. Clause 65 states that

> A person is guilty of an offence if he makes to another a threat to cause the death of, or serious personal harm to, that other or a third person, intending that other to believe that it will be carried out.

Not only would implementation extend the scope of the offence to serious personal harm; it also replaces the word 'fear' with 'believe'.

Protection from harassment

9.29 The Protection from Harassment Act 1997 created a novel approach to deal with those who harass others. Sections 2 and 4 create offences of harassment. Thus, s 4:

> A person whose course of conduct causes another to fear, on at least two occasions, that violence will be used against him is guilty of an offence if he knows or ought to know that his course of conduct will cause the other so to fear on each of those occasions.

There are three statutory defences to these offences: prevention of crime; lawful excuse or that the pursuit of the course of conduct was reasonable (for the offence under s 4, the conduct must be reasonable for the protection of himself or another or for the protection of property). Do you think that piecemeal changes in the law in this way can make up for the inadequacies in the OAPA 1861 highlighted earlier in this chapter?

Under s 3, civil courts can make non-harassment injunctions, and under s 3(6) breach of such an injunction is a criminal offence punishable with up to five years' imprisonment. We will return to the question whether the civil law should be used for what would normally be described as criminal behaviour in chapter 13 on crimes against the environment, an area where it is notoriously difficult to separate civil from criminal law.

Administering poison

9.30 The original OAPA 1861 contained many surprisingly specific offences (see **9.1**), many of which have now been repealed. Two which seem somewhat archaic are still regularly enforced. First, s 23:

> Whosoever shall unlawfully and maliciously administer to or cause to be administered to be taken by any other person any poison or other destructive or noxious thing, so as thereby to endanger the life of such person, or so as thereby to inflict upon such person any grievous bodily harm, shall be guilty of an offence.

See also s 24:

> Whosoever shall unlawfully and maliciously administer to or cause to be administered to or taken by any other person any poison or other destructive or noxious thing, with intent to injure, aggrieve, or annoy any such person, shall be guilty of [an offence].

The maximum penalty for an offence under s 23 is 10 years' imprisonment, for an offence under s 24, five years. Section 23 penalises those who endanger life or inflict grievous bodily harm by poisoning; Section 24 requires no such consequence, but there must be an intent to injure.

9.31 *Administer* Something can be administered directly or indirectly, and administration may even consist of causing the victim to administer the substance to himself. *Cunningham* (1957) (still the basic case on subjective recklessness: see **3.18**) was a case under s 23 where D 'administered' gas by breaking off the gas meter and allowing escaping gas to fill the next door house.

> *Gillard* (1988) D bought CS gas to attack the doorman of a wine bar. He appealed from his conviction for 'conspiracy to cause to be administered a noxious thing …' on the ground that administer does not encompass spraying CS gas. CA: upheld his conviction. Administer was an ordinary word which should be left to the jury. There was no need to postulate entry into the body: bringing a noxious thing into contact with the body, directly or indirectly, was enough.

Would assault be a more appropriate charge in the case of someone who sprays CS gas at someone else? Do we need this extra offence?

9.32 *Reform* There is considerable doubt as to the *mens rea* for an offence under s 23; for s 24, there is clearly a need for an ulterior intent. The Law Commission (in Law Com No 218) agree with the CLRC (1980) that conduct of the type penalised in s 23 is anyhow covered by their proposed offence of intentionally or recklessly causing serious injury, but they nonetheless propose a variation on the s 24 offence:

> (1) A person is guilty of an offence if, knowing that the other does not consent to what is done, he intentionally or recklessly administers to or causes to be taken by another a substance which he knows to be capable of interfering substantially with the other's bodily functions.

> (2) For the purposes of this section a substance capable of inducing unconsciousness or sleep is capable of interfering substantially with bodily functions.

This would replace the current need to prove an 'intent to injure, aggrieve or annoy' with a need to prove simply knowledge that what D administers was capable of interfering with V's bodily functions. Is this offence necessary, or again in all serious cases coming within the clause be covered by intentionally or recklessly causing injury (or attempting to do so)?

Torture

9.33 Section 134 of the CJA 1988 added an offence of torture to English law. This was to implement the Convention on Torture adopted by the UN in 1984. There have so far been no prosecutions under this, but it is still worth considering how (if at all) it fits in within a framework of offences against the person:

> (1) A public official or person acting in an official capacity, whatever his nationality, commits the offence of torture if in the UK or elsewhere he intentionally inflicts severe pain or suffering on another in the performance or purported performance of his official duties.
>
> (2) A person not falling within subsection (1) above commits the offence of torture, whatever his nationality, if -
> (a) in the UK or elsewhere he intentionally inflicts severe pain or suffering on another at the instigation or with the consent or acquiescence -
>   (i) of a public official; or
>   (ii) of a person acting in an official capacity; and
> (b) the official or other person is performing or purporting to perform his official duties when he instigates the commission of the offence or consents to or acquiesces in it.
>
> (3) It is immaterial whether the pain or suffering is physical or mental and whether it is caused by an act or omission.

Section 134(4) gives a defence of 'lawful authority, justification or excuse for that conduct'. The maximum penalty is life imprisonment. The Law Commission propose to reproduce this offence within their codification of non-fatal offences against the person since it belongs more appropriately there rather than tucked away in a CJA.

The Law Commission's proposals

9.34 There can be little argument that the law is in desperate need of reform. As Lord Mustill points out in *Mandair* (1995; see **9.4**)

> the reappearance of s 20 before your Lordships' House barely two years after it was minutely examined in *Savage; DPP v Parmenter* (1992) demonstrates once again that this unsatisfactory statute is long overdue for repeal and replaced by legislation which is soundly based in logic and expressed in language which everyone can understand.

This point is echoed in Law Com No 218, para 12.34, where the Law Commission state that:

> The interests both of justice and social protection would be much better served by a law that was
> (i) clearly and briefly stated;
> (ii) based on the injury intended or contemplated by the accused, and not on what he happened to cause; and
> (iii) governed by clear distinctions, expressed in modern and comprehensible language, between serious and less serious cases.

9.35 They therefore propose three new offences:

(i) intentionally causing serious injury – maximum sentence life

(ii) recklessly causing serious injury – five years

(iii) intentionally or recklessly causing injury – three years

As was mentioned in **9.14**, the meaning of recklessly would be *Cunningham*-type subjective recklessness. The Law Commission have no doubt that this should involve a test in terms of awareness of risk of injury of the type that occurred, and not one based on the results of conduct which D neither intended nor foresaw. This requires only 'a fairly low level of awareness of risk, rather than prolonged reflection and deliberate decision-making'. Nor does it require D to have foreseen all the details of what occurred, but 'merely to have been conscious of a danger of injury of that sort occurring' (see para 14.12 of the Report).

9.36 Students may like to ponder whether they prefer the concept of 'personal harm' proposed in the DCC or 'injury'. The recent proposals (1993) propose injury, defined in cl 18:

(a) physical injury, including pain, unconsciousness, or any other impairment of a person's physical condition, or

(b) impairment of a person's mental health.

This seems both very wide, and somewhat narrow. For example, does it include mental anguish? And would it include liability for the transmission of diseases? Should the word serious be defined or left up to the common sense of juries? The Law Commission accept that, however the offences are defined, a lot will be left up to the courts to interpret. Difficulties in reaching agreement on drafting should not be allowed to divert attention from the basic need: any new Code is likely to be a vast improvement on the OAPA 1861. Finally, it should be remembered that many of the problems in this area concern the applicability of defences (particularly self-defence and consent): re-read chapter 5.

Racially aggravated offences

9.37 The Crime and Disorder Act 1998 introduced four new offences of racially aggravated assaults. The meaning of racially aggravated is explained in s 28: P must prove, beyond reasonable doubt, either

(a) the existence of racial hostility at or around the time the offence was committed, or

(b) that the offence was motivated by racial hostility.

The four new offences of racially aggravated assaults are:

- racially aggravated wounding

- racially aggravated grievous bodily harm

- racially aggravated actual bodily harm

- racially aggravated common assault.

These offences do not make illegal what was previously legal, but simply make the existing offences under the OAPA 1861 more serious. How this will work in practice remains to be seen: sentencers have in any case long given increased sentences for offences which involve racism. And as Malik suggests (1999), it is a mistake to over-estimate the role that the criminal law has in addressing the consequences of racism.

Further reading

Law Commission (1993) Legislating the Criminal Code: Offences against the Person and General Principles (Law Com No 218)

Alldridge, 'Threats Offences – a Case for Reform' [1994] Crim LR 176

Gardener, 'Rationality and the Rule of Law in Offences against the Person' (1994) Camb LJ 502

Bronitt, 'Spreading Disease and the Criminal Law' [1994] Crim LR 21

Malik, 'Racist crime: racially aggravated offences in the Crime and Disorder Act 1998', Part II (1999) 62 MLR 409

Self-test questions

1. In a drunken fight, Dee stabs Phil in the hand with her penknife. She told the police she thought the knife was so blunt that it could only cause a tiny scratch. Unfortunately she almost severs his finger and he has to undergo a series of operations.

2. Dee deliberately hits Phil on the head with a wooden spoon, but she does not foresee any harm resulting to him. Surprised, he slips and fractures his skull. What offence(s) has Dee committed?

3. After a filthy row, Dee locks Phil in an upstairs room, telling him that he can 'wait there while I go and get something that will really sort you out'. Phil tries to escape through the window but falls and breaks both his legs. Dee says that she had had no intention of injuring Phil but had merely wanted to frighten him. Discuss.

4. Dee fires her gun wildly into the air at night in a public park not thinking about the risks involved. She tells the police later that she was sure that no-one normally wanders through the park at night. Phil is badly wounded in the chest.

5. Dee points a toy pistol at Phil, who does not realise the gun is a toy and is very frightened. He is a weapons expert and therefore should have known that it was a toy.

CHAPTER TEN

Sexual offences

SUMMARY

Problems of perception and definition: what is a sexual offence?

Rape: Defined as non-consensual sexual intercourse, the main problems here are often evidential: the word of one person against another. Can you distinguish consent from submissions? Until recently neither wives nor men were protected by the offence of rape. Recklessness as to V's lack of consent is enough, but there is some doubt as to whether this is simply *Cunningham*-type recklessness (see *Satnam Singh*).
cf procuring a woman by threats or false pretences.

Other offences discussed:
- buggery and non-consensual homosexual acts: illustrates the uncomfortable relationship between law and morals. Is the distinction between private and public places appropriate?
- indecent assault: difficult to assess whether an assault is indecent: see *Court*
- offences connected with prostitution
- bigamy: a problem for polygamous marriages?
- incest: note the DCC's proposals for change.

Introduction

10.1   There are a wide variety of offences which can be loosely classified as sexual:

rape; offences related to prostitution such as soliciting and kerb-crawling; incest; bigamy; sexual intercourse with girl under 16; sexual intercourse with girl under 13; buggery; indecent assault; indecent exposure ...

What do these offences have in common? Clearly they have a sexual element. Some sexual offences are offences whether or not the parties consent (prostitution-related offences), whilst the essence of others (eg rape) is that one party was not consenting. By concentrating on the sexual element of an offence, one might be ignoring other, more important, elements in it. Many crimes, especially those of violence, may include sexual elements. For example, in the sado-masochism case of *Brown* (1994; see **1.7**), although the defendants were tried for offences under s 20 and s 47 of the OAPA 1861, it is clear from the speeches in the HL that their Lordships found it difficult to separate sex from violence. Lord Templeman in his majority speech said that 'In my opinion sado-masochism is not only concerned with sex. Sado-masochism is also concerned with violence'. Lord Mustill opens his dissenting speech with 'My Lords, this is a case about the criminal law of violence. In my opinion, it should be a case about the criminal law of private sexual relations, if anything at all'. Thus the majority say this is about sex and violence, so Ds are guilty; the minority say it is primarily about sex and should not be prosecuted as offences of violence. Can the distinction between sex and violence be usefully maintained?

10.2   Look at rape: why do we classify it as a sexual offence and not as a crime of violence? There is a danger that in labelling it simply as a sexual offence, we dilute the seriousness of the offence. In Canada, the Criminal Code was radically overhauled in 1982: the offences of indecent assault and rape were replaced by the offence of sexual assault and aggravated sexual assault. Look at these three reasons given by the Law Reform Commission of Canada in 1978 for abolishing rape:

(i)   the predominant legal and behavioural characteristic of rape is not for the offender its sexual but rather its aggressive aspect, its violation of the physical integrity of the human person;

(ii)   the use of the word 'rape' attaches a profound moral stigma to the victims and expresses an essentially irrational folklore about them;

(iii) all acts of penetration, vaginal, oral or anal, and all acts of sexual aggression regardless of form should come within the same scope of legal sanction.

In England, there have been few calls to abolish rape: it is an offence well understood and abhorred by the public. But some of the Canadian arguments are strong. As we shall see in **10.7**, a man who carries out a frenzied sexual attack but who does not intend actual penetration can only be convicted of indecent assault. Rather than extend the meaning of the word rape, Canada substituted the term aggravated sexual assault. However, does this sound as serious as rape? At the end of the day, whether a 'rapist' is convicted of rape in England or of aggravated sexual assault in Canada, he will still be subject to a lengthy custodial sentence. Does the label matter (see **1.2**)?

10.3 Even if we accept the classification 'sexual offences', do the individual offences fall into appropriate categories? The term 'domestic violence' may in its popular sense conjure up ideas of sexual and physical violence, but finds no place in the criminal law. Neither does the term 'child abuse', although this is well understood by ordinary people. Below we look at the offence of buggery: Parliament has slowly been loosening the prohibition on homosexuality, and perhaps buggery (an offence which does not exist in Scotland) should be re-labelled to fit in better with contemporary attitudes to homosexuality? The Law Commission has recommended that the crime of incest should be significantly narrowed (see **10.26**). How does one decide the proper ambit of the criminal law in these areas?

10.4 In chapter 1, we looked briefly at the relationship between law and morals (see **1.5**). It seems to have become accepted that the law should not concern itself too much with people's private morality. Yet this causes major difficulties: people are probably in greater need of protection from violence and sexual attack in the privacy of their own home than they are on the open street. The family home is often portrayed as a haven of peace; personal safety campaigns concentrate on safety in open places. Yet it is vital to 'open up' sexual offences to allow victims of 'private' sexual offences to gain better protection from the law (see Zedner (1996)). Read again the second Canadian argument for abolishing rape: victims of rape may be unfairly stigmatised. Is this really an argument for abolishing the offence, or simply for improving the procedural safeguards for victims?

10.5 Many of the difficulties in this area are procedural and evidential: if there are only two people present, how does one balance the presumption of innocence with the need to protect the public from dangerous offenders? The fundamental principle of autonomy was highlighted 1.2, yet, as Lacey, Wells and Meure (1998) point out, the principle is a loose one and it pulls in two directions: 'Bodily autonomy can demand protection in two senses: first, protection of one's own choices, and second, protection against interference by others' (at page 307). Although most Ds in sexual cases are male, many writers have pointed out that while the law formally penalises men, the reality is often that it seems to reinforce male domination over women: women giving evidence in rape trials for example often end up feeling more defiled, more guilty than does D himself. The Youth Justice and Criminal Evidence Act 1999 creates more protection for vulnerable witnesses, but at a cost for those defending themselves. Other measures such as those introduced in Part I of the Sex Offenders Act 1997 which require certain sex offenders to notify the police of their address, or the provisions for extended sentences for sex offenders, may do something towards reassuring the public, but also illustrate the balance which has to be drawn between respecting the rights of the offender and the desire to protect the public.

Rape

10.6 Rape is the offence of having sexual intercourse without consent. Until 1994 a man was not guilty of rape if he had non-consensual sex with another man. A new s 1 of the Sexual Offences Act 1956 was substituted by s 142 of the Criminal Justice and Public Order Act 1994:

(1) It is an offence for a man to rape a woman or another man.

(2) A man commits rape if (a) he has sexual intercourse with a person (whether vaginal or anal) who at the time of the intercourse does not consent to it; and (b) at the time he knows that the person does not consent to the intercourse or is reckless as to whether the person consents to it.

The maximum sentence is life imprisonment, though sentences vary enormously. It is still an offence which can only be committed by men (though a woman may be convicted of aiding and abetting rape (see **6.5**)). Rape remains one of the most under-enforced crimes, with a low conviction rate. Only recently has 'domestic violence' started to be treated adequately seriously: what more should be done?

10.7 *Sexual intercourse* The order of the words in s 1(2)(a) is very odd, but it is clear that anal or vaginal intercourse is sufficient. As s 44 of the SOA 1956 makes clear, the slightest degree of penetration is all that is required:

> Where, on the trial of any offence under this Act, it is necessary to prove sexual intercourse (whether natural or unnatural) it shall not be necessary to prove the completion of the intercourse by the emission of seed, but the intercourse shall be deemed complete on proof of penetration only.

If at any stage during the intercourse the other party withdraws his or her consent, the act becomes unlawful. Thus Lord Scarman made it clear in the PC in *Kaitamaki v R* (1985) that although the act of rape was complete upon penetration, it is a continuing act only ending with withdrawal. Thus, if a man realises that she is not consenting half way through the act, he may still be guilty of rape. Does this mean that this is a case of rape by omission? Do the ordinary rules covering liability for omissions apply (see **2.8**)? Should rape extend to non-consensual oral sex, or to the D who violently inserts a bottle or broomstick into V's vagina with sexual intent? The CLRC (1980) concluded that it would be undesirable that the definition of such a serious offence should become out of step with popular understanding. As we saw at **10.2**, Canada has renamed the offence 'aggravated sexual assault' partly because it was felt that the definition of the offence was too narrow.

10.8 *Absence of consent* The *actus reus* of rape involves not only sexual intercourse, but also the absence of consent. If consent is gained through force, fear or fraud it will not count as valid consent. However, fraud only vitiates consent if it is a deception as to the nature of the act or as to the identity of the man. One would hope that there are few women in the UK today who do not understand the nature of sexual intercourse; it is also extremely rare that someone will have sex with someone believing that they are someone else (despite cases such as *Elbekkay* (1995) and *Collins* (1973)). Thus, fraud only very rarely vitiates consent. However, those who submit out of fear should not be taken to have consented:

Olugboja (1982) D had sex with V after she had already been raped by his friend. She did not struggle or scream until he penetrated her, when she thought he was going to ejaculate inside her. He then withdrew. CA: dismissed his appeal against his conviction for rape. Dunn LJ:

> It is not necessary for the P to prove that what might otherwise appear to have been consent was in reality merely submission induced by force, fear or fraud, although one or more of these factors will no doubt be present in the majority of cases of rape. [The jury] should be directed that consent, or the absence of it, is to be given its ordinary meaning and if need be, by way of example, that there is a difference between consent and submission; every consent involves a submission, but it by no means follows that a mere submission involves consent.

Do you think that this distinction between consent and submission is adequately clear to juries?

10.9 *Mens rea* The fault element in rape is intentional sexual intercourse combined with knowledge that the other person does not consent or recklessness as to the other's consent. Most of the difficulties in this area concern the issue of consent. It is not surprising that if a man genuinely believes that the other person is consenting, he should not be guilty. But what if he makes an unreasonable (but genuine) mistake?

> *DPP v Morgan* (1976) M invited other RAF officers to have sex with his wife. The trial judge had summed up to the jury that they should acquit the Ds if they honestly believed that V was consenting and had reasonable grounds for that belief. HL: held that a man cannot be convicted of rape if he believed that the woman was consenting, even if that belief was unreasonable. There had been a misdirection, but no miscarriage of justice so the convictions were upheld. Lord Hailsham:

> > the mental element is and always has been the intention to commit that act, or the equivalent intention of having intercourse willy-nilly, not caring whether the victim consents or no.

Lord Cross distinguished bigamy where D's belief that he or she is single must be both honest and reasonable (see **10.25**) since bigamy is an absolute offence.

10.10 After the controversy surrounding *Morgan*, Parliament intervened. Section 1(2) of the SOA 1976 provides:

> It is hereby declared that if at a trial for a rape offence the jury has to consider whether a man believed that a woman or man was consenting to sexual intercourse, the presence or absence of reasonable grounds for such a belief is a matter to which the jury is to have regard, in conjunction with any other relevant matters, in considering whether he so believed.

Is this appropriate? It is merely a declaration of the law (a public relations provision?), but in reality, is it fair that an unreasonable but genuine belief should result in an acquittal? Would you rather argue that the risk should lie on the man that his partner really is consenting? After some hints that *Caldwell* recklessness (see **3.22**) might apply to rape, the debate seems to have been put to rest in

Satnam Singh (1983) Both Ds had sex with a girl in the back of a car, and were convicted of rape. CA (Bristow J): quashed their convictions.

> Any direction as to the definition of rape should ... be based upon s 1 of the 1976 Act and upon *DPP v Morgan*, without regard to *R v Caldwell* or *R v Lawrence*, which were concerned with recklessness in a different context and under a different statute ... In summing-up a case of rape which involves the issue of consent, the judge should, in dealing with the state of mind of the D, first of all direct the jury that before they could convict of rape the Crown had to prove either that the D knew the woman did not want to have sexual intercourse, or was reckless as to whether she wanted to or not. If they were sure he knew she did not want to they should find him guilty of rape knowing there to be no consent. If they were not sure about that, then they would find him not guilty of such rape and should go on to consider reckless rape. If they thought he might genuinely have believed that she did want to, even though he was mistaken in his belief, they would find him not guilty. In considering whether his belief was genuine, they should take into account the relevant circumstances (which could at that point be summarised) and ask themselves whether, in the light of those circumstances, he had reasonable grounds for such a belief. If, after considering these circumstances, they were sure he had no genuine belief, they would find him guilty. If they came to the conclusion that he could not care less whether she wanted to or not, but pressed on regardless, then he would have been reckless and

201

could not have believed that she wanted to, and they would find him guilty of reckless rape.

10.11 Of course, courts are reluctant to accept a defence based on mistaken belief in consent. This may put defence counsel in a quandary. If the primary line of defence is that she was consenting, then the defence will not want to weaken their case by raising as a subsidiary defence that even if she was not consenting, D mistakenly believed that she was. In such cases, trial judges are unlikely to mention mistake in their summing up. This can prove quite hard on Ds (compare the rules on provocation, where if there is any evidence of provocation, the judge must put the defence to the jury: **8.23**).

Taylor (1984) V came to D's house to cook and serve D's dinner while his wife went out. After dinner they had sex on the sitting room floor: D said it was consensual, V said it was rape. CA (Lord Lane CJ): dismissed his appeal. A question for the jury was: Was D's attitude one of 'I could not care less whether she is consenting or not, I am going to have intercourse with her regardless'. Once the jury came to the conclusion that the complainant did not in fact consent, that she was telling the truth about that, there was little, if any, room for the conclusion that D might have been labouring under any honest but mistaken belief despite his protestations. Therefore no such direction was necessary by the judge.

Haughian and Pearson (1985) Ds gave V a lift home from pub. Both had sex with her in the back of car. CA (O'Connor LJ): upheld their convictions. The facts were such that once the jury had found that she had not consented, there was no room for a mistaken but genuine belief. Since mistake had never been an issue at the trial, there was no obligation on the judge to give a direction.

10.12 *Marital rape* These cases illustrate the problems often found in rape cases: only the parties immediately concerned are present and they give very different versions of history. This was one of the reasons why it took so long for the law to recognise that husbands should in appropriate circumstances be guilty of raping their wives. The law became 'frozen' in outdated social conditions. Sir Matthew Hale wrote in 1736:

But the husband cannot be held guilty of a rape committed by himself upon his lawful wife, for by their mutual matrimonial consent and contract the wife hath given herself up in this kind unto her husband which she cannot retract.

This statement was still seen in the 1990s as a major source of the 'rule' that a man could not be convicted of raping his wife. It was a dubious statement of the law even in 1736, and times have changed.

> *R* (1992) D and his wife, V, separated, and agreed to seek a divorce. Three weeks later D forced his way into V's parents' home, where she was now living, and attempted to rape her. He pleaded guilty after a ruling from the judge that a husband could be guilty after a wife had clearly revoked her consent to sex, and he was sentenced to three years' imprisonment. HL (Lord Keith): dismissed his appeal. Section 1(1) of the SOA 1976 presents no obstacle to this House declaring that in modern times the supposed marital exception in rape forms no part of the law in England.

10.13 This case was very controversial, not because many people wanted to argue that a husband should be immune from a rape prosecution, but because the HL was accused of usurping the role of Parliament. The CLRC (1980) had recommended against the extension of rape to husbands who had ceased cohabitation for the rather doubtful reason of the difficulty in defining 'cohabitation', and the word 'unlawful' remained even in the SOA 1976. This argument seems to have missed the point: who would argue that even cohabiting wives should be excluded from protection from genuinely non-consensual intercourse? As we saw at **1.24**, R took his case unsuccessfully to the ECHR. At last Parliament acted and the current (CJPOA 1994) statement of the law makes clear that any man may be convicted of the rape of any woman. Many of the controversies have now switched to the sentencing of rapists as courts struggle to find the 'appropriate' length of sentence in cases where the parties knew each other at the time of the rape, and to the need to protect the victim from aggressive cross-examination in court. Sometimes 'date rape' or 'marital rape' may be seen as less serious than 'stranger rape'; at other times it will be seen as more serious because of the breach of trust involved. Perhaps too the time has come too when the law should penalise any person who has non-consensual intercourse, and not merely men.

Procuration by threats or false pretences

10.14 Whilst s 1 of the SOA 1956 deals with rape, ss 2 and 3 deal with two offences where V's consent is not freely given. Section 2 of the SOA 1956 provides that:

> It is an offence for a person to procure a woman, by threats or intimidation, to have sexual intercourse in any part of the world.

Section 3 of the SOA 1956 provides that:

> It is an offence for a person to procure a woman, by false pretences or false representations, to have sexual intercourse in any part of the world.

Both offences carry a maximum penalty of merely two years. The CLRC (1984) suggested that the maximum for s 2 should be five years. If you compare the ingredients of the offence with blackmail (see **11.32**), with its maximum of 14 years' imprisonment, it is difficult to see the justification for the difference. It would be interesting to know whether the dearth of prosecutions under these sections is due to simply to the reluctance of victims to go to the police, or also to the reluctance of the police to prosecute. As we have seen (**10.8**), fraud rarely vitiates consent to rape: it is worth considering whether a man who obtains a woman's consent by fraud should be guilty of rape. Thus, if a middle-aged man falsely promises his employee a pay rise, or promises a naive 17-year-old a Caribbean holiday which he cannot provide, if she will have sex with him, should he be guilty of an offence? If so, what offence should it be?

Unlawful sexual intercourse with a minor

10.15 By s 5 of the SOA 1956

> It is an offence for a man to have unlawful sexual intercourse with a girl under the age of thirteen.

This offence is punishable with life imprisonment, but the offence under s 6:

> (1) It is an offence [triable either way], subject to the exceptions

mentioned in this section, for a man to have unlawful sexual intercourse with a girl under the age of 16 ...

(3) A man is not guilty of an offence under this section because he has unlawful sexual intercourse with a girl under the age of 16, if he is under the age of 24 and has not previously been charged with a like offence, and he believes her to be of the age of 16 or over and has reasonable cause for the belief.

Clearly here the word 'unlawful' is not surplusage, despite the different position in rape cases pre-R (**10.12**): if the girl was his lawful wife, it would not be an offence (but no-one can marry lawfully under the age of 16 in this country). Note *Prince* (1875) and *B (a minor) v DPP* (2000); **3.40**: a belief that the girl is over 13 (or 16) may now be a defence.

Buggery

10.16 Until 1967 homosexual sex was criminal: an act of anal intercourse even between consenting adults constituted the offence of buggery. Now the law is less intolerant, but also more complicated. Section 12 of the Sexual Offences Act 1956 now provides that:

(1) It is [an offence] for a person to commit buggery with another person otherwise than in the circumstances described in subsection (1A) below.

(1A) The circumstances referred to in subsection (1) are that the act of buggery takes place in private and both parties have attained the age of eighteen.

(1B) An act of buggery by one man with another shall not be treated as taking place in private if it takes place -
(a) when more than two persons take part or are present; or
(b) in a lavatory to which the public have or are permitted to have access, whether on payment or otherwise.

(1C) In any proceedings against a person for buggery with another person it shall be for the prosecutor to prove that the act of buggery took place otherwise than in private or that one of the parties to it had not attained the age of eighteen.

Why has the age of consent to heterosexual sex remained different from that to male homosexual sex? Parliament has specified different penalties according to the nature of the specific offence of buggery: if it is with a person under 16 or with an animal, the maximum penalty is life imprisonment; if D is 21 or over, and the other person is under 18, the maximum penalty is five years; in other circumstances, the maximum penalty is two years' imprisonment. Given that there is a higher penalty for some offences of buggery, should there be a separate offence of 'aggravated buggery' (see the discussion on incest under **10.28**)?

10.17 The Sexual Offences (Amendment) Bill 2000 will make three changes to the law on sexual offences. First, it reduces the minimum age at which a person, whether male or female, may lawfully consent to buggery and certain homosexual acts. This reduction is from 18 to 16 in England and Wales and Scotland, and from 18 to 17 in Northern Ireland. This will equalise the age of consent for sexual activity so that it is the same for male homosexuals as for heterosexuals and lesbians ie 16 in England, Wales and Scotland and 17 in Northern Ireland. Second, in all jurisdictions, a person under the age of consent will no longer commit an offence themselves if they engage in buggery (not Scotland) or certain homosexual acts with a person over the age of consent. Third, the Bill introduces a new offence where a person aged 18 or over has sexual intercourse or engages in any other sexual activity with or directed towards a person under that age, if the person aged 18 or over is in a position of trust (curiously defined) in relation to the younger person in circumstances specified in the Bill. A person convicted of such an offence, unless they are under 20 years old, will be subject to the notification requirements of the Sex Offenders Act 1997. Any person convicted of the offence may also be made the subject of an 'extended sentence' by the court.

Indecent assault

10.18 Indecent assaults on women and on men are dealt with by different sections of the SOA 1956. Section 14 makes it an offence for a person to make an indecent assault on a woman. The penalty was raised from a maximum of two years to a maximum of 10 years by the SOA 1985. To avoid any doubt, s 14(2) provides that a girl under the age of 16 cannot in law give any consent. Section 15 provides that it is an offence to make an indecent assault on a man. This has been subject to a maximum sentence of 10 years' imprisonment since 1956. Presumably the higher maximum for assaults on men in 1956 was explained by the fact that at that time Parliament felt that it was more unnatural and therefore 'worse' for a man to assault a man. Offences of indecent assault range from the extremely minor to near-rape, as illustrated in the following case:

> *Kowalski* (1988) D forced his wife at knife point to commit an act of fellatio and have *sexual intercourse*. He could not be convicted of the rape of his wife at that time (see **10.12**), but was nonetheless convicted of indecent assault and assault occasioning actual bodily harm, and was sentenced to four years' imprisonment. CA (Ian Kennedy J) upheld his conviction.

Common to both indecent assaults on men and women is the need for an assault (see **9.20**).

> *Fairclough v Whipp* (1951) D, who was urinating near a river bank, invited a nine-year-old girl who was passing by to touch his penis. She did so. KBD (Lord Goddard CJ): there was no assault since D had not used force or the threat of force on the victim. (Since this case Parliament passed the Indecency with Children Act 1960, but the case is still a good authority on indecent assault.)

10.19   More difficult to assess is the circumstances of indecency required. The test is primarily objective: if the circumstances of the assault are incapable of being regarded as indecent, the assault does not become indecent simply because of some secret motive of the accused.

> *George* (1956) D attempted to removed girl's shoe as it gave him sexual gratification. Streatfield J: Here there was no indecency: an assault only becomes indecent if it is accompanied by circumstances of indecency towards the victim.

> *Court* (1989) D spanked a 12-year-old girl in the shop where he worked 12 times outside her shorts. He pleaded guilty to assault, but not to indecent assault. He admitted that he had a buttock fetish, but this was only his secret motive. He was sentenced to three years' probation on the condition that he receive psychiatric treatment for 12 months. HL (4-1): dismissed D's appeal. Evidence of D's secret motive was

admissible. Lord Ackner distinguished three types of case: first, where the conduct would not be considered indecent by any right-minded observer, there could be no conviction whatever D's motivation; secondly, where every right-minded observer would consider the behaviour indecent, whatever D's actual motivation, it would be an indecent assault. Thirdly, if the right-minded individual would be unsure, the court should look at D's motive: if that was indecent, the offence would be made out.

10.20　Note Lord Goff's dissent: he argued that if P cannot establish that the assault is objectively indecent, they should not be allowed to justify the case by calling evidence of a secret indecent intention. Only if the assault is *prima facie* indecent, should D be able to show that it was not in fact indecent by calling evidence of his purpose. Is there a clearer way of distinguishing between those assaults which are indecent and those which aren't? Who is a right-minded person? Is she the same as a reasonable person? Has the time come to re-name these offences sexual assaults, or is the wider term 'indecent' useful?

Indecency with children

10.21　The Indecency with Children Act 1960 created a specific offence of gross indecency involving a child:

> 1(1) Any person who commits an act of gross indecency with or towards a child under the age of 14, or who incites a child under that age to such an act with him or another shall be liable on conviction on indictment to imprisonment for a term not exceeding ten years ...

The phrase 'with or towards a child' includes the person who masturbates in front of a child, as long as D gains satisfaction from the fact the child is watching. Indeed, it has been held that passively permitting a child to keep her hand on his penis constitutes the offence (*Speck* (1977)). There is a clear overlap here with the common law offences of outraging public decency and indecent exposure. The age of the victim is clearly an essential ingredient of the offence, though a mistaken belief may now constitute a defence.

B (a minor) v DPP (2000) D, aged 15, sat next to V, a 13-year-old girl on a bus. He asked her several times to perform oral sex with him, and she repeatedly refused. His defence was that he honestly believed she was over 14, but when the magistrates ruled that this was no defence to a charge under s 1 of the 1960 Act, he changed his plea to guilty. Div Ct (this was an appeal by way of case stated): upheld his conviction. HL (unanimously): allowed D's appeal. Where Parliament failed to specify the mental element required, it was not a necessary implication that it was the intention of Parliament that liability should be strict so that an honest belief as to the age of the child would not be a defence. *Prince* (1875) was a 'relic from an age dead and gone' (Lord Hutton) and could be ignored as concerning a different offence and a different statute. They rely on the principle of legality as spelt out by Lord Hoffman in *R v Secretary of State for the Home Department, ex p Simms* (1999):

> The principle of legality means that Parliament must squarely confront what it is doing and accept the political cost. Fundamental rights cannot be overridden by general or ambiguous words.

Offences connected with prostitution

10.22 It is not illegal to be a prostitute in this country, but many activities connected with prostitution are criminal. Thus, the SOA 1956 specifies an offence (for a man) of living on the earnings of prostitution (s 30), an offence of keeping a brothel (s 33), an offence of knowingly allowing premises to be used for purposes of prostitution (s 36). The SOA 1959 was largely concerned with criminalising soliciting by prostitutes. The SOA 1967 then added new offences such as an offence (for a man or woman) to live on the earnings of a male prostitute (s 5), and also extended the definition of a brothel to include premises people resort to for the purpose of 'lewd homosexual practices' . The SOA 1985 concentrated on further criminalising various offences connected with soliciting. Thus, s 1 proscribes kerb-crawling:

> (1) A man commits an offence if he solicits a woman (or different women) for the purpose of prostitution -
> (a) from a motor vehicle while it is in a street or public place; or
> (b) in a street or public place while in the immediate vicinity of a vehicle that he has just got out of or off,
> persistently or in such manner or in such circumstances as to be likely to cause annoyance to the woman (or any of the women) solicited, or nuisance to other persons in the neighbourhood.

10.23 There is a large literature on prostitution (see, for example, Lacey, Wells and Meure (1998)), and in considering the rightful ambit of the criminal law you might like to consider whether you think the law is cast too wide. Here is one example:

> *Paul v DPP* (1989) D picked up a known prostitute in his car. There were no other pedestrians or cars around at the time, apart from the police car which followed him. He was convicted of an offence under s 1 SOA 1985, and fined £200. CA (Woolf LJ): dismissed his appeal. There was no need for evidence that anyone was actually offended. A likelihood of nuisance to others in the neighbourhood was sufficient. In determining that issue, the magistrates could use their knowledge of the locality as a residential area, its frequentation by prostitutes, and its population density.

Bigamy

10.24 Bigamy, while not a common offence, is worth mentioning since it is an example of an offence where the circumstances surrounding the act (of marrying) are more important than the act itself. What is the rationale for the offence: protection of the victim, or upholding the institution of marriage? The OAPA 1861, s 57 provides:

> Whosoever, being married, shall marry any other person during the life of the former husband or wife, whether the second marriage shall have taken place in England or Ireland or elsewhere, shall be guilty of [an offence], and being convicted thereof shall be liable to [imprisonment] for any term not exceeding seven years ...: provided, that nothing in this section contained shall extend to any second marriage contracted elsewhere than in England and Ireland by any other than a subject of Her Majesty, or to any person marrying a second time whose husband or wife shall have been continually absent from such person for the space of seven years then last past, and shall not have been known by such person to be living within that time, or shall extend to any person who, at the time of such second marriage, shall have been divorced from the bond of the first marriage, or to any person whose former marriage shall have been declared void by the sentence of any court of competent jurisdiction.

10.25 Thus P needs to prove that D got married when he or she was already married; that the first spouse was alive; and in respect of certain categories of people, that the second marriage took place in England or Ireland. The section does not specify the requisite *mens rea*, and this may cause difficulties in relation to the various different circumstances.

> *Tolson* (1889) D believed in good faith and on reasonable grounds, but mistakenly, that her husband was dead, and remarried. CCCR: held by a majority of 9-4 that her conviction for bigamy should be quashed. Cave J:

>> At common law, an honest and reasonable belief in the existence of circumstances, which, if true, would make the act for which a prisoner is indicted an innocent act has always been held to be a good defence.

This decision, that mistaken beliefs should excuse, was confirmed in *DPP v Morgan* (1976) (see **10.9**), though since *B (a minor) v DPP* (2000) (see **5.25**) it is no longer necessary that the mistake should have been reasonable.

Incest

10.26   Section 10 of the SOA 1956 provides that:

> (1) It is an offence for a man to have sexual intercourse with a woman whom he knows to be his granddaughter, daughter, sister or mother.

> (2) In the forgoing subsection 'sister' includes half-sister, and for the purposes of that subsection any expression importing a relationship between two people shall be taken to apply notwithstanding that the relationship is not traced through lawful wedlock.

and s 11:

> (1) It is an offence for a woman of the age of 16 or over to permit a man whom she knows to be her grandfather, father, brother or son to have sexual intercourse with her by her consent.

> (2) In the foregoing subsection 'brother' includes half-brother, and for the purposes of that subsection any expression importing a relationship between two people shall be taken to apply not withstanding that the relationship is not traced through lawful wedlock.

10.27   Why is incest a crime? If it is simply a question of enforcing a moral belief that incest is wrong, this raises the same issues which led the Wolfenden Committee (see **1.5**) to recommend the de-criminalisation of consensual homosexuality. It is sometimes argued that it is not simply a question of morality, but that there are also more practical reasons for criminalising it: the risk of handicapped babies. But if this were the true reason, would it also be an argument for saying that it should be a criminal offence for haemophiliacs or those who are HIV positive to have sex?

10.28 The DCC recommended various modifications to the existing law:

(i) that the offence should extend to adoptive as well as to blood relationships between father and daughter and mother and son. If the offence were extended beyond blood relationships, then the rationale would not seem to be the public health issue raised above.

(ii) that it should cease to be an offence for a brother and sister to have intercourse where they have both reached the age of 21. This controversial recommendation received more coverage in the popular press than any other at the time that the DCC was published. Yet the argument of the Law Commission is that the logic of the Wolfenden Committee (see **1.5**) which resulted in the legalisation of homosexuality should also prevent the law inquiring into the bedrooms of other consenting adults.

(iii) that daughters, granddaughters and sons under the age of 21 should be exempted from liability.

10.29 The DCC also included a separate offence of 'aggravated incest'. The Law Commission argued that if it was agreed that incest by a man with a girl under the age of 13 should carry a higher penalty, this would require a separate offence. Is this really a requirement: if so, should buggery be sub-divided into different offences of 'buggery' and 'aggravated buggery' in the statute (see **10.15**)?

Further reading

Adler, *Rape on Trial* (1987)

Lacey, Wells and Meure, *Reconstructing Criminal Law* (1998, 2nd edn)

Temkin *Rape and the Legal Process* (1987)

Zedner, 'Regulating Sexual Offences within the home' in *Frontiers of Criminality* (ed Loveland)(1995)

Self-test questions

1. What offences are committed in the following circumstances:
   (i) Dee persuades Phil aged 15 to have sex with her.
   (ii) Dee encourages Dave to have sex with Viola (aged 15). Dave presumes without thinking that Viola is consenting. In fact, Viola only allows him to have sex with her because Dee has threatened to beat her up if she does not.

2. Dave, angry that one of his lovers has infected him with the AIDS virus, has sex with as many people as he can. Discuss his liability in the following circumstances:
   (i) He informs Ann that he has AIDS, and she decides to have sex with him anyhow.
   (ii) He does not tell his wife, Beth, that he has the virus, and she says that she would not have consented to have sex had she known the truth.
   (iii) He has anal sex with Charles, who says that while he consented to rough sexual play with Dave, he never consented to the intercourse.

3. At a wild party, Dee encourages Dave to have sex with Violet. Violet is dragged screaming and kicking by Dave into a bedroom, where he pulls off most of her clothes. Dee stands around laughing, but others arrive to save Violet before intercourse takes place.

4. In what respects, if at all, does the law of sexual offences need reform?

CHAPTER ELEVEN

Theft and offences of deception

SUMMARY

Theft: The main problems centre on the meaning of the words 'appropriation' (does it imply consensual appropriation? can you steal your own property?) and 'dishonesty' (the *Feeley* test).

There is also an enormous overlap with other offences: eg TA 1968 s 15 and TA 1978 s 1.

Robbery: only minimum 'force' is required.

Burglary: distinguish the two separate offences under TA 1968 s 9. Are either or both of these offences necessary?

Blackmail: unwarranted demands with menaces.

Handling stolen goods and offences of deception: does the overlap between the various offences (and theft) matter?

Introduction

11.1   Most of the offences which we are studying in this chapter concern 'property'. Some of the problems are not caused by unclear criminal law, but by civil law uncertainties concerning ownership. Criminal law adapts to the civil framework: land law, contract, gift, succession, intellectual property issues may all be relevant here. This reflects a key difficulty – where the line is to be drawn between those who are sufficiently 'naughty' to be criminally liable and those who are not. If I ask a plumber to mend my dripping tap and then say (falsely) that I cannot pay him this month, should I be guilty of a crime? Should all those people who delay paying their bills as long as possible be guilty of a crime?

Starting afresh, how would you distinguish different crimes in this field? The basic one would probably be stealing. In ordinary language this involves 'taking' other people's property. But theft involves something much wider than this: you may be guilty of theft without taking anything, just because you infringe one of someone's property rights (as long as you have the appropriate dishonest intent): see **11.7**. Property itself is a difficult concept: what is the property involved in a mortgage fraud, for example? Working on from here, would you specify various aggravated forms of theft (eg burglary, robbery), or would you merely give those thieves who use violence, or who steal from houses, higher sentences for theft? Then you have to face the problem of whether thieves and cheats are different: how does or should the law of deception vary from the law of theft? You also face the same problem with offences of deception as you faced with theft: do you break deception into a number of different offences, or should there be just one offence of 'obtaining a benefit by deception'? How does 'white collar crime' fit into this picture? Should we be concerned that it seems to be easier to convict petty thieves and con-men than those who defraud the tax and social security systems, or who carry out major commercial frauds? Finally in this chapter we will come to those who help or encourage thieves. They are normally convicted not of aiding and abetting theft, but of a separate (and more serious) offence of handling stolen goods. Why?

Theft

11.2   Despite the fact that we have a statement of the law of theft in s I of the Theft Act 1968, the law is far from clear. Theft replaced larceny (grand and petit), which could be defined as 'the felonious taking and carrying away of personal goods'. The CLRC (1966) sought to bring common sense, clarity, comprehensiveness, coherence and consistency to the law. You may judge to what extent they succeeded! Section I provides a general definition:

> (1) A person is guilty of theft if he dishonestly appropriates property belonging to another with the intention of permanently depriving the other of it; and 'thief' and 'steal' shall be construed accordingly.

It is an offence triable either on indictment or summarily, and is subject to a maximum penalty of seven years' imprisonment (though only six months if tried summarily: see **1.12**). The *actus reus* may be seen as 'the ·

216

appropriation of property belonging to another' and the *mens rea* as 'dishonesty + an intention to permanently deprive'. Most elements have proved difficult to interpret.

11.3 *Meaning of property* Property is partially defined in s 4 of the TA 1968:

> (1) 'Property' includes money and all other property, real or personal, including things in action and other intangible property.

Money (coins and bank notes) are clearly property which can be stolen. Land in general can't be stolen (see s 4(2)), unless a trustee or some other authorised person sells it in breach of the confidence reposed in him. Picking wild mushrooms, fruit or flowers from land is not theft unless done for commercial reasons (s 4(3)). Personal property includes goods such as the piece of paper on which a cheque or exam paper is written. A thing in action (or 'chose in action') is a property right which can only be claimed by action and not physically taken. The most common thing in action is a debt for a fixed sum. An account held at a bank or building society is a thing in action: but once the account is overdrawn there is no thing in action which is capable of being stolen. Intangible property which can be stolen includes patents, copyrights, and electronic transfers (see *Mensah-Lartey* (1996)).

> *Oxford v Moss* (1978) D, a civil engineering student, copied an exam paper and then returned it. CA: quashed his conviction for theft since confidential information cannot be stolen.

11.4 The Law Commission's Consultation Paper No 150 (1997), *Misuse of Trade Secrets*, provisionally proposed that it should be an offence to use or disclose a trade secret without authority (the Law Commission point out that theft of a board room table is currently punished more severely than theft of board room secrets!). Other property which cannot be stolen include electricity and human bodies, but other specific offences cover those who abuse those two things (for the former see **11.30** and for the latter, the Human Tissue Act 1961; Anatomy Act 1984 etc). The Computer Misuse Act 1990 created specific offences related to those who dishonestly enter other people's computer systems.

11.5 *Belonging to another* According to s 5 of the TA 1968:

(1) Property shall be regarded as belonging to any person having possession or control of it, or having in it any proprietary right or interest (not being an equitable interest arising only from an agreement to transfer or grant an interest).

The following subsections raise specific situations where property may be deemed to belong to another: where property is subject to a trust, the persons to whom it belongs shall be regarded as including any person having a right to enforce the trust (s 5(2)); where a person receives property for or on account of another and is under an obligation to deal with it in a particular way, the property shall be regarded as belonging to the other (s 5(3)); where a person gets property by mistake and is under an obligation to make restoration (in whole or in part) the property shall be regarded as belonging to the person entitled to restoration (s 5(4)).

11.6 Thus although a classic case of theft involves taking something from the owner, it can also be committed against those with lesser interests. A partner can steal from his co-partners, or a director can steal from his company. D may even steal from himself:

> *Turner (No 2)* (1971) D took his car home from a garage where it had been repaired without paying for the repairs. He was convicted of theft. CA: dismissed the appeal. It was sufficient that the person from whom the property was appropriated was in fact at the time in possession or control.

> *Hinks* (2000) D befriended a middle-aged and vulnerable man who took large sums out of his bank account and gave them to D. CA: upheld her conviction for theft. The recipient of a valid indefeasible gift may commit theft if she receives it 'dishonestly'. The Vice President (Rose LJ) concluded:

>> Despite the strictures of Professor Sir John Smith QC in [1997] Crim LR 359, we respectfully agree with the approach of the differently constituted division of this Court in *Kendrick and Hopkins* [1997] 2 Cr App R 524. Civil unlawfulness is not a constituent of the offence of theft, and we are unpersuaded that Lord Browne-Wilkinson's analysis in *Gomez* was flawed in the way which Professor Smith there suggests. We derive some comfort in this conclusion from the article by Simon Gardener in [1998] Crim LR 35. Professor Smith's response to that

article by letter, at page 80 of [1998] Crim LR is, in our view, not perhaps the most cogent of his outstanding contributions to the criminal law.

The CA in *Hinks* seem to accept that there can be theft where there are no stolen goods. Yet, as JC Smith (1998) says, 'the TAs assume the existence of the civil law of property ... TA offences exist for the purpose of protecting those interests'. Gardener (1998), on the other hand, argues that there may be good reasons for contract and criminal law not to coincide: the civil law is there to protect property rights, even if they were unsatisfactory acquired, whereas the criminal law rightly concentrates on the unsatisfactory manner of acquisition. As this book goes to print, the decision of the HL in this case is anxiously awaited.

Compare these decisions with *Preddy* (1996) discussed at **11.36**, and

A-G's Reference (No 1 of 1985) (1986) A publican sold his own beer in a tied house, keeping the profit. CA (Lord Lane CJ): upheld his acquittal. The manager had a civil obligation to the brewery, but there was no theft. Despite the wording of s 5(2), the concept of theft by importing the equitable doctrine of constructive trust is so obtuse and so far removed from ordinary people's understanding of what constitutes stealing, that it should not amount to it.

11.7   *Actus reus: Appropriation* Section 3 provides:

(1) Any assumption by a person of the right of an owner amounts to an appropriation, and this includes, where he has come by the property (innocently or not) without stealing it, any later assumption of a right to it by keeping or dealing with it as owner.

(2) Where property or a right or interest in property is or purports to be transferred for value to a person acting in good faith, no later assumption by him of rights which he believed himself to be acquiring shall, by reason of any defect in the transferor's title, amount to theft of the property.

Appropriation involves any usurpation of the rights of the owner. It is much wider than merely 'taking'. If you give me your chocolate to look after and I eat it, I have usurped your rights as the owner. In that case, I have usurped all your rights, but any interference with your rights as the owner may constitute usurpation. Even if all I do is fail to return your chocolate to you when you ask for it (having dishonestly decided to keep it) I have stolen it. This is a form of liability by omission, which as we saw in **2.5** is rare in criminal law.

11.8 *Appropriation and consent* The HL has made a difficult issue more difficult:

> *Lawrence* (1971) An Italian tourist on his first visit to the UK was taken by taxi from Victoria Station to an address in central London. The taxi driver, when offered £1 from V's wallet, took a further £6 from the wallet, although the correct fare should have been less than £1. D's conviction was upheld by both CA and HL. Viscount Dilhorne:
>
>> I see no ground for concluding that the omission of the words 'without the consent of the owner' was inadvertent and not deliberate, and to read the subsection as if they were included is, in my opinion, wholly unwarranted. Parliament by the omission of these words has relieved the prosecution of the burden of establishing that the taking was without the owner's consent. That is no longer an ingredient of the offence.
>
> *Morris; Anderton v Burnside* (1984) In both these cases Ds took price labels from lower priced articles and substituted them for the price labels on higher priced articles. In one case, D paid the lower price at the checkout and was then arrested; in the other, D was arrested before he reached the check out. HL (Lord Roskill): upheld their convictions, but introduced a narrower view of appropriation: the concept involves 'an act by way of adverse interference with or usurpation of' any of the rights of the owner. Thus a shopper was not appropriating goods by taking the goods from the shelf: he was doing what the shop wanted him to do. Only when the interference was 'adverse' was it an appropriation.

11.9 To many commentators this case was a disappointment. Spencer (at (1984) 43 CLJ 10) called it a depressing decision 'not even competent in technical respects'. Here, he suggests, was the HL, clearly bored by theft, concurring in a single speech which flatly contradicted *Lawrence* without saying whether that decision was distinguished or overruled. There followed a whole series of cases which added confusion upon confusion. For example, in *Fritschy* (1985) the CA held that a man who

220

agreed to take kruggerands from London to Geneva for the owner only appropriated the money once he had deviated from the authorised route, even though from the beginning he had never intended to deliver them to their correct destination. In *Dobson v General Accident Fire and Life Assurance Corpn* (1990), a civil case, the CA drew a distinction between authorisation and consent in order to try and reconcile the cases: an act which is authorised could constitute appropriation (following *Morris*) but an act which was consented to could not (following *Lawrence*). The best thing about the next decision is that it has at least clarified the law:

> *Gomez* (1991) D persuaded the manager of the shop where he worked to sell £16,000 worth of electrical goods to a rogue by accepting a cheque that was subsequently dishonoured. He pleaded guilty to theft when the judge refused to accept a submission that there was no appropriation since the manager had expressly authorised the removal of the goods. CA: allowed D's appeal, but HL (4-1) allowed the Crown's appeal. Lords Jauncey, Browne-Wilkinson and Slynn agreed with the speech of Lord Keith. Lord Keith accepted that no 'sensible distinction can be made in this context between consent and authorisation', and that *Lawrence* was authoritative and correct. This speech should be contrasted with the vociferous dissent of Lord Lowry. He relied heavily on the 8th Report of the CLRC (1966), and also on the fact that s 15 becomes redundant if s 1 is given the meaning accepted by the majority.

11.10 The *Gomez* solution has the merit of simplifying the law. It has also, though, widened the law quite extraordinarily. Any assumption of a right of an owner, even with her consent, may constitute the *actus reus* of theft (see *Hinks* (2000) at **11.6**). Nor has the decision solved all the possible problems:

> *Gallasso* (1992) D, a nurse caring for mentally handicapped adults, had the responsibility of drawing money from their bank accounts for their living expenses. She opened a separate bank account for V, a patient, and subsequently transferred some of the money in it into her own account and some into a cash card account. CA: quashed her conviction for theft based on the opening of the account in V's name, since paying the cheque into a trust account could not be regarded as an appropriation since it was evidence of D affirming V's rights rather than assuming them for herself.

Is this an appropriate interpretation of *Gomez*? Surely merely by handling the cheque she was 'appropriating' it: the question then remains as to whether she was dishonest.

11.11 Can property be appropriated more than once? Section 3(1) appears to say that where someone has come by property without stealing it, he may still commit theft by some later act. Can one person therefore commit theft of an item more than once? If so, this may pose problems for the law of handling (see **11.44**) since handling can only be committed once the stealing is complete. For the complex overlap between handling and theft, see **11.45**. Even larger is the overlap between theft and obtaining property by deception (see **11.34**). Does this matter? Glazebrook (1991) argues (supporting the approach taken by the majority in *Gomez*) that it should not. He points out that if one accepted the argument of Lord Lowry's dissent in *Gomez*, D would not be guilty of theft simply because he was guilty of a more serious offence. Many cases of theft nowadays involve D obtaining goods by trickery. In strict contract law, D becomes the owner of the goods in these circumstances: the contract is valid until and unless the victim chooses to avoid the contract. In which case, can one argue that D is appropriating his own property?

11.12 Another problem is whether appropriation is one-off, or a continuing event.

> *Atakpu* (1994) Ds hired cars in Belgium and Germany using false documents. They then brought them to England intending to sell them. They were arrested within the hire period, and charged with conspiracy to steal. CA: quashed their conviction. If goods have once been stolen, they cannot be stolen again by the same thief. Courts should 'leave it for the common-sense of the jury to decide that the appropriation can continue for so long as the thief can sensibly be regarded as in the act of stealing or, in more understandable words, so long as he is "on the job" as the editors of *Smith and Hogan* ... suggest the test should be'. There was therefore no conspiracy to steal in England.

Note that this particular problem would not arise today: s 5 CJA 1993 provides that conspiracies to defraud may be tried in this country if some part of the conspiracy arose in this country (see **7.3**).

11.13 *Mens rea: Dishonesty* Section 2 of the TA 1968 provides no definition of dishonesty, simply some examples of behaviour which is not dishonest:

(1) A person's appropriation of property belonging to another is not to be regarded as dishonest -

(a) if he appropriates the property in the belief that he has in law the right to deprive the other of it, on behalf of himself or a third person; or

(b) if he appropriates the property in the belief that he would have the other's consent if the other knew of the appropriation and the circumstances of it; or

(c) (except where the property came to him as trustee or personal representative) if he appropriates the property in the belief that the person to whom the property belongs cannot be discovered by taking reasonable steps.

(2) A person's appropriation of property belonging to another may be dishonest notwithstanding that he is willing to pay for the property.

This gives no guidance on whether the test for dishonesty should be subjective or objective, nor whether it is a matter of fact for the jury or a question of law for the judge.

Feely (1973) D, a branch manager of a firm of bookmakers, borrowed £30 from the 'float'. Four days later he was transferred to another branch, and the new manager discovered the loss. D then gave an IOU to cover the deficiency and, when questioned by the police, he said that he intended to pay it back and that he was owed by the firm in wages more than he had borrowed. CA (5 judges, but only Lawton LJ gave a judgement): quashed his conviction. Because the word dishonestly is in common use, judges should not define it.

Jurors when deciding whether an appropriation was dishonest can be reasonably expected to, and should, apply the current standards of ordinary decent people. In their own lives they have to decide what is and what is not dishonest. We can see no reason why, when in a jury box, they should require the help of a judge to tell them what amounts to dishonesty.

It was a defence that should have been left to the jury that he intended to repay the money and that he had reasonable grounds for believing that he would be able to do so.

11.14 Thus the test for dishonesty is left as a question of fact for juries to apply, using ordinary standards and with no help from the judge. Griew (1985) is highly critical of this, giving a long list of criticisms such as the danger of inconsistent verdicts, the fiction of community norms, the danger of longer and more expensive trials and the problem of the ordinary dishonest juror. Guest (1987) goes further, arguing that if the judge hands over a question of interpreting the law to the jury he is abdicating his constitutional responsibility. It is for judges to identify the state of affairs which were envisaged to be within the scope of the relevant law. Particular difficulties arise where D says he did not think that his act was dishonest:

> *Ghosh* (1982) D, a locum hospital consultant, falsely claimed that money was owing to him for an operation, but later explained that the money was in any case owing to him in fees. CA (Lord Lane only): upheld his conviction. Dishonesty describes a state of mind, not conduct and therefore the test is subjective. However the standard to be applied is that of the reasonable and honest man, not that of the accused.

>> It is no defence for a man to say 'I know that what I was doing is generally regarded as dishonest, but I do not regard it as dishonest. Therefore I am not guilty'. What he is however entitled to say is 'I did not know that anybody would regard what I was doing as dishonest'. He may not be believed ... but if he is believed, or raises a real doubt about the matter, the jury cannot be sure that he was dishonest.

11.15 Thus the *Ghosh* test is a two stage test. First the jury asks itself whether D's behaviour was dishonest by the standards of the honest and reasonable person. Only if the answer to the first question is yes, should they then ask whether D realised it was dishonest in this sense. Spencer (at (1982) CLJ 222) criticises the test for being too sophisticated ('clearly intelligence tests for juries will soon be needed'), and for allowing in effect a mistake of law to act as a defence. The CA has made clear (in *Price* (1989), for example) that the *Ghosh* test should only be applied in *Ghosh*-like situations, ie where D might have believed that what he is alleged to have done was in accordance with the ordinary person's idea

224

of honesty. Otherwise all that is necessary is a *Feely* direction. But if you think that a definition of dishonesty would be useful, what would it say? Glazebrook (1993) has a proposal:

> A person's appropriation of property belonging to another is to be regarded as dishonest unless -
> (a) done in the belief that he has in law the right to deprive the other of it, on behalf of himself or a third person; or
> (b) done in the belief that he would have the other's consent if the other knew of the appropriation and the circumstances of it; or
> (c) done (otherwise than by a trustee or personal representative) in the belief that the person to whom the property belongs is unlikely to be discovered by taking reasonable steps; or
> (d) he received it in good faith and for value;
> (e) the property is money, some other fungible, a thing in action or intangible property, and is appropriated with the intention of replacing it, and in the belief that it will be possible for him to do so without loss to the person to whom it belongs; or
> (f) it consists in picking (otherwise than for reward or for sale or other commercial purpose) mushrooms, flowers, fruit or foliage growing wild.

Would this resolve the difficulties? Would the person who keeps a £50 note found in the gutter be dishonest under this test? The Law Commission (1999) seem to want to go yet further: in exploring the proper role of dishonesty in the law, they point out that the CLRC in their Eighth Report (1966) intended that the word 'dishonesty' should do little more than preserve the old defence of claim of right, they criticise both the *Feeley* [1973] QB 530 and the *Ghosh* [1982] QB 1053 tests for 'their assumption of, and dependence on, a shared moral standard' (para 5.8). 'The fact-finders are required not merely to place the defendant's conduct at an appropriate point on the scale, but to construct their own scale' (para 5.13). They provisionally conclude that dishonesty should not be a separate element in deception offences (see **11.36**).

11.16   *Intention permanently to deprive* The biggest problems here are evidential: all rogues when caught are likely to say that they intended to pay back/give back the property in due course. But add to this evidential difficulty the huge legal problem of interpreting s 6, which in Spencer's words 'sprouts obscurity at every phrase':

> (1) A person appropriating property belonging to another without

225

meaning the other permanently to lose the thing itself is nevertheless to be regarded as having the intention of permanently depriving the other of it if his intention is to treat the thing as his own to dispose of regardless of the other's rights; and a borrowing or lending of it may amount to so treating it if, but only if, the borrowing or lending is for a period and in circumstances making it equivalent to an outright taking or disposal.

(2) Without prejudice to the generality of subsection (1) above, where a person, having possession or control (lawfully or not) of property belonging to another, parts with the property under a condition as to its return which he may not be able to perform, this (if done for purposes of his own and without the other's authority) amounts to treating the property as his own to dispose of regardless of the other's rights.

11.17 Spencer (1977) traces the uncomfortable passage of this section through Parliament: the moral of the story seems to be that a criminal code should not be over-specific. The approaches taken to the interpretation of this section by different courts, too, have not been entirely consistent:

Lloyd (1985) D, a cinema projectionist, borrowed films from the cinema where he worked in order to make unlawful copies of them. He was convicted of conspiracy to steal. CA (Lord Lane CJ): quashed his conviction. Section 6

> must mean, if nothing else, that there are circumstances in which a D may be deemed to have the intention permanently to deprive, even though he may intend the owner eventually to get back the object which has been taken ... A mere borrowing is never enough to constitute the necessary guilty mind unless the intention is to return the thing in such a changed state that it can be truly said that all its goodness or virtue has gone.

Here the films were not diminished in value at all, so there could have been no theft.

11.18 If I borrow your football season ticket and return it after I have seen the first match of the season, have I stolen it?

Coffey (1987) D obtained machinery by a worthless cheque in order to put pressure on V to resolve a dispute between them. He was convicted of obtaining property by deception. CA: quashed his conviction. If the jury thought that D might have intended to return the goods, they would not have convicted unless they were sure that he intended that the period of detention should be so long as to amount to an outright taking. Even if the jury concluded that D had in mind not to return the goods if V failed to do what he wanted, they would still have to consider whether he had regarded the likelihood of this happening as being such that his intended conduct could be regarded as equivalent to an outright taking.

> ... the reference in s 6(1) to 'borrowing' (plainly used in a loose sense to denote non-consensual assumption of possession coupled with an intention ultimately to restore the object taken) shows that the 'deprivation' can be 'permanent' even if it is meant to be temporary.

DPP v Lavender (1994) D took two doors from one council house and installed them in another. CA: upheld his conviction for theft.

11.19 Are these cases satisfactory? One conclusion is to argue that Parliament would have been wiser to leave the interpretation of an 'intention permanently to deprive' to case law. Some statutory provisions create more problems than they solve. Is this concept not one that is safely left to juries or magistrates as a question of fact? However, Glazebrook (1993) proposes a new definition:

> A person is to be regarded as having the intention of permanently depriving the person to whom the property belongs of it if he realises that
> (a) the person may be permanently deprived of it, or
> (b) it may not be returned to that person before it has become worthless.

11.20 Perhaps the requirement of an intent to deprive permanently should simply be removed, and the law of theft should include unlawful borrowings. Parliament decided in 1968 that such unlawful borrowings could be dealt with under the civil law, or by specific crimes such as removal of articles from places open to the public (s 11 of the TA 1968) and taking a motor vehicle without authority (s 12). However, Ashworth (at p 393, PCL) argues that since the value of many objects lies in their use, and that they may have relatively short lives, there is a strong argument for penalising temporary deprivations generally: see also Glanville Williams (1981).

Robbery

11.21 Robbery is stealing with force. It could be as easily classified as an offence of violence as a property offence. Section 8 of the TA 1968 provides:

> (1) A person is guilty of robbery if he steals, and immediately before or at the time of doing so, and in order to do so, he uses force on any person or puts or seeks to put any person in fear of being then and there subjected to force.

> (2) A person guilty of robbery, or of an assault with intent to rob, shall on conviction on indictment be liable to imprisonment for life.

11.22 Thus the *actus reus* of robbery is that of theft combined with the use of force or fear of subjection to force. The courts have accepted that only minimal force is required:

> *Dawson* (1976) Three men, including D, approached V who was 'nudged' by one of them. As V stumbled, his wallet was stolen. CA: the word force had been deliberately used in the TA 1968 rather than the word violence which had appeared in the Larceny Act 1916. It was a word in ordinary use which juries could apply appropriately.

> *Clouden* (1987) D pulled on a lady's shopping bag in order to wrench it from her. He appealed from his conviction for robbery on the basis that he had not used force on any person. CA: dismissed his appeal. Whether force was 'used on any person' should be left to the jury. It may be sufficient for the appellant to use force on V's possessions in a way which affects V.

The CLRC (1966) had said that they 'would not regard mere snatching of property, such as a handbag, from an unresisting owner as using force for the purpose of definition'. Do you think that the decision in *Clouden* dilutes the offence of robbery too much, offending the principle of fair labelling (see **1.2**)? It is after all a very serious offence, subject to a maximum of life imprisonment and triable only on indictment. The Crime (Sentences) Act 1997 includes robbery with a firearm (including an imitation forearm) amongst those offences, which for a second conviction, result in an automatic life sentence.

11.23 The *mens rea* of robbery is the *mens rea* for theft: dishonesty (see **11.13**) + an intention permanently to deprive V of the property (see **11.16**), as well as at least recklessness as to the force used: since D must use the force in order to steal, more than accidental or negligent use of force is necessary.

Burglary

11.24 Stealing from buildings has long been treated differently to other forms of stealing. The word burglary, deriving from 'burge breche', an old English term, used to mean breaking into a house by night with intent to commit a felony. Section 9 of the TA 1968 creates two distinct offences:

(1) A person is guilty of burglary if -
(a) he enters any building or part of a building as a trespasser and with intent to commit any such offence as is mentioned in sub-s (2) below; or
(b) having entered any building or part of a building as a trespasser he steals or attempts to steal anything in the building or that part of it or inflicts or attempts to inflict on any person therein any grievous bodily harm.

(2) The offences referred to in subsection (1)(a) above are offences of stealing anything in the building or part of a building in question, of inflicting on any person therein any grievous bodily harm or raping any person therein, and of doing unlawful damage to the building or anything therein.

The two separate offences are (i) entering a building with the necessary intent and (ii) having entered a building as a trespasser, committing one of the specified offences. Both are triable either way, though burglary is generally tried summarily (unless the unrecovered value of property is at least £10,000). When it comes to sentencing, burglary from domestic premises is taken more seriously than burglary from shops or businesses: the maximum penalty for domestic burglary is 14 years; whereas if the burglary is from a non-dwelling the maximum penalty is only 10 years' imprisonment. It is not clear whether D has to know he is in a dwelling to incur a higher penalty.

11.25 *The meaning of 'building'* Something will not qualify as a building unless it has a certain degree of permanence. Thus a 25-foot long freezer weighing three tons which had sat in a farmyard for more than two years qualified as a building (*B and S v Leathley* (1979)) whilst a disconnected articulated container did not (*Norfolk Constabulary v Seekings and Gould* (1986)).

Walkington (1979) D walked into the till area in a department store but found it to be empty. CA: dismissed his appeal against conviction for an offence under s 9(1)(a) TA 1968. The jury was entitled to conclude that the counter area was a 'part of a building' from which members of the public were excluded. He also had an intention to steal, although this was conditional upon him finding something worth stealing.

11.26 *'Trespasser'* Perhaps the greatest difficulty of the pre-1968 law on burglary was the requirement of a 'breaking and entry'. In order to get rid of these difficult and somewhat technical rules, Parliament introduced a new test that entry must be as a trespasser. The courts have been keen to avoid all the technicalities of the tort of trespass:

Collins (1973) D, who was drunk, saw a ladder leaning against a house at 3.30 am. He climbed the ladder and saw V, a naked woman, asleep. He descended, removed his clothes, and climbed up again. As he climbed on to the window sill, V woke up and invited him in, believing him to be her boyfriend. They had sexual intercourse before V realised her mistake. CA (Edmund Davies LJ): quashed his conviction for s 9(1)(a) burglary. There cannot be a conviction for entering premises as a trespasser unless the person entering does so knowing that he is a trespasser and nevertheless deliberately enters, or, at the very least, is reckless whether or not he is entering the premises of another without the other party's consent.

Smith and Jones (1976) D1 and D2 were arrested having removed two television sets from D1's father's house. D1 argued that since he had a general permission to enter his father's house, he could not be a trespasser. Both Ds were convicted of s 9(1)(b) burglary. CA (James LJ): dismissed their appeal. A person is a trespasser if he enters premises knowing that he is entering in excess of the permission that has been given to him, or being reckless as to whether he is entering in excess of the permission that has been given to him to enter,

230

provided the facts are known to D which enable him to realise that he is acting in excess of the permission given.

Does *Smith and Jones* widen the law of burglary too far? It suggests that all shop-lifters are in fact burglars: why then are they charged with theft? Presumably burglary has a higher penalty than theft because Parliament felt that people need especial protection from intruders in their own homes. Should this protection be limited to uninvited intruders?

11.27   *'Entry'* Not all of the burglar's body need enter the building:

Brown (1985) D broke a shop window and rummaged around with the top half of his body inside the window. CA: dismissed his appeal. His entry had been both effective and substantial.

JC Smith in his commentary to this case suggests that the words effective and substantial should be in the alternative, otherwise the law requires too much.

11.28   The *mens rea* of burglary depends on which offence is charged: for s 9(1)(a) an intention to commit one of the ulterior offences must be proved; for s 9(1)(b) the *mens rea* for the ulterior offence must be proved. In both cases, D must know or be reckless as to whether he is entering as a trespasser. The main problem that has arisen in the case-law is whether conditional intent is sufficient. If D only has a conditional intent, he may still be liable for attempted burglary. Why is a person who enters with intent to do an ulterior offence not guilty simply of an inchoate offence (whether attempted burglary or an attempt at the ulterior offences specified in s 9(2))? This raises another fair labelling question (see **1.2**): is the crime of burglary necessary, or could we rely simply on prosecutions for the ulterior offence, or an attempt at these offences? Parliament's answer is clear where the ulterior offence is theft: burglary is a more serious version of theft since the thief has intruded into V's home. However, it is difficult to suggest that burglary is more serious than rape. The fact that D raped someone in her own home may make it a more aggravated form of rape, but should it turn the offence into burglary?

Aggravated burglary

11.29   Section 10 of the TA 1968 creates an aggravated form of burglary

> ... if he commits any burglary and at the time has with him any firearm or imitation firearm, any weapon of offence, or any explosive ...

Aggravated burglary is triable only on indictment and has a maximum penalty of life imprisonment. The offence poses few problems, except perhaps in defining a 'weapon of offence'. The maximum penalty for 'plain' domestic burglary is 14 years' imprisonment (see **11.24**), and sentences of more than 14 years are extremely rare even for aggravated burglary. If the burglar has real weapons with him, and uses them, he will be charged with offences against the person as well as (or rather than) burglary. It is therefore questionable whether aggravated burglary is required as a separate offence.

Abstracting electricity

11.30   As we saw at **11.4**, electricity is not property so the TA provides a separate (triable either way) offence of abstracting electricity in s 13:

> A person who dishonestly uses without due authority, or dishonestly causes to be wasted or diverted, any electricity shall on conviction on indictment be liable to imprisonment for a term not exceeding five years.

A person is guilty of an offence under s 13 if she abstracts electricity by tampering with a meter, or by diverting electricity in any way without the consent of the owner. It looks as though merely leaving the lights on wastefully could be an offence! Would it be more straightforward to decide that electricity was property which could be stolen?

Blackmail

11.31   A close cousin to robbery is blackmail, the extortion of money by threats rather than by violence. Section 21 of the TA 1968 provides

> (1) A person is guilty of blackmail if, with a view to gain for himself or another or with intent to cause loss to another, he makes any

232

unwarranted demand with menaces; and for this purpose a demand with menaces is unwarranted unless the person making it does so in the belief-

(a) that he has reasonable grounds for making the demand; and

(b) that the use of the menaces is a proper means of reinforcing the demand.

(2) The nature of the act or mission demanded is immaterial, and it is also immaterial whether the menaces relate to action to be taken by the person making the demand.

(3) A person guilty of blackmail shall on conviction on indictment be liable to imprisonment for a term not exceeding 14 years.

The meaning of the words 'unwarranted demands with menaces' causes some difficulties. Menaces are serious threats, but when are they unwarranted demands? Where a person who takes back his own property from someone who borrowed it is not guilty of stealing it, if he threatens violence in order to recover it, he may be guilty of assault but is not guilty of robbery. However, since his threats of violence are improper, he may still be guilty of blackmail.

> *Lawrence and Pomroy* (1971) D1 and D2 went round to V's house to obtain money that V was refusing to pay for building repairs which he said had been inadequately carried out. D1 said 'Step outside the house and we will sort this out, and D2 said menacingly, 'Come on mate come outside'. A flick-knife was later found in D1's coat pocket. CA: affirmed D1 and D2's convictions for blackmail.

The word 'menaces' is an ordinary English word which any jury can be expected to understand and only in exceptional cases where, because of special knowledge in special circumstances, what would be a menace to an ordinary person is not a menace to the person to whom it is addressed, or where the converse applies, is it necessary for the trial judge to spell out the meaning of the word.

11.32 The gain or loss concerns only money or other property (see s 34(2) of the Act). If D by menaces gains other benefits, then there is no blackmail. If the benefit is sexual intercourse, then D may be charged with an offence under s 2 of the SOA 1956 (see 10.14), or even rape. What about other favours? Suppose D manages to gain a place at his chosen school for his child by threatening to reveal secrets about the head teacher: should this be blackmail? The demand may take any form and need not be explicit. It need not even reach the intended victim.

11.33 *Mens rea* D must intend to make an unwarranted demand with menaces, with a view to gain for himself or another or with intent to cause loss to another. The section provides that a demand is not unwarranted if the use of menaces is a proper way of reinforcing the demand. In deciding what is 'proper', the court faces the ambiguity and potential for inconsistency of the *Ghosh* test (see **11.14**).

Deception offences

11.34 In the original TA 1968, the two main offences of deception were found in s 15 (obtaining property by deception: maximum sentence, 10 years' imprisonment) and s 16 (obtaining a pecuniary advantage by deception: maximum sentence, five years' imprisonment). However, there were major problems with the interpretation of s16: Edmund-Davies LJ in *Royle* (1971) called it 'a judicial nightmare' and asked for it to be replaced by a simpler provision. The most significant part of it (s 16(2)(a)) has been repealed, but the TA 1978, passed to plug the gap, is certainly no simpler. We will start by briefly considering four different offences of deception:

11.35 *(i) Obtaining property by deception (TA 1968 s 15)*

> (1) A person who by any deception dishonestly obtains property belonging to another, with the intention of permanently depriving the other of it, shall on conviction on indictment be liable to imprisonment for a term not exceeding 10 years.

The section defines obtaining property as obtaining ownership, possession or control of it, and 'obtain' includes obtaining for another or enabling another to obtain or to retain. Thus enabling another person to retain property is an offence. 'Deception' means any deception (whether deliberate or reckless) by words or conduct as to fact or as to law, including a deception as to the present intentions of the person using the deception or any other person. It seems that someone can be deceived by silence:

Silverman (1987) D charged elderly customers excessive amounts for

234

repairs to their flat. He had not pressurised them to accept his quotation. CA: quashed his conviction because of an inadequate summing up, yet stressed that where there is a situation of mutual trust, an excessively high quotation could constitute a representation of the D's state of mind, that he did not intend to make an excessive profit (and see *Firth* (1989) at **11.39**).

This commonsense approach may add fuel to the argument for wider liability for omissions generally (see **2.12**).

11.36 As it was pointed out in **11.11**, there is now enormous overlap between theft and obtaining by deception. Many of the problems which apply in theft also apply here. First, dishonesty. Although the deception offences are not governed by s 2 (see s 1(3)), the courts have applied the *Ghosh* test (see **11.14**). As we saw at **11.15**, the Law Commission (1999) provisionally conclude that dishonesty should not be a separate element in deception offences. Secondly, the same problems arise in deciding whether a deceiver can be guilty of obtaining the same property more than once as applied to deciding whether theft was a continuing act. Since obtaining may be obtaining ownership, possession or control, it would appear that a thief who obtains control may subsequently become guilty of an offence under s 15 when he obtains ownership.

Rozeik (1996) D applied to two finance companies for funds by way of hire purchase agreements to purchase equipment for limited companies which he owned or controlled. He was convicted on 12 counts of dishonestly obtaining property (cheques) by falsely representing that the information in the agreements was true. CA: quashed his convictions. The deception had to operate on the mind of an employee from whom the cheque was obtained and who had authority to provide it; a cheque could not be obtained from an employee who merely typed it out: an employee whose state of mind stood as that of the company had to be deceived. D should have been charged with theft or conspiracy to defraud.

Preddy (1996) D supplied false information on a mortgage application to a building society. HL, reversing CA: quashed his conviction under s 15, since nothing which had belonged to V now belonged to D. A thing in action belonging to V had been diminished or extinguished, and a thing in action belonging to D had been enlarged or created.

Lord Jauncey: 'In Scotland common law and common sense rather than Parliamentary wisdom still prevail'.

The decision in *Preddy* created an important gap in the law. The Law Commission looked at the problem immediately and in Law Com No 243, *Offences of Dishonesty: Money Transfers,* recommended the enactment of two new offences: obtaining a money transfer by deception, and retaining credits from dishonest sources. This recommendation was accepted and sped through Parliament in record time becoming the Theft (Amendment) Act 1996. Section 1 inserts a new s 15A into the 1968 Act:

> (1) A person is guilty of an offence if by any deception he dishonestly obtains a money transfer for himself or another.
>
> (2) A money transfer occurs when -
> (a) a debit is made to one account,
> (b) a credit is made to another, and
> (c) the credit results from the debit or the debit results from the credit.
>
> (3) References to a credit and to a debit are to a credit of an amount of money and to a debit of an amount of money.

11.37 *(ii) Obtaining a pecuniary advantage by deception* (TA 1968 s16)

> (1) A person who by any deception dishonestly obtains for himself or another any pecuniary advantage shall on conviction on indictment be liable to imprisonment for a term not exceeding five years.
>
> (2) The cases in which a pecuniary advantage within the meaning of this section is to be regarded as obtained for a person are where -
> (a) [this has been repealed: see earlier, at **11.34**]
> (b) he is allowed to borrow by way of overdraft, or to take out any policy of insurance or annuity contract, or obtains an improvement of the terms on which he is allowed to do so; or
> (c) he is given the opportunity to earn remuneration or greater remuneration in an office or employment, or to win money by betting.

Students are sometimes tempted to think of money as a pecuniary advantage. No: it is of course property. The section creates one offence. The only pecuniary advantages which result in an offence under s 16 since the repeal of s 16(2)(a) are those very limited circumstances

236

described in s 16(2)(b) and (c): overdrafts, insurance and annuities, or opportunities to earn or win money.

McNiff (1986) D denied that he had previous convictions and gave inaccurate personal details in order to obtain the tenancy of a pub. CA: quashed his conviction under s 16(2)(c) since the obtaining of the tenancy was not an office or employment. Having obtained the tenancy, D was able to apply for a justices' license after which he would have the opportunity to earn remuneration, but the tenancy itself was not the equivalent of an opportunity to earn remuneration.

Callender (1993) D, a self-employed accountant, obtained work from clients by falsely claiming to hold CIMA qualifications. CA: upheld his conviction under s 16(2)(c). Employment was to be given its ordinary and natural meaning and not any narrow technical sense.

11.38   *(iii) Obtaining services by deception.* (TA 1978 s1)

(1) A person who by any deception dishonestly obtains services from another shall be guilty of an offence.

(2) It is an obtaining of services where the other is induced to confer a benefit buy doing some act, or causing or permitting some act to be done, on the understanding that the benefit has been or will be paid for.

The maximum penalty for this offence is five years' imprisonment. Note that if someone deceives someone into providing free benefits which they would otherwise have charged for then there is no offence.

In *Halai* (1983) the CA had held that obtaining a mortgage advance was not obtaining services, and the Law Com No 228 Conspiracy to Defraud (1994) recommended that this should be reversed. They proposed a new subsection to s 1 which would provide that

it is an obtaining of services where [a person] is induced to make a loan, or to cause or permit a loan to be made, on the understanding that any payment (whether by way of interest or otherwise) will be or has been made in respect of the loan.

However, this proposal has now been superseded by the Theft (Amendment) Act 1996, which introduced the new s 15A which covers the *Halai* situation (see **11.36**).

11.39   *(iv) Evasion of liability by deception* (TA 1978 s 2)

(1) Subject to subsection (2) below, where a person by any deception -

(a) dishonestly secures the remission of the whole or part of any existing liability to make a payment, whether his own liability or another's; or

(b) with intent to make permanent default in whole or in part on any existing liability to make a payment, or with intent to let another do so, dishonestly induces the creditor or any person claiming payment on behalf of the creditor to wait for payment (whether or not the due date for payment is deferred) or to forgo payment; or

(c) dishonestly obtains any exemption from or abatement of liability to make a payment; he shall be guilty of an offence.

(2) For purposes of this section 'liability' means legally enforceable liability; and subsection (1) shall not apply in relation to a liability that has not been accepted or established to pay compensation for a wrongful act or omission.

(3) For purposes of subsection (1)(b) a person induced to take in payment a cheque or other security for money by way of conditional satisfaction of a pre-exiting liability is to be treated not as being paid but as being induced to wait for payment.

(4) For purposes of subsection (1)(c) 'obtains' includes obtaining for another or enabling another to obtain.

Much the most difficult task for the student here is distinguishing the three ways that this offence may be committed. As JC Smith (1997) says, the section 'probably' creates three offences which are 'probably' not mutually exclusive:

For instance, D who secures the remission of a liability contrary to para (a) and who has an intent to make permanent default is almost certainly also guilty of inducing his creditor to forego payment contrary to para (b). If D has no intention to make permanent default, he may be guilty under (a) but not under (b); and if he induces P merely to forego payment (as distinct from remitting the liability – whatever that distinction may be) with intent to make permanent default, he is guilty under (b) but not under (a). The three offences overlap but it must be assumed that they are not coincident and that no one of them includes the whole of another (at page 136, para 4.88).

Thus, s 2(1)(b) requires an intention to make permanent default, but where there is such an intent it would seem that s 2(1)(a) overlaps with s 2(1)(b). Section 2(1)(c) is the only one not to require P to prove an existing liability. Another challenging question is why the behaviour in question needs to be criminalised: why is the civil law not adequate to deal with these offences?

> *Firth* (1989) D, a consultant obstetrician, omitted to inform his hospital that he had been treating private patients at his NHS hospital and had therefore avoided being billed for NHS beds and facilities. CA (Lord Lane CJ): upheld his conviction for an offence under s 2(1)(c) TA 1978. If it was incumbent upon him to give the information to the hospital and he deliberately refrained from doing so, with the result that no charge was levied either upon the patients or upon himself, the wording of the section is satisfied. 'It mattered not whether it was an act of commission or omission' (see **2.13**).

11.40 *The nature of deception* The CLRC (1966) preferred the term deception to 'false pretence'. It must be proved that D actually deceived someone and that this caused V to act. Only people can be deceived, not machines. Thus it appears that if you use someone else's PIN number to obtain money from the bank you may be guilty of theft but not of obtaining the money by deception. The ordinary meaning of 'to deceive' is 'to induce someone to believe that a thing which is false is true'. However, in the criminal law it may be a deception to falsely persuade someone that something only *may* be true

> *Lambie* (1982) D had been asked by the bank to return her credit card having exceeded her credit limit. Instead she continued to use it. She bought goods in a shop with it, the assistant having made the usual checks against the credit card. The shop manager gave evidence that she was not concerned about what went on between D and Barclaycard. HL, reversing CA: upheld her conviction under s 16. By tendering the credit card D was making a representation of actual authority to make the contract with the shop on the bank's behalf that the bank would honour the voucher when it was presented by the shop. Had the assistant known that the customer did not have the authority to make such representation, the inference was irresistible that she would not have allowed D to take the goods away.

The HL were obviously concerned by the enormous potential for fraud created by credit cards, but does this overcome the logical difficulty that the victim of the deception was genuinely indifferent whether or not she was deceived? The shop knew that they would be paid as long as they checked the signature, the current 'stop-list' etc. The banks introduced credit cards not for the convenience of their customers but because they knew that they were a wonderful way in which the bank could make more profit. Should it not be for the bank to control the abuse of their own inventions? The case of *Lambie* illustrates well the difficulty of drawing a line between civil and criminal law. Mrs Lambie never pretended to the bank that she was anyone but Mrs Lambie, nor did she deny her civil debt to the bank. What is it that makes her conduct criminal? If I lie to the plumber who comes and mends my dripping tap that I have lost my cheque book and have no cash on me, and I ask him to come back next week for the money, am I criminal? If he contacted the police, they would probably tell him that it sounded simply like a non-payment of a debt and that the plumber should sue me through the small claims court (at his own expense). What is it that is different about *Lambie* which allows the banks to sue for their bad debts at taxpayers' expense through the mechanism of the criminal justice process?

11.41 Another difficulty here is the overlap between these various offences, and indeed the student should be aware that there are many other offences beyond those raised in this book. Thus, not only may obtaining services by deception constitute an offence of theft or of obtaining property by deception, it may also be the obtaining of an unauthorised overdraft, or the procuring of a valuable security by deception (contrary to s 20 of the TA 1968). Does the principle of fair labelling (**1.2**) demand that these various offences be separated one from the other? Could the law be made simpler?

Law Comm Consultation Paper No 155 on *Fraud and Deception* (1999) considers, amongst other things, 'whether a general offence of fraud would improve the criminal law'. We noted their comments on dishonesty (**11.15**), which led them to conclude that proof of dishonesty should not be a separate element in deception offences. This would (of course) necessitate a new defence that the defendant secured the requisite consequence in the belief that he or she is legally entitled to do so, whether by deception or otherwise.

240

The Law Commission recommend a number of reforms: The *Preddy* - problems (**11.36**) could be avoided if for the purposes of the offence of obtaining property by deception, it was sufficient that the person to whom the property belongs is deprived of it by deception, whether or not anyone else obtains it. They propose that the 'intention permanently to deprive' in theft should be removed. This would inevitably criminalise certain trivial conduct and would increase reliance on prosecutorial discretion not to prosecute in appropriate cases.

They deprecate the association of deception with false representations: they argue that the question should simply be: did the defendant, by what he did, induce in the other a mistaken belief. Non-disclosure alone should not count as deception, whether or not there is a legal duty to disclose. Similarly, they criticise the 'constructive deception' applied in cases such as *Lambie*: 'we believe that deception should be understood as the inducing of a false belief – a psychological fact – rather than as something which by abstract analysis can be *deemed* to have occurred' (para 8.16). They therefore propose that the misuse of payment cards should form the subject matter of a new offence, adopting the suggestion of JC Smith (1996):

> A person commits an offence if he intentionally causes a legal liability to pay money to be imposed on another, knowing that the other does not consent to his doing so and that he has no right to do so (at page 40-41).

The Law Commission question whether the *mens rea* of this proposed offence should be intention, or whether recklessness would suffice. The development of internet commerce re-inforces the difficulties that arise from the fact that a machine cannot be deceived. The Law Commission provisionally conclude that it should be criminal to obtain a service without the permission of the person providing it, albeit without the deception of a human mind. This change, they suggest, should be effected by extending the offence of theft, rather than by extending the concept of deception. Do you agree?

Making off without payment

11.42 Section 3 of the Theft Act 1978 defines the offence of making off without payment:

(1) Subject to subsection 3 below, a person who, knowing that payment on the spot for any goods supplied or service done is required or expected from him, dishonestly makes off without having paid as required or expected and with intent to avoid payment of the amount due shall be guilty of an offence.

(2) For purposes of this section 'payment on the spot' includes payment at the time of collecting goods on which work has been done or in respect of which service has been provided.

(3) Subsection (1) above shall not apply where the supply of goods or the doing of the service is contrary to law, or where the service done is such that payment is not legally enforceable.

(4) Any person may arrest without warrant anyone who is, or whom he, with reasonable cause, suspects to be, committing or attempting to commit an offence under this section.

Making off without payment is triable either way, and has a maximum penalty when tried on indictment of two years' imprisonment. Since no deception need be proved it is a more minor offence than those discussed above. However, there is clearly a wide overlap with theft and obtaining by deception: where someone leaves a restaurant without paying, he may be prosecuted for theft or obtaining by deception if it can be proved that he never intended to pay. However, if D does not admit the offence, or does not admit that it was his intention at the time he obtained the food not to pay, P may instead charge him with making off without payment.

11.43 The *mens rea* of the offence is dishonesty + knowledge that payment on the spot is required + an intent to avoid payment permanently. It was not clear from s 3 whether D has to intend to avoid payment permanently but the HL decided that this was so:

Allen (1985) D left a hotel leaving an unpaid bill of £1,286. He rang the hotel two days later to explain that he was in financial difficulties but hoped to pay the bill a month later. When he returned a month later to collect his possessions he was arrested. HL (Lord Hailsham): upheld the CA's decision to quash his conviction for an offence under s 3. Whilst there might be something to say for a summary offence to punish those who abscond without paying as required, this was not what this offence did. At the very least it provided an equivocation which had to be resolved in D's favour.

242

Handling stolen goods

11.44 By s 22 of the Theft Act 1968:

(1) A person handles stolen goods if (otherwise than in the course of the stealing) knowing or believing them to be stolen goods he dishonestly receives the goods, or dishonestly undertakes or assists in their retention, removal, disposal or realisation by or for the benefit of another person, or if he arranges to do so.

Figure 5

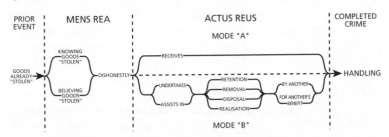

Reproduced with permission from (1983) 13 NLJ 844

Tunkel's diagram (figure 3) illustrates the different modes that handling can be committed. The penalty for this triable either way offence is up to a maximum of 14 years' imprisonment. Why is the maximum double the maximum for theft? The rationale is that some handlers are particularly culpable: those who commission specific offences of theft for example, or who are professional organisers or distributors of stolen goods. Without handlers, it is often said, there would be few thieves.

11.45 As Ashworth points out the offence of handling is drafted so widely as to 'cast a net around the main Theft Act offences' (PCL, p 410). He points out that in doing so, the offence assumes the role normally played by the doctrine of complicity and the inchoate offences, and since these doctrines still apply here, the scope of criminal liability is widened yet further.

Pitham (1976) M decided to steal and to sell an acquaintance's furniture, knowing the acquaintance was in prison. D1 and D2 paid a sum considerably less than they knew the furniture was worth. CA (Lawton LJ): as soon as M had assumed the rights of the owner, the appropriation was complete and the Ds were not dealing with the goods in the course of stealing.

243

Bloxham (1983) D innocently purchased a car, and then later realised that it must be stolen so sold it on to someone else. He was charged with . HL (Lord Bridge): a purchaser could not be 'another person' for whose benefit goods were realised or sold since it was the purchase, not the sale, that was for the purchaser's benefit. The purchase of goods by a person could not be described as a disposal or realisation of the goods 'by' him.

11.46 *Money laundering* Cases of 'money laundering' are now covered by a range of provisions inserted into the CJA 1988 by the CJA 1993, part III. These provisions were originally devised to deal with the proceeds of drug trafficking, but have now been extended to cover the proceeds of crime generally. The Money Laundering Regulations 1993 require those carrying on financial businesses to take various procedures to avoid involvement in money laundering. It may well be that where crooks arrange for the transfer, concealment and investment of the proceeds of crime, they will nowadays be prosecuted for 'assisting another to retain the benefit of criminal conduct' under s 93A of the CJA 1988. The T(A)A 1996 (see **11.36**), s 2 inserts a new s 24A into the TA 1968: dishonestly retaining a wrongful credit. These are both examples of the recent proliferation of criminal offences to deal with 'new' problems as perceived by the Government and Parliament. While it may be very important to be tough on those who profit from their own or other people's crimes, is the appropriate response to create new offences? (See also **11.41**.)

11.47 *Serious fraud* Much publicity has been given in recent years to the Serious Fraud Office's failures: set up in 1987 to investigate and to prosecute serious frauds, the SFO has a disappointing record in securing convictions in high profile (and costly) cases. These failures however are not so much a result of inadequate criminal law, but stem from difficulties in securing convincing evidence, despite the fact that the Office has wide powers to compel suspects to answer questions (which have recently been struck down by the ECHR in *Saunders v UK* (1996)). There are also arguments for abolishing trial by jury in this area, as was recommended by the Roskill Committee on Fraud Trials (1986), but would the abolition of juries in this area lead to their abolition altogether? In any case, is fraud innately more 'difficult' than, say, rape? It is worth considering what constitutes 'serious' fraud: if it is just the amount of money involved, why does this merit a different criminal procedure?

Further reading

Beatson and Simester, 'Stealing One's Own Property' (1999) 115 LQR 372

Criminal Law Revision Committee, Eighth Report, *Theft and Related Offences*, (1966) Cmnd 2977

Gardener, S, 'Property and Theft', [1998] Crim LR 35

Glanville Williams, 'Temporary appropriation should be theft' [1981] Crim LR 129

Glazebrook, 'Thief or Swindler: who cares?' (1991) CLJ 389

Glazebrook, 'Revising the Theft Acts' (1993) CLJ 191

Griew, 'Dishonesty: the Objections to Feeley and Ghosh' [1985] Crim LR 341

Guest, 'Law, Fact and Lay Questions' in *Criminal Law and Justice* (1987)

Law Commission Consultation Paper No 155 on Fraud and Deception (1999)

Smith, J C (1996) 28 Bracton LJ 27

Smith, J C (1997) *The Law of Theft* (8th ed)

Spencer, 'The Metamorphosis of s 6 Theft Act 1968' [1977] Crim LR 653

Spencer, 'The Theft Act 1978' [1979] Crim LR 24

Spencer, 'Theft – Appropriation and Consent' (1984) 43 Camb LJ 7

Self-test questions:

What offences have been committed in the following scenarios:

(i) Dee persuades Jo to buy Phil's hot-dog stand for £1,000 by persuading her that it is Dee's own. Phil, knowing nothing about the agreement, takes the stand around to Jo's house where he leaves it, believing that Jo is going to carry out some minor repairs for him. Dee meanwhile enters Phil's house because she is curious to see whether he has a large supply of hot-dogs. She trips and breaks a vase.

(ii) Dee takes Phil's season ticket for the football club, uses it twice and then returns it, but Phil has missed the match he most wanted to see.

(iii) Dee promises to mend Phil's bicycle tyre and asks for £5 in advance. She spends the money on beer and never does the repair. Would it make any difference if she had asked Phil for the £5 saying that she needed it to buy materials?

(iv) Dee breaks into Phil's office, and removes a copy of an exam paper that Phil has just set for the forthcoming exams. She photo-copies it and returns the original. She shows the copy to her friend Ann. She then makes an imaginary paper, and sells a copy of it to Belinda for £5, pretending that it is a copy of the real paper.

(v) Dee obtains a student railcard by falsely representing that she is a student.

(vi) Dee finds Phil's credit card and takes it to the bank. She inserts it into the cash machine and the first PIN number she invents works. She asks the machine to £100 cash which it gives her, and then transfers £50 from Fred's account to her own at the same bank.

CHAPTER TWELVE

Criminal damage and public order offences

SUMMARY

Criminal damage and arson: distinguish simple and aggravated criminal damage. If the offence is committed by fire, it is arson. Wide definition of destroying or damaging property. *Mens rea* – objective recklessness.

Offences under the Public Order Act 1986: but what is public order?

Riot: 12 or more people using or threatening unlawful violence for a common purpose

Violent disorder: three or more people using or threatening unlawful violence for a common purpose

Affray: using or threatening violence in a group

Other offences (eg fear or provocation of violence; causing harassment, alarm or distress): are they necessary or could public order be maintained simply by the enforcement of other criminal laws?

12.1 A discussion of criminal damage could as easily have sat in a chapter on theft, since it is an offence against property. Yet criminal damage in every day speech is often simply vandalism, which can be seen as an offence against good order. Not all syllabi include public order offences (so check!), but they are included briefly in this book in order to provide a comparison with other offences of violence. Given the existence of the offences of violence discussed in chapter 9, do we need these substantive public order offences? Whilst the offences found in

247

the Public Order Acts (POA) are primarily designed to deal with group offending, there is nothing to stop the prosecution of 'rioters' under the OAPA 1861. A rioter who seriously injures someone, for example, will be guilty of an offence under s 20 of the OAPA 1861 (see **9.8**). The POA 1986 consolidated and strengthened existing public order law. It abolished a number of common law offences (including riot, unlawful assembly and affray) and replaced them with statutory offences. It also extended controls over processions and public assemblies. The language of the POA seems somewhat confrontational. It starts: Part I: New Offences. Part II then deals with the new rules surrounding processions and assemblies. Think how you would draw up such a statute. For example, the Immigration Act 1971, whilst severely limiting immigration into this country, started with a section of 'General Principles' which specifies that all those who have the right of abode in the UK shall be free to live in, and to come and go into and from the UK (subject of course to the limitations described later in the Act). Should the POA have started with a general right to process and to demonstrate, before proceeding to the limitations on these rights?

12.2 Whilst it is clearly a vital police function to maintain public order, do they have sufficient powers to prevent disorder without the need for these additional offences? You might argue that what the POA adds to the 'armoury' of criminal law is more symbolic than real: the police will often choose to rely on other powers. Their common law powers include the power to arrest for a breach of the peace, and they have other statutory powers beyond the offences in the OAPA: the power to ban wilful obstructions of the highway, contrary to s 137 of the Highways Act 1980, for example. It is also an offence under s 89 of the Police Act 1996 to assault a constable in the execution of his duty. One 'weapon' frequently used has been to 'bind people over to be of good behaviour' but this power of the magistrates has recently been struck down by the ECHR:

Hashman and Harrup v UK (2000) Ds, who had been disrupting a hunt by shouting and sounding horns, were bound over to keep the peace and to be of good behavior for 12 months. ECHR: 16-1: There was a violation of art 11 of the ECHR (see **1.23**). Ds did not breach the peace, and it could not be said that what they were being bound over not to do must have been apparent to them.

Law Comm No 22 (1994) had recommended that binding over orders should be abolished without replacement. The Government has yet to take action.

12.3 The POA 1986 has been reinforced by a welter of additional provisions in the Criminal Justice and Public Order Act 1994. Many people, including police officers, argued at that time that what was needed were not more powers but greater resources. The 'criminals' in this area are often football hooligans, travellers, strike pickets, and those generally at the bottom of the social hierarchy. Here we are in the most obviously political area of criminal law: who is to define what is order and what is not, who is acting lawfully and who unlawfully? The POA and the CJPOA 1994 were 'political' measures: do you think they are reactions to people's legitimate fears of public disorder, or do the media and politicians create a moral panic? This latter viewpoint is adopted by Lacey, Wells and Meure (1998), who describe the principal actors in the social construction of the 'law and order problem' as the news media and their intended audience, the police and political institutions. At **9.29**, we asked whether the Protection from Harassment Act 1997 was an appropriate response (with its mixture of civil and criminal sanctions) to the public's concern about harassment. Then at **9.37** the racially aggravated offences added to the Crime and Disorder Act 1998 were discussed: s 30 introduces a new offence of racially-aggravated criminal damage; and s 31 creates three racially aggravated offences based on the offences in ss 4,4A and 5 of the Public Order Act 1986 (see **12.17-12.20**), ie:

- racially aggravated fear or provocation of violence

- racially aggravated intentional harassment, alarm or distress

- racially aggravated harassment, alarm or distress.

Would better community policing deal with the problem more effectively than the enactment of more legislation?

12.4 Many of the most interesting cases are not strictly criminal, but have involved people using judicial review proceedings to challenge the decisions of the police, or other bodies, to use their powers in what is considered by another person or body to be an improper way. Consider how you would have decided the following cases:

R v Somerset County Council, ex p Fewings (1995) A group of huntsman sought judicial review of a local authority's decision to ban fox hunting on their land, arguing that the local authority was acting on moral grounds, which were outside their statutory powers to 'benefit, improve or develop' their local area. CA (by a majority of 2-1): upheld the judge's decision to quash the local authority's decision. There were three judgements, with Simon Brown LJ dissenting on the main issue of whether the local authority had acted unlawfully; Swinton Brown LJ dissenting on the question whether a cruelty argument is necessarily irrelevant to a consideration of what is for the benefit of the area.

R v Coventry City Council, ex p Phoenix Aviation(1995) In three separate applications for judicial review the question arose whether public authorities operating air and sea ports were entitled to ban the flights or shipment of livestock by animal exporters in order to avoid the disruptive consequences of animal rights demonstrations. DC (Simon Brown LJ): ordered the port authorities to accept the livestock trade. 'One thread runs consistently throughout all the case law: the recognition that public authorities must beware of surrendering to the dictates of unlawful pressure groups ... If ever there were cases demanding the court's intervention in support of the rule of law, these are they'.

12.5 These cases illustrate the fundamental dilemma. Who is acting unlawfully? Why did Simon Brown LJ in the *Phoenix Aviation* case talk of 'unlawful' pressure groups? Drawing the line between who is and who is not acting lawfully in these situations is a near impossible task. In *R v Chief Constable of Devon and Cornwall, ex p Central Electricity Board* (1982) Lord Denning MR said

There is a breach of the peace whenever a person who is lawfully carrying out his work is unlawfully and physically prevented by another from doing it.

Of course people have a right to go about their lawful business. But you also have a right to demonstrate. If your demonstration is to bring your cause successfully to the public attention it may well be inevitable that people are prevented from crossing the road for a minute or two, or are prevented from taking their lorry where they want for a short while. Are you inevitably breaking the law? Anyone who attends a peaceful demonstration should be aware that they are at risk of finding themselves

250

the wrong side of the criminal law. Where does this leave the right to demonstrate lawfully?

Criminal damage and arson

12.6 The Malicious Damage Act 1861 was replaced by the Criminal Damage Act 1971. Section 1 provides:

> (1) A person who without lawful excuse destroys or damages any property belonging to another intending to destroy or damage any such property or being reckless as to whether any such property would be destroyed or damaged shall be guilty of an offence.

An aggravated form of the offence is to be found in s 1(2):

> A person who without lawful excuse destroys or damages any property, whether belonging to himself or another -
> (a) intending to destroy or damage any property or being reckless as to whether any property would be destroyed or damaged; and
> (b) intending by the destruction or damage to endanger the life of another or being reckless as to whether the life of another would be thereby endangered;
> shall be guilty of an offence.

If the offence is committed by fire, it is charged as arson (s 1(3)). The maximum penalty for simple or aggravated arson is life imprisonment; whereas the maximum sentence for 'simple' criminal damage is 10 years' imprisonment.

12.7 *Actus reus* Destroying or damaging property has been defined very widely: in *Whiteley* (1993), which concerned interference with a computer disc, Lord Lane CJ said that 'any alteration to the physical nature of the property concerned may amount to damage within the meaning of the section'. Property is defined for the purpose of this Act in s 10: it is wider than the definition in the TA 1968 in that it does not exclude land, but it is narrower in that it does not include things in action or intangible property.

12.8 The *mens rea* of criminal damage is objective recklessness. As Lord Diplock said in *Metropolitan Police Comr v Caldwell* (1982: see **3.22**):

a person charged with an offence under s 1(1) of the CDA 1971 is 'reckless as to whether any such property would be destroyed or damaged' if (1) he does an act which in fact creates an obvious risk that property will be destroyed or damaged and (2) when he does the act he either has not given any thought to the possibility of there being any such risk or has recognised that there was some risk involved and has nonetheless gone on to do it ...Neither state of mind seems to me to be less blameworthy than the other; but if the difference between the two constituted the distinction between what does and what does not in legal theory amount to a guilty state of mind for the purpose of a statutory offence of damage to property, it would not be a practicable distinction for use in a trial by jury.

12.9 *The defence of lawful excuse* We saw at **4.23** that s 5 provides a defence of lawful excuse. By s 5(2), D has a lawful excuse for causing criminal damage

(a) if at the time of the act or acts alleged to constitute the offence he believed that the person or person whom he believed to be entitled to consent to the destruction of or damage to the property in question had so consented, or would have so consented to it if he or they had known of the destruction or damage and its circumstances; ...

This leads to the acquittal of those whose mistaken beliefs may be caused by their own drunkenness, particularly since s 5(3) states that

For the purposes of this section it is immaterial whether a belief is justified or not if it is honestly held.

Jaggard v Dickinson (1981) D, who had been drinking, mistook V's house for that of her friend, with whom she had planned to stay. Finding the house locked and no-one at home, she broke a window in order to get in. She was convicted of criminal damage. DC (Mustill J): quashed her conviction. The defence under s 5(2)(a) of the CDA 1971 was still available although D was drunk.

The court is required by s 5(3) to focus on the existence of the belief, not its intellectual soundness; and a belief can be just as much honestly held if it is induced by intoxication, as if it stems from stupidity, forgetfulness or inattention.

See **4.24** for a discussion of this defence.

252

Public order offences

12.10 Public order offences typically penalise group offending. Does this offend against the principle that criminal responsibility is generally personal and individual? Compare these offences with comments made in the chapter on accomplices on the common purpose rules (see **6.20**). You might have thought that another characteristic of public order offences would have been that they must take place in public but this is not so: *DPP v Orum* (1988) (see **12.20**) is an example of the POA 1986 being enforced in a domestic matter, and against one single offender. Is this appropriate?

Riot

12.11 Section 1 of the Public Order Act 1986 provides:

(1) Where 12 or more people who are present together use or threaten unlawful violence for a common purpose and the conduct of them (taken together) is such as would cause a person of reasonable firmness present at the scene to fear for his personal safety, each of the persons using unlawful violence for the common purpose is guilty of riot.

(2) It is immaterial whether or not the 12 or more use or threaten unlawful violence simultaneously.

(3) The common purpose may be inferred from conduct.

(4) No person of reasonable firmness need actually be, or be likely to be, present at the scene.

(5) Riot may be committed in private as well as in public places.

Riot is triable only on indictment and the maximum sentence is 10 years' imprisonment or a fine, or both. The *mens rea* is intention or awareness. Should this awareness be replaced by a subjective form of recklessness as recommended by the DCC (in clause 198)? This would involve in addition to awareness of the relevant risk an awareness that it is unreasonable to take it. However, it is difficult to see how a person could claim that it was reasonable for him to take the risk that his conduct might be violent or his behaviour threatening, so the difference is not great. It was noted at **4.24** that s 6(5) of the POA 1986 makes clear that awareness impaired by self-induced intoxication is no defence. This avoids the need to apply the difficult *Majewski* rule (see **4.17**). The section places on D the burden of proving that his intoxication was involuntary: is this appropriate?

12.12   How does riot vary from an offence under the OAPA? The key must be the concept of collective violence. An offender is only guilty under the POA 1986 if the 12 were together using or threatening violence. Should the fact that several people are involved make it a different offence or should it merely affect the sentence? While it is clearly an aggravating feature of an offence that there was a group of people who put others in fear, these factors would justify a higher sentence if the offender were simply charged under the OAPA.

> *Sallis* (1993) D prisoners were convicted of riot after disturbances at a prison remand centre, during which two prison officers were badly injured and damage of £1.3 million was caused. CA: upheld sentences of four and a half and five years on two prisoners who had been ring leaders.

Do you think riot was the appropriate offence in this case?

Violent disorder

12.13   Section 2 of the Public Order Act 1986 provides:

> (1) Where three or more people who are present together use or threaten unlawful violence for a common purpose and the conduct of them (taken together) is such as would cause a person of reasonable firmness present at the scene to fear for his personal safety, each of the persons using or threatening unlawful violence is guilty of violent disorder.

> (2) It is immaterial whether or not the three or more use or threaten unlawful violence simultaneously.

> (3) No person of reasonable firmness need actually be, or be likely to be, present at the scene.

254

(5) Violent disorder may be committed in private as well as in public places.

Although violent disorder is triable either way (see 1.12), it is generally committed for trial in the Crown Court. The maximum penalty is five years' imprisonment, a fine or both. The key again is the number of people present: three of more people using or threatening violence. Section 6(7) provides that where one or more Ds are acquitted because they lack *mens rea*, the determination of the number of people involved is unaffected.

Affray

12.14   Section 3 of the Public Order Act 1986 provides:

(1) A person is guilty of affray if he uses or threatens unlawful violence towards another and his conduct is such as would cause a person of reasonable firmness present at the scene to fear for his personal safety.

(2) Where two or more persons use or threaten the unlawful violence, it is the conduct of them taken together that must be considered for the purposes of subsection (1).

(3) For the purposes of this section a threat cannot be made by the use of words alone.

(4) No person of reasonable firmness need actually be, or be likely to be, present at the scene.

(5) Affray may be committed in private as well as in public places.

The maximum punishment for affray is three years' imprisonment, but since it is a triable either way offence, which is normally tried summarily, the penalties are usually much less.

12.15   Since a threat cannot be made by words alone (see s 3(3)), there must be some conduct on the part of the accused but this may be minimal.

Dixon (1993) When the police arrived at a domestic incident, D ran

255

away accompanied by his alsatian-type dog. He encouraged the dog to attack the policemen who eventually cornered him. Two officers were bitten before reinforcements arrived and the man was arrested. CA: upheld his conviction for an offence under s 3 POA 1986.

If the dog had not attacked, do you think that the court would have held that the order to the dog constituted conduct?

12.16 Note in s 3(4) that no person of reasonable firmness need be present at the scene.

> *Davison* (1992) The police were called to a domestic incident at a house. D waved an 8 inch knife at a police officer saying 'I'll have you'. CA: upheld his conviction for an offence under s 3 POA 1986.

Is this a suitable case for the application of s 3? The common law offence of affray had typically been charged in cases of street battles between gangs or fights outside pubs. JC Smith suggests (at (1992) Crim LR 33) that the OAPA 1861 should be used for the protection of those at whom the violence is aimed, whereas affray should be used for the protection of a bystander who would have been frightened.

Fear or provocation of violence

12.17 Section 4 of the POA 1986 states:

> (1) A person is guilty of an offence if he:
> (a) uses towards another person threatening, abusive or insulting words or behaviour, or
> (b) distributes or displays to another person any writing, sign or other visible representation which is threatening, abusive or insulting,
> with intent to cause that person to believe that immediate unlawful violence will be used against him or another by any person, or to provoke the immediate use of unlawful violence by that person or another, or whereby that person is likely to believe that such violence will be used or it is likely that such violence will be provoked.
>
> (2) ...

This offence is triable summarily only, and is subject to a maximum of six months' imprisonment (though the racially aggravated version of the offence, mentioned at **12.3** has a maximum sentence of two years' imprisonment). It can be committed in four different ways. D uses threatening words or behaviour, or distributes or displays such threatening, abusive or insulting material and, either:

(i) D may intend his victim to believe that immediate unlawful violence will be used against him or another person; or

(ii) D may intend to provoke immediate unlawful violence by that person; or

(iii) the victim is likely to believe that violence will be used; or

(iv) simply, it is likely that violence will be provoked.

12.18 The phrase 'threatening, abusive or insulting words or behaviour' is not defined. However, the words are not the creation of this Act.

> *Brutus v Cozens* (1973) D ran onto a tennis court during a match at Wimbledon blowing a whistle and distributing leaflets against apartheid in South Africa. The whole protest lasted two or three minutes. He argued that he had no intention to break the law: it was an entirely peaceful protest. He was charged (and acquitted by magistrates) of insulting behaviour, whereby a breach of the peace was likely to be occasioned, contrary to s 5 of the POA 1936 (since repealed). HL: 'insulting' was to be given its ordinary meaning and the question whether words or behaviour are insulting is a question of fact.

It has been held that masturbating in a public lavatory in the sight of another person, or homosexuals kissing at a bus stop can constitute insulting behaviour. Whilst these acts may be offensive to some people, does this mean they are 'insulting'? Should the judge or jury decide the issue? Remember Guest's argument discussed at **11.14**, in relation to the meaning of the word 'dishonesty, that judges should identify the state of affairs which were envisaged to be within the scope of the relevant law. A judge who hands over a question of interpreting the law to the jury is abdicating her constitutional responsibility.

Intentionally causing harassment, alarm or distress

12.19   Section 4A (inserted by s 154 of the CJPOA 1994)

(1) A person is guilty of an offence if, with intent to cause a person harassment, alarm or distress, he -

(a) uses threatening, abusive or insulting words or behaviour, or disorderly behaviour, or

(b) displays any writing, sign or other visible representation which is threatening, abusive or insulting,

thereby causing that or another person harassment, alarm or distress.

This too is a summary offence, punishable with up to six months imprisonment or a fine (though the racially aggravated version of the offence, mentioned at **12.3** has a maximum sentence of two years' imprisonment). The offence is similar to the offence under s 5, except that s 4A is more serious: D must be proved to have intended to cause harassment, alarm or distress.

Harassment, alarm or distress

12.20   Section 5 of the POA 1986 provides that:

(1) A person is guilty of an offence if he -

(a) uses threatening, abusive or insulting words or behaviour, or disorderly behaviour, or

(b) displays any writing, sign or other visible representation which is threatening, abusive or insulting, within the hearing or sight of a person likely to be caused harassment, alarm or distress thereby.

The maximum sentence is a level 3 fine, with a guideline fine of £180 (though the racially aggravated version of the offence, mentioned at **12.3** has a maximum sentence of a level 4 fine). The person who is likely to be caused harassment, alarm or distress may be the police officer called to the scene of a domestic disturbance:

DPP v Orum (1988) D was having an offensive and public argument with his girlfriend. He was abusive to a police officer who intervened and was arrested for breach of the peace. He assaulted the police officer in the back of the police van, and was later charged with, and convicted of, offences under s 5 POA 1986 and with assaulting a police officer in the execution of his duty. DC (Glidewell LJ): a police officer may be a person who would be likely to be harassed, alarmed or distressed for the purposes of s 5(1).

Is this a surprising use of a pubic order offence? Brown and Ellis (1994) doubt whether grossly insulting abuse would cause alarm and distress except to unduly sensitive officers. Their study of the policing of low level disorder suggests that many incidents follow a spiral of warning/ abuse/arrest, and they conclude that s 5 should not be used merely to restore order by removing drunk participants from the streets: for that purpose, the police should arrest people for being drunk and disorderly or for causing a breach of the peace. They argue that it is more efficacious if s 5 is reserved for cases in which the public genuinely suffer significant harassment.

Other offences of public order

12.21 The POA is far from comprehensive. There are many offences which pre-date it such as obstruction of the highway contrary to the HA 1980, public nuisance, outraging public decency, seditious and criminal libel. Not all the POA 1936 has been repealed: for example, it remains an offence under s 1 POA 1936 to wear a uniform for a political objective. There are also other offences which have been created since the POA 1986, such as those enacted in the CJPOA 1994. Thus ss 70 and 71 insert into the POA 1986 new sections 14A, 14B and 14C, creating offences in connection with organising or participating in a trespassory assembly, or incitement to an offence.

> *DPP v Jones* (1999) In 1995 the Chief Constable of Wiltshire obtained an order banning trespassory assemblies within four miles of Stonehenge for four days. On the last day, 21 people gathered on the grass verge on the main road near Stonehenge. Ds were convicted of an offence under s 14B(2) of the 1994 Act. HL (3-2): the assembly had not been shown to be trespassory, largely because Ds had not exceeded the public's right of access but also because of their right to peaceful assembly protected by art 11 of the ECHR (see **1.23**).

The CJPOA 1994, s 68 creates an offence of aggravated trespass:

> (1) A person commits the offence of aggravated trespass if he trespasses

259

on land in the open air and, in relation to any lawful activity which persons are engaging in or are about to engage in on that or adjoining land in the open air, does there anything which is intended by him to have the effect-

(a) of intimidating those persons or any of them so as to deter them or any of them from engaging in that activity,

(b) of obstructing that activity, or

(c) of disrupting that activity.

This summary offence, subject to a maximum sentence of three months' imprisonment or a fine or both, is designed to deal with people who are interrupting such activities as hunting or the construction of controversial roads. Section 63 creates offences in relation to raves: it is an offence for a person who knows that the police have given a direction ordering people to leave land to fail to leave as soon as is reasonably practicable.

12.22 In conclusion, reconsider these offences. If you were drawing up a Criminal Code would you include a separate category of 'public order offences'? Note that the DCC gathers together offences concerned with the preservation of public order and safety under the title 'Offences against public peace and safety'. Is this a better description? Criminal damage and arson are included by the drafters of the DCC in a separate chapter called 'Other offences relating to property' (immediately following the chapter on theft, fraud and related offences, as in this book).

Further reading

Smith ATH *Offences against public order* (1987)

Brown and Ellis *Policing Low Levels of Disorder* (HMSO, 1994; HORS No 135)

Self-test questions

1. Are the offences in the Public Order Act 1986 necessary?

2. A large crowd gathers at the docks to protest against the export abroad of young animals in small crates. Dee and Bee, peace-loving vegetarians, wave banners saying 'You lorry drivers are murderous

bastards' and 'Anyone who works in this trade deserves to be eaten'. Many others in the crowd, including Fee, throw bottles at lorries which arrive at the dock. Discuss the criminal liability of Dee, Bee and Fee.

CHAPTER THIRTEEN

Crimes against the environment

SUMMARY

This brief chapter looks at an unusual area of criminal law in order to conclude a review of the general principles of criminal law.

The use of the criminal law to protect the environment has developed in a piecemeal way, as a response to specific problems: see the Public Health Act 1875; the Town and Country Planning Act 1947. Now, the whole subject of environmental protection has moved centre stage and it is appropriate to review the use of the criminal law in this field: see the Water Resources Act 1991; the Environment Act 1995. This leads us to end where we started: with a search for first principles.

Introduction

13.1 It is unusual in a book of this kind to include a chapter on environmental crimes. Indeed, the subject as such is rarely on criminal law syllabi. Beware: you may not need to 'know' this chapter! However, it provides a useful way of concluding a review of criminal law:

(i) identifying crimes against the environment raises fundamental questions about the nature of crime generally. The criminal law may be particularly useful here where there are no obvious victims who might otherwise sue in tort, and of course a criminal prosecution may generate more publicity than a civil action, thus reinforcing the educative message. But what happens when the criminal law is widely flouted? In the last 10 years, for example, water companies have been prosecuted more than 300 times for water quality offences.

(ii) these crimes, lying as they do at the edge of traditional ideas of crime cause us to re-assess our views on key issues: strict liability, causation, corporate liability etc.

13.2 *History of environmental protection* With the industrialisation of Britain in the last century, an awareness slowly developed that many of the features of economic growth brought with them large problems. Uncontrolled industrialisation was likely to lead to public health disasters. Legal controls were slowly introduced in order to protect people's health as well as the health of the environment in which they lived. A landmark was the Public Health Act 1875, designed to protect health and improve standards of housing in the fast growing and filthy urban slums. This Act included criminal sanctions, often on a strict liability basis. At **3.39** various 19th century cases under the Licensing Act 1872 were used to illustrate the fundamental problems of strict liability: the problems live with us today. Legal controls over town planning and the environment developed more slowly than public health legislation; here the landmark statutes might include the Town and Country Planning Act 1947, the Clean Air Act 1956 (passed as a response to London smog), and the Control of Pollution Act 1974 which perhaps marked the beginning of modern environmental thinking. Not all criminal offences are found only in primary legislation: see, by way of example, the Producer Responsibility Obligations (Packaging Waste) Regulations 1997, which requires businesses to achieve minimum levels of recycling.

13.3 In the last 20 years there has been a huge increase in the awareness of the devastating impact of many activities (especially industrial activities) on the environment, and the result has been a number of statutes aiming to achieve a new balance between the advantages of industrial development and the need to protect the environment. The Water Act 1989, the Environmental Protection Act 1990, the Water Resources Act 1991, the Clean Air Act 1993, and the Environment Act 1995 all reflect the strengthening of Government commitment in this area. In 1996 the Environment Agency took over the work of three previously independent bodies, Her Majesty's Inspectorate of Pollution, the National Rivers Authority and the Waste Regulation Authorities. Its principal aim is to secure protection of the environment so as to achieve sustainable development. How well it achieves its aims will, of course, depend largely on the resources allocated to it, but it is worth considering here the extent to which it should (and does) use the criminal law.

13.4 The law can be used to protect the environment in many ways, and it is not obvious that criminal sanctions are always appropriate. Thus, environmental protection may be achieved through civil claims for damages in tort (particularly negligence, nuisance and *Rylands v Fletcher* (see Hedley (2000), chapter 7). From the perspective of the Environment Agency, the main routes to environmental protection are likely to be education, advice, Codes of Practice and administrative regulations, such as permits and licenses for exploiting the environment. Civil sanctions may be more appropriate than criminal ones, especially since the burden of proof is lower. Even where the criminal law is seen to be a suitable weapon, the emphasis will remain on prevention before the event rather than on punishment after the event. For example, Hutter analysed the work of Environmental Health Officers (1988), exploring how the criminal law is used to regulate business activities. Where the offender is seen as basically 'good and respectable', the enforcement agency concerned tends to adopt what may be described as an accommodative approach, seeking compliance through negotiation. Only where the alleged offender is seen as 'bad' does the agency need to enforce compliance. Compliance is also necessary since if the regulator does not get the co-operation of the offender, they will often not discover offending, until 'accidents' happen. The aim of this compliance strategy is prevention, not punishment. The agency negotiates with the firms against whom they are enforcing the law.

13.5 *Sources of environmental criminal law* Domestic legislation is far from the only source of environmental law. In 'traditional' areas of criminal law we are beginning to see a more global thinking: the Sexual Offence (Conspiracy and Incitement) Act 1996 was noted at **7.3** and the problem of enforcing thefts and frauds abroad was discussed at **11.12**. Similar problems arise with environmental protection, much of which has been perceived to be global for a long time. There are a vast number of international treaties governing the environment: from the Treaty banning Nuclear Tests in the Atmosphere, in Outer Space and Under Water (1963), to the International Convention on the Prevention of Marine Pollution by Dumping of Wastes and other matter (1972), to the more recent Directives of the European Union. According to Hughes (1996 at page 142), there were well over 400 EU legislative instruments on the environment between 1967 and 1994. Globalisation is doubtless to be a feature of criminal law in the future.

Examples of environmental crimes

13.6 Although the emphasis today has shifted from simple pollution control towards more positive environmental management, more integrated pollution prevention and control, here we will look simply at two examples of the criminal law being used to protect the environment: one in relation to water, the other in relation to air.

13.7 *Criminal sanctions under the Water Resources Act 1991* This Act consolidated various enactments relating to the National Rivers Authority, which itself was the creation of the Water Act 1989, which provided for the privatisation and restructuring of the water industry in England and Wales. Thus, water abstraction is now governed by a licensing system which controls the amount of water removed from streams and rivers. Section 24 creates an offence of abstracting water illegally. Perhaps more importantly, Part III of the Act is entitled Control of Pollution of Water Resources, and Chapter II of Part III contains 'Principal Offences'.

Section 85(1) provides that

> a person contravenes this section if he causes or knowingly permits any poisonous, noxious or polluting matter or any solid waste matter to enter any controlled waters.

The section continues by setting out various circumstances in which it may be contravened. The penalty is set out in sub-s (6):

> Subject to the following provisions of this Chapter, a person who contravenes this section or the conditions of any consent given under this Chapter for the purpose of this section shall be guilty of an offence and liable –
> (a) on summary conviction, to imprisonment for a term not exceeding three months or to a fine not exceeding £20,000 or to both;
> (b) on conviction on indictment, to imprisonment for a term not exceeding two years or to a fine or to both.

13.8 The section therefore creates two offences: causing pollution and knowingly permitting pollution. Look back at our discussion of *Alphacell Ltd v Woodward* (1972) (at **2.23**). The HL's 'common sense' approach involved deciding whether someone 'causes' something when they do nothing. Since then there have been many other prosecutions. For example,

National Rivers Authority v Yorkshire Water Services Ltd (1995) D owned and operated sewage works, which operated largely by gravity: from the settlement tanks, sewage flowed through filter beds and settlement tanks until it was eventually discharged into a river. D had permission to discharge sewage in accordance with certain conditions. They in turn granted consent to their industrial customers to discharge effluent into the sewers. These conditions excluded the discharge of iso-octonal, which is very dangerous to river life. An unauthorised and undiscovered person made a large discharge of iso-octonal into the sewer. D was convicted by the magistrates of causing pollution, their appeal was allowed by CC, which held that as a matter of law the water authority did not cause the iso-octonal to enter controlled waters. DC (Buckley J): reversed decision of CC, applying the 'common sense approach of the HL in *Alphacell*'. HL (Lord Mackay): allowed D's appeal, since Yorkshire Water had a due diligence defence under s 108(7) of the Act.

13.9 The case provides an excellent example of conflicting policy interests: the DC's judgement, whilst disappointing for those who care primarily for environmental control, had put an extraordinary burden on industry. The appeal in the DC turned on whether causation was a question of law or fact. Buckley J, applying *Brutus v Cozens* (1973; see **12.18**) held that 'I am satisfied that once the facts have been established, whether any party may be said to have 'caused' a certain result is itself a factual conclusion for the tribunal'. Despite the fact that, as Buckley J pointed out, 'Yorkshire Water could not reasonably be expected to prevent the discharge of iso-octonal into the sewer or indeed into the works', he concluded that the question of causation should simply be left to the jury or magistrates, allowing them to use their 'common sense'. But the decision of the HL may be hardly less satisfactory: many of the key questions were left unexplored. The Lord Chancellor held that Yorkshire Water Services could not reasonably have been expected to prevent the discharge of the iso-octanol. They could not have known of its presence until it had entered the works, at the earliest. Thereafter its discharge into controlled water was 'inevitable'. With respect, this conclusion is surely open to challenge. Yorkshire Water could monitor all sewage entering its works, and could provide a shut-down system (albeit at great expense). Many of the key questions were left unexplored.

13.10 This case has been superceded by another in which the magistrates, Crown Court , Div Ct and HL all agreed:

Empress Car Co (Abertillery) Ltd v National Rivers Authority (1998) D company maintained a diesel tank in a yard. The tap to the tank was opened by a person unknown (who could have been an employee or a complete stranger) and the entire contents of the tank ran into a drum, overflowed into the yard and passed down a drain into a river. D's defence to a   charge under s 85 of the Water Resources Act 1991 was that 'causing' required some positive act and that the escape could not be said to have been caused by the company. HL (Lord Hoffman): dismissed D's appeal. It was open to the magistrates to hold that Ds caused the oil to enter the controlled waters. It is wrong and distracting to ask 'what caused the pollution?'. The only question is 'did D cause the pollution'

> One cannot give a common sense answer to a question of causation for the purpose of attributing responsibility under some rule without knowing the purpose and scope of the rule ... If D did something which produced a situation in which the polluting matter could escape but a necessary condition of the actual escape which happened was also the act of a third party or a natural event, the justices should consider whether that act or event should be regarded as a normal fact of life or something extraordinary. If it was in the general run of things a matter of ordinary occurrence, it will not negative the causal effect of D's acts, even if it was not foreseeable that it would happen to that particular D or take that particular form. If it can be regarded as something extraordinary, it will be open to the justices to hold that D did not cause the pollution.

Contrast this 'common sense' approach to causation with that taken in homicide cases. At **2.16** we distinguished factual causation from legal or imputable causation. There the conclusion was that the main justification for these complicated rules on causation was the law's concern to say that D only 'caused' a death if he was blameworthy. The same concerns do not appear in this area. Which approach do you prefer? Another question is who should decide if D 'caused' an event, whether the event is a death or an act of pollution: a professional, or a body of lay people. The evidence in a pollution case may be highly technical, and a verdict may have to strike a balance between economic and environmental factors. Is a jury the right body to decide these issues? The same question was asked in relation to serious fraud [**11.47**].

13.11   *Fire and smoke* The Clean Air Act 1993 was passed to prevent air pollution and creates a number of offences. Thus, for example, s 2:

(1) Dark smoke shall not be emitted from any industrial or trade premises and if, on any day, dark smoke is so emitted the occupier of the premises and any person who causes or permits the emission shall be guilty of an offence.

This is drafted similarly to the water protection offences described above. It raises similar questions of causation and strict liability.

O'Fee v Copeland Borough Council (1995) D, a farmer, was prosecuted for emitting dark smoke from a fire more than 600 meters from the boundary of his farm. The question was whether it was necessary to prove that the smoke emitted over and beyond the farmer's own land. D argued that ownership of land gives rights in the space above that land, and that a penal statute should not be construed as limiting those rights unless plain language is used. DC (Pill LJ): dismissed the appeal. Section 2 applies to black smoke in the air within the boundaries of the relevant premises. Thus it was not necessary for P to prove that dark smoke emitted beyond the territorial boundary of the land.

Do you think that D in this case should feel aggrieved? In chapter 1, we discussed the nature of a crime. Fundamental was the principle of autonomy. Yet in this area we seem happy to say that the principle of social responsibility [1.2] outweighs the farmer's freedom of choice.

13.12 In this area it is particularly difficult to see where criminal law ends and civil law starts. In *Sherras v de Rutzen* (see **3.39**), Wright J spoke of acts which 'are not criminal in any real sense, but are acts which are in the public interest are prohibited under a penalty'. Is it true to say that some criminal acts are more 'criminal' than others, or has the time come to recognise that these offences are just as much criminal as any other offence? One answer is to introduce a third category, of quasi-crime. In recent years, a new sort of an intermediate offence has evolved in the form of the fixed penalty notice. A recent example is provided by the Noise Act 1996. Possible sanctions under this Act include criminal liability and a fine of up to £100 (under s 4) or a fixed penalty of £100 without the imposition of criminal liability (under s 8). This fixed penalty gives the offender the chance to avoid criminal liability, and the procedure is based on the provision in relation to litter in the Environmental Protection Act 1990. However, the danger with this sort of quasi-crime

269

is that D may not have full due process safeguards. Look at this recent decision of the ECHR:

> *Schmautzer v Austria* (1995) D was fined by the federal police authority for not wearing a seatbelt while driving. In default of payment, he was committed to prison for 24 hours. D argued that the administrative criminal offence of which he had been accused gave rise to a criminal charge and that his being sentenced to imprisonment in default by an administrative authority infringed his rights under the ECHR, art 6. ECHR: The criminal nature of the offence with which D had been charged was determined by the language used in describing it. The police authority was an administrative authority which should be subject to control by a judicial body having full jurisdiction. D was entitled to significant damages for this breach of art 6.

We noted at **1.24** that incorporation of the European Convention on Human Rights may well lead to a proliferation of litigation. The 'mixing' of criminal and civil sanctions is an example of a recent development in the law may be challenged. It has been used not only in environmental law, but also, for example, controversially, in the Protection from Harassment Act 1997 (see **9.29**).

13.13   How wide should the criminal law be? Let us return to where we started in chapter 1 with Ashworth's principle of autonomy. Perhaps the answer lies in saying that the essence of what makes an act criminal is the *mens rea* behind it. Those who dump chemicals in rivers intentionally or recklessly should be prosecuted. In which case, am I arguing for the abolition of all strict liability offences? At **3.43** we weighed the advantages and disadvantages of strict liability. Closely related is the question of whether companies, and not simply the individuals within the company should be liable. At **4.33** we noted the courts recent line in favour of corporate liability: but is the answer really a need for punitive damages in civil courts? Another question is the correct way of drafting environmental offences: are result or act-oriented offences better (**2.2**)? How do we measure 'better'?

Conclusion

13.14   Changes in this area are happening fast. It is very difficult to draw conclusions about their success or otherwise. Fundamental questions like 'how clean can we afford to be' are openly asked: as important in the context of burglary may be the question 'How burglary free can we afford to be?', but such questions are less openly asked. One conclusion of this book is that whilst criminal law may at one level be a jumble of rules, it is vital that these rules are based on clear goals and philosophies.

Another conclusion is that enforcement issues may cause more difficulties in theory and practice than the law itself. The first advice published by the Sentencing Advisory Panel, created in the Crime and Disorder Act 1998 to give advice to the Court of Appeal on sentencing guidelines, was on environmental offences. Yet, the CA in *Milford Haven Port Authority* (2000) did not choose to issue a sentencing guideline, simply reducing the fine imposed from £4m to £750,000. This illustrates the fact that it makes little sense to study substantive criminal law outside the context in which it is applied. Substantive criminal law, whether it is in a specific area such environmental protection or in a broader Criminal Code, should only be seen as the beginning of the story: be aware of criminal justice in a wider context, including sentencing and punishment, procedure and evidence, if you want to evaluate the substance of the criminal law.

Further reading

Butterworths *Environmental Regulation: A Guide to the Powers of the Environmental Agency and Local Authorities* (1996)

Elsworthy and Holder *Environmental Protection: Text and Materials* (1997)

Hedley *Tort* (2000, 2nd ed)

Hughes *Environmental Law* (1996, 3rd ed)

Hutter *The Reasonable Arm of the Law?* (1988)

Thornton and Beckwith *Environmental Law* (1997)

Self-test questions

1. D1, a company which runs a leather factory on the banks of a large river, allows chemicals to escape into the river killing fish. D2 is the manager of the factory. Both are prosecuted under s 85 of the Water Resources Act 1991. Explain the principles involved in deciding questions of criminal liability.

2. Write a memorandum of advice to the Home Secretary on the advantages and disadvantages of using the criminal law to enforce environmental protection legislation.

Index

Abortion
generally 8.42-8.43
necessity, and 5.20
see also FOETUS
Accomplices
accessories 3.35, 6.3-6.4
acting with purpose of limiting
harmful consequences 6.18
actus reus 6.6-6.8
'aid, abet, counsel or procure' 6.1,
6.3, 6.6-6.7
distinguishing 6.7
aiding unlawful sexual intercourse
with a minor 5.20, 6.18,
6.30
assisting crime, proposed offence
of
actus reus 6.32
generally 6.11, 6.27, 6.28, 7.33,
7.35
mens rea 6.29-6.31
attempt, to 6.2, 7.13
concealing offences 6.33
defences to accomplice liability
6.15-6.19
derivative liability 6.26
encouraging crime, proposed
offence of 6.11, 6.27, 7.33-
7.36
essential matters, knowledge of
6.14
failure to exercise control 6.12,
6.32
generally 6.1-6.2
informers 6.17
innocent agents 6.5
children as 4.4, 6.26
joint enterprise/common purpose
6.20-6.25
law enforcement defence 6.17
legal obligation, belief in 6.19

Accomplices—*contd*
liability by mere presence 6.9-6.11
mens rea 6.13-6.14
motive, and 6.16
principals 6.3-6.4
rape, and 6.9
reckless driving 6.12, 6.32
reform 6.27
riot 6.2
terrorist offences 6.14
transferred malice, and 3.35
violent disorder 6.2
see also JOINT ENTERPRISE/COMMON
PURPOSE
Acquittal
reference to Attorney-General
1.20
Actus reus
accomplices, and 6.6-6.8
arson 12.7
assisting crime, proposed offence
of 6.32
attempt 7.5-7.7
automatism, and 2.3, 4.16
causation *see* CAUSATION
conspiracy 7.16-7.17
criminal damage 12.7
defence, and 5.1
generally 2.1-2.2, 5.1
incitement 7.28
manslaughter 8.3
meaning 2.1
murder 2.2, 8.3
omissions 2.9
rape 10.8
robbery 11.22
sexual offences 2.2, 2.25
state of affairs 2.24-2.25
theft *see under* THEFT
voluntary acts 2.3-2.4
see also AUTOMATISM